THE POWERPUFF GIRLS™

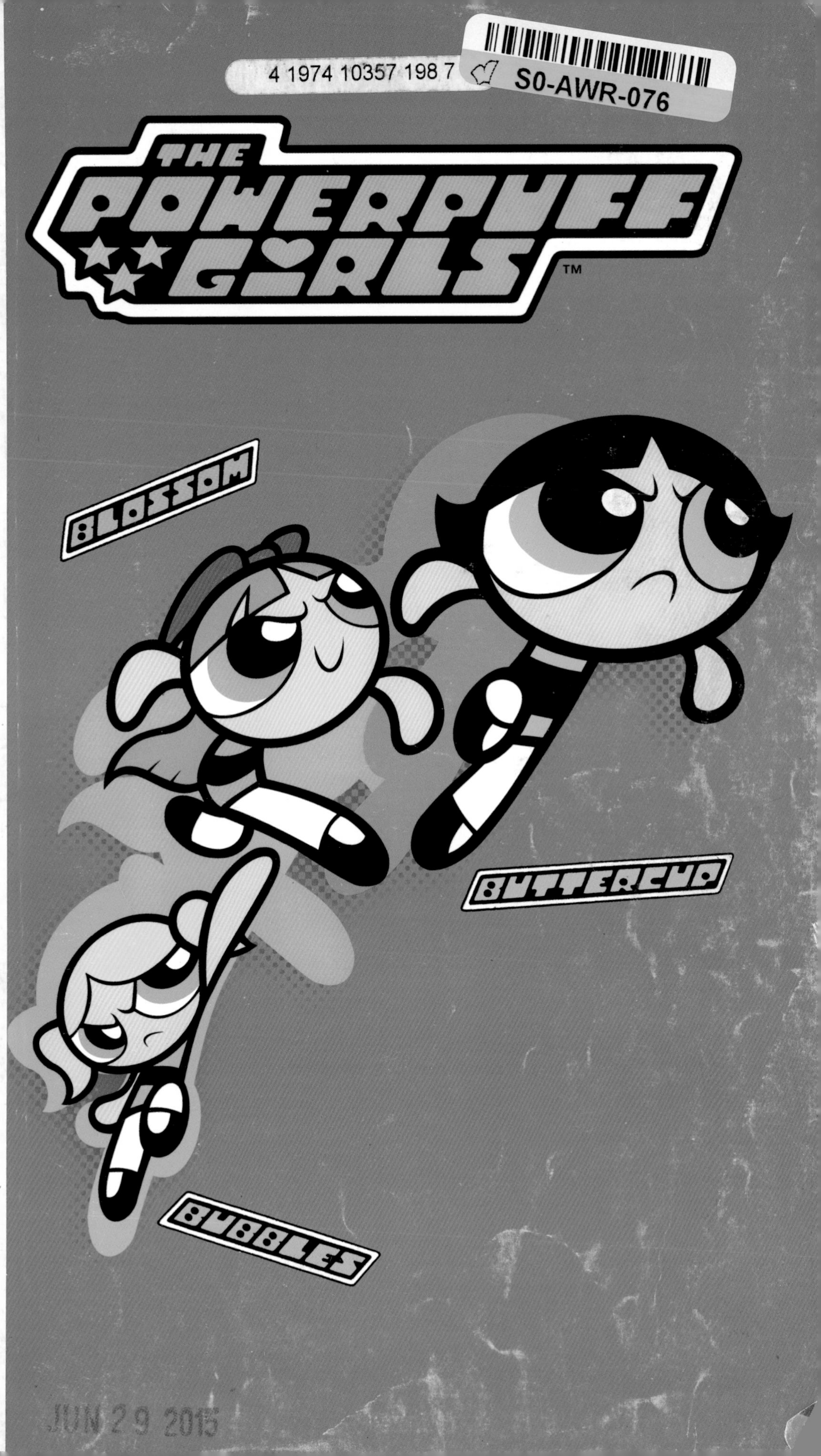
BLOSSOM
BUTTERCUP
BUBBLES

front cover art by
Derek Charm

back cover art by
Phil Moy

series edits by
Sarah Gaydos

collection edits by
Justin Eisinger & Alonzo Simon

collection design by
Claudia Chong

Special thanks to Jeff Parker, Laurie Halal-Ono and Marisa Marionakis of Cartoon Network.

ISBN: 978-1-63140-107-7

THE POWERPUFF GIRLS CREATED BY CRAIG McCRACKE

17 16 15 14   1 2 3

IDW CN
CARTOON NETWORK.
www.IDWPUBLISHING.com
IDW founded by Ted Adams, Alex Garner, Kris Oprisko, and Robbie Robbins

Ted Adams, CEO & Publisher
Greg Goldstein, President & COO
Robbie Robbins, EVP/Sr. Graphic Artist
Chris Ryall, Chief Creative Officer/Editor-in-Chief
Matthew Ruzicka, CPA, Chief Financial Officer
Alan Payne, VP of Sales
Dirk Wood, VP of Marketing
Lorelei Bunjes, VP of Digital Services
Jeff Webber, VP of Digital Publishing & Business Development

Facebook: facebook.com/idwpublishing
Twitter: @idwpublishing
YouTube: youtube.com/idwpublishing
Instagram: instagram.com/idwpublishing
deviantART: idwpublishing.deviantart.com
Pinterest: pinterest.com/idwpublishing/idw-staff-fave

Originally published as POWERPUFF GIRLS issues #7-10.

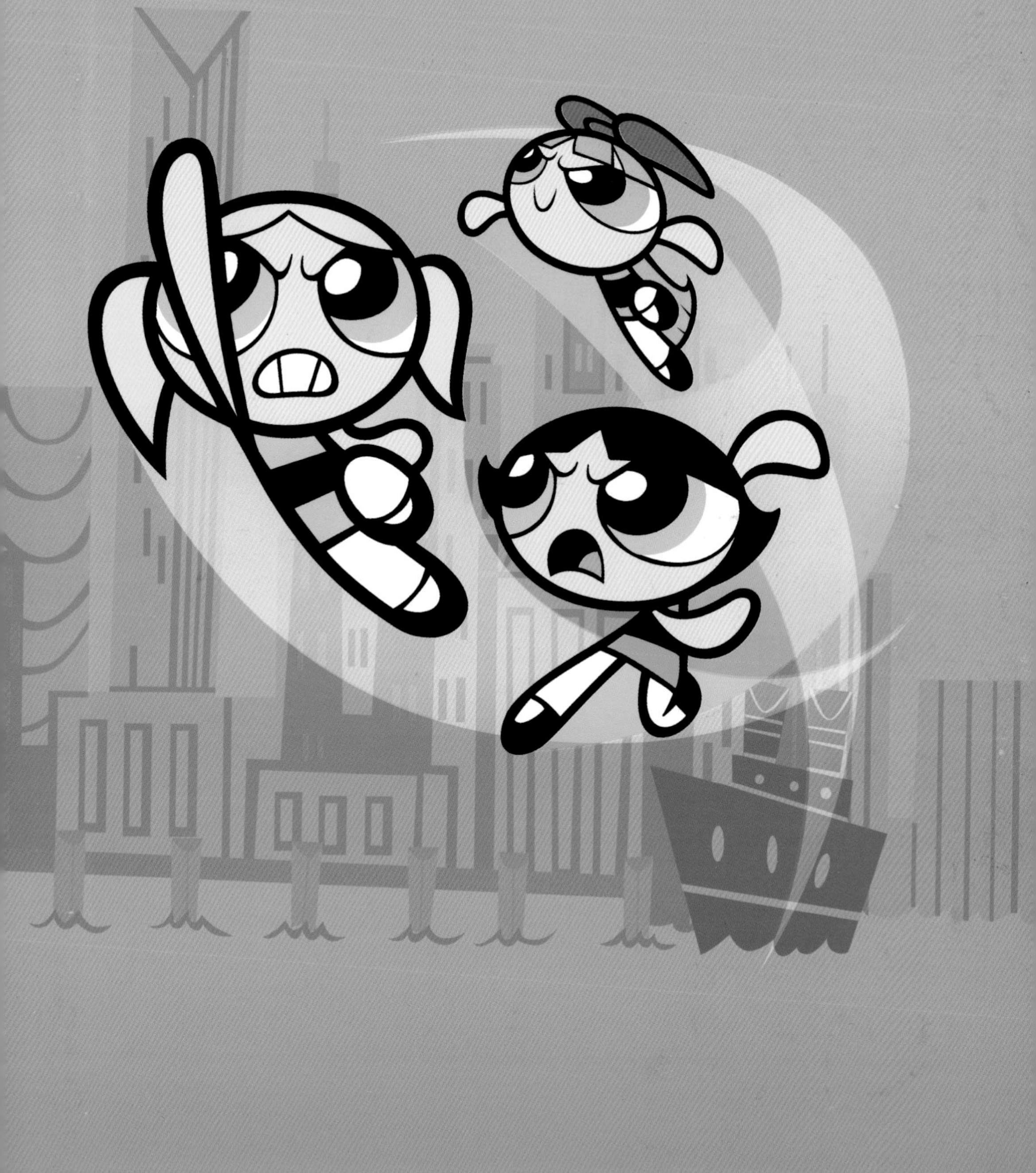

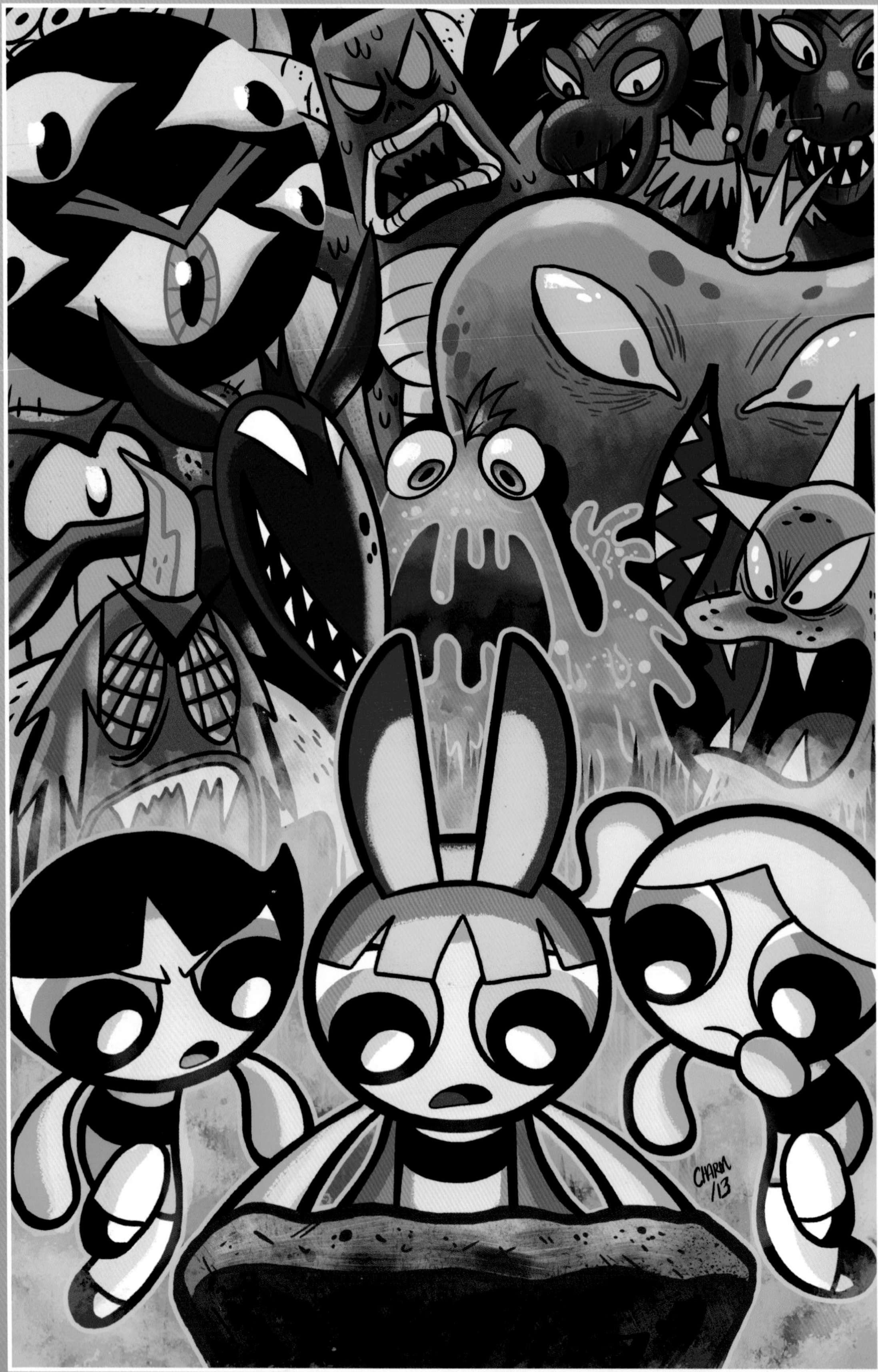
CHARM
/13

Cover by Derek Charm

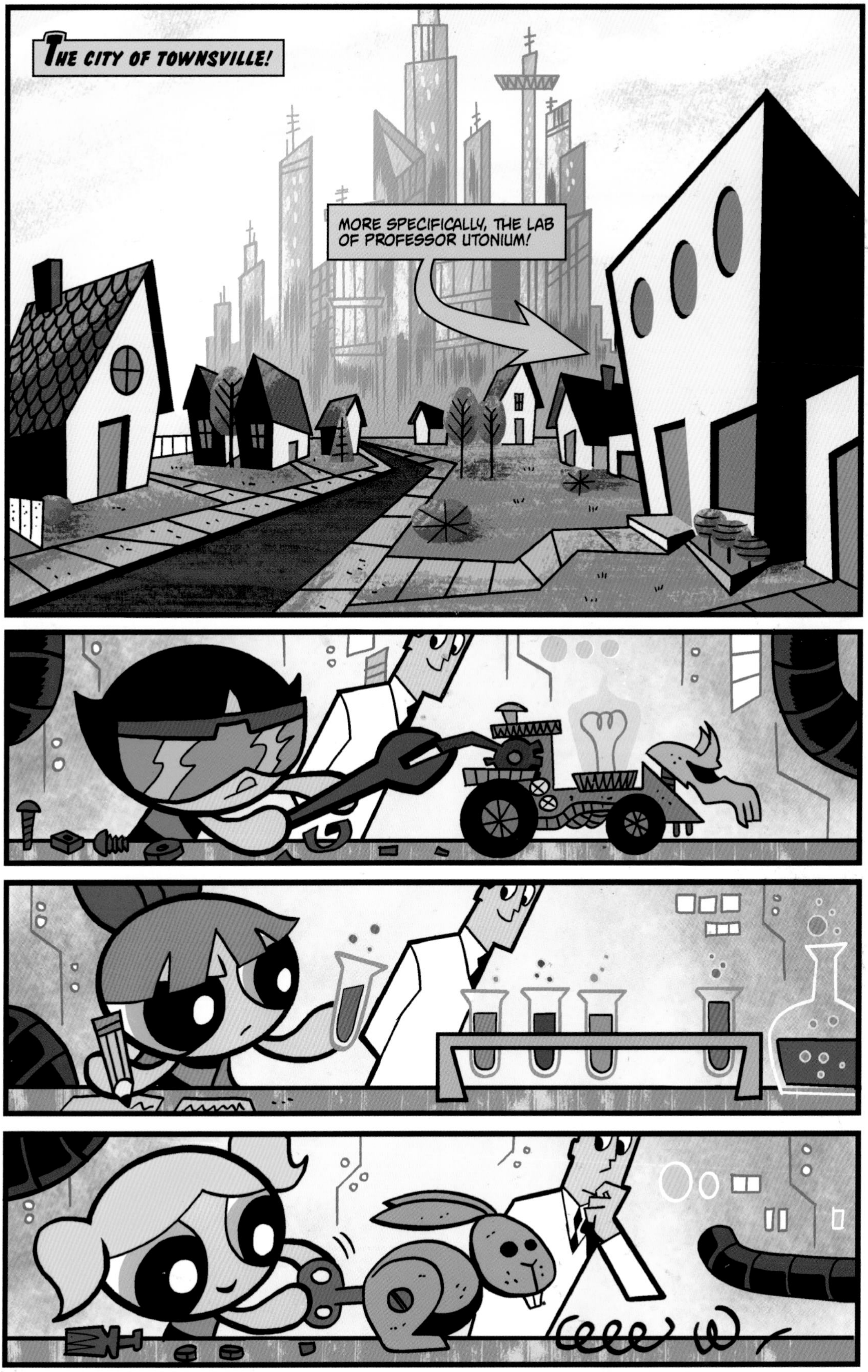
THE CITY OF TOWNSVILLE!
MORE SPECIFICALLY, THE LAB OF PROFESSOR UTONIUM!

Story and Art by Derek Charm · Lettering by Neil Uyetake

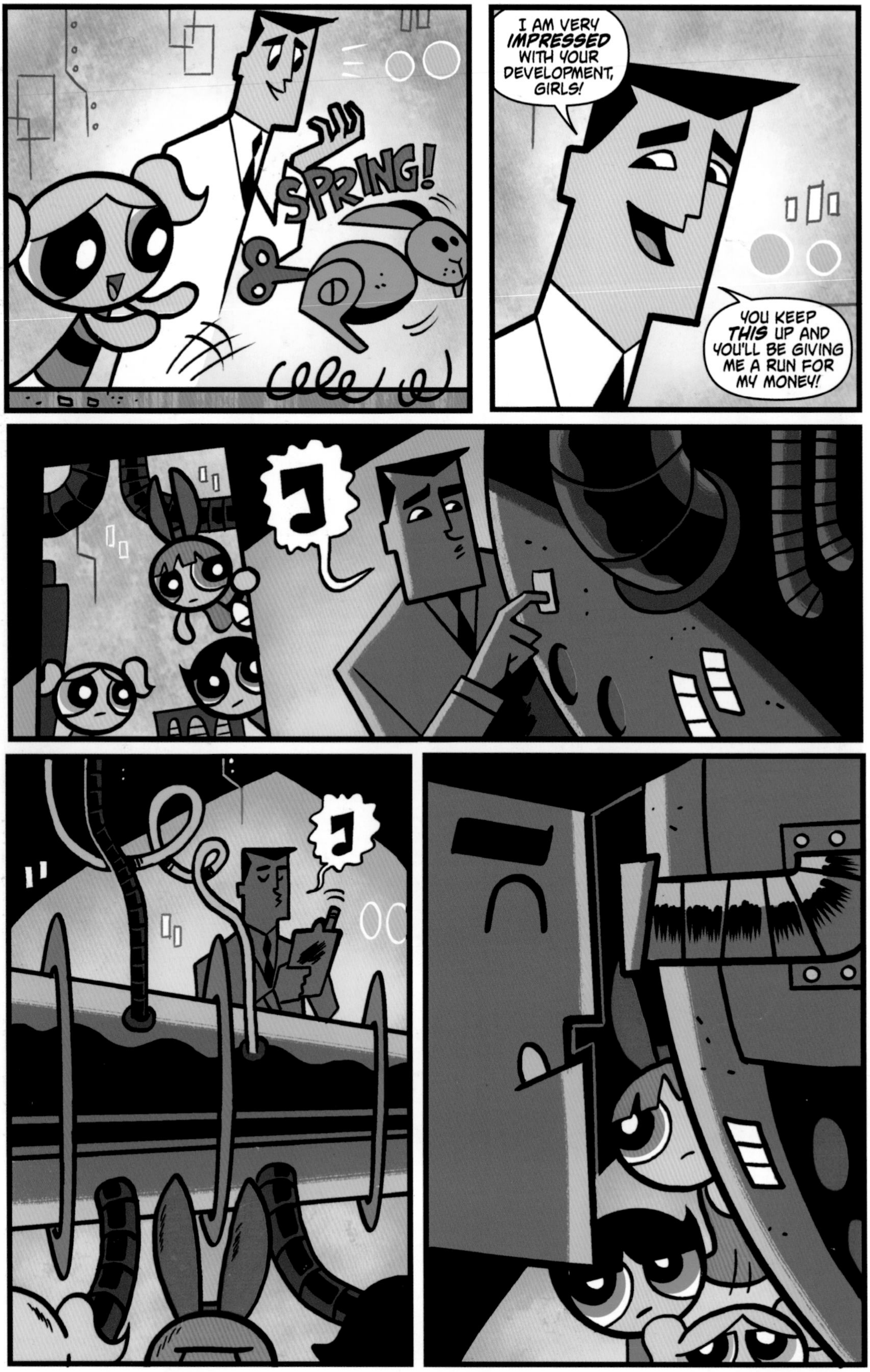
SPRING!
I AM VERY IMPRESSED WITH YOUR DEVELOPMENT, GIRLS!
YOU KEEP THIS UP AND YOU'LL BE GIVING ME A RUN FOR MY MONEY!

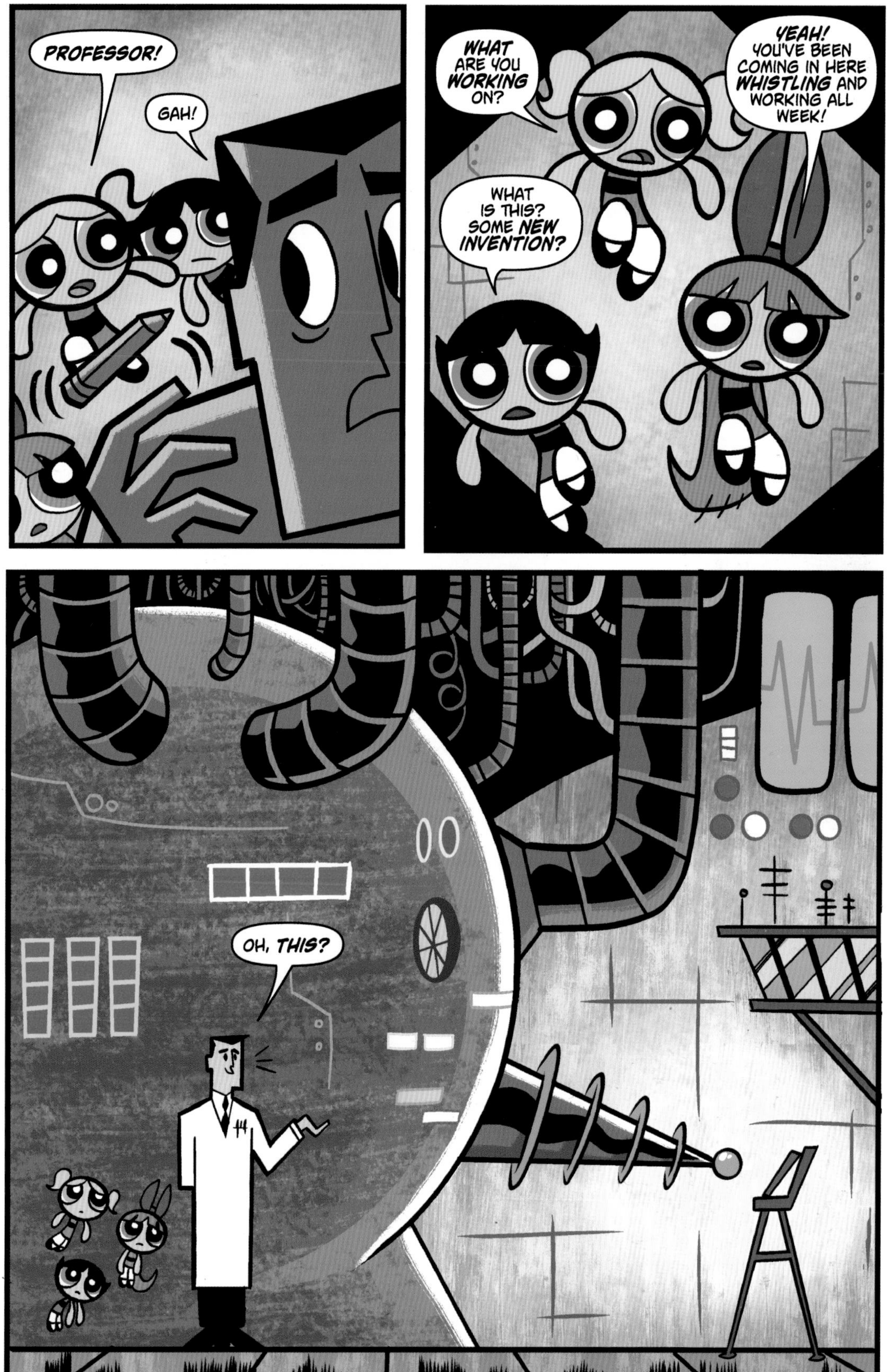
PROFESSOR!
GAH!
WHAT ARE YOU WORKING ON?
YEAH! YOU'VE BEEN COMING IN HERE WHISTLING AND WORKING ALL WEEK!
WHAT IS THIS? SOME NEW INVENTION?
OH, THIS?

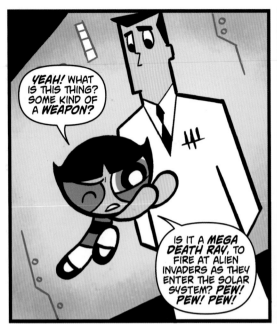

YEAH! WHAT IS THIS THING? SOME KIND OF A *WEAPON*?

IS IT A *MEGA DEATH RAY*, TO FIRE AT ALIEN INVADERS AS THEY ENTER THE SOLAR SYSTEM? *PEW! PEW! PEW!*

DOES IT SHOOT OUT LITTLE PUFFS OF *COTTON CANDY* THAT COME TO LIFE AND START TO HOP AROUND LIKE *LITTLE BUNNIES* LOOKING FOR—

ENOUGH!

WELL, PROFESSOR?

I'M AFRAID IT'S NOTHING SO EXCITING, GIRLS. DO YOU SEE THAT *STONE SLAB* ACROSS THE ROOM?

YEAH...

LOOKS OLD!

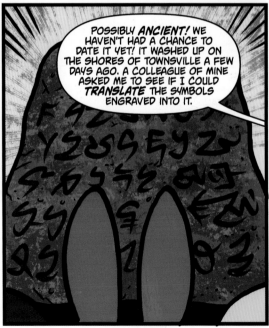

POSSIBLY *ANCIENT!* WE HAVEN'T HAD A CHANCE TO DATE IT YET! IT WASHED UP ON THE SHORES OF TOWNSVILLE A FEW DAYS AGO. A COLLEAGUE OF MINE ASKED ME TO SEE IF I COULD *TRANSLATE* THE SYMBOLS ENGRAVED INTO IT.

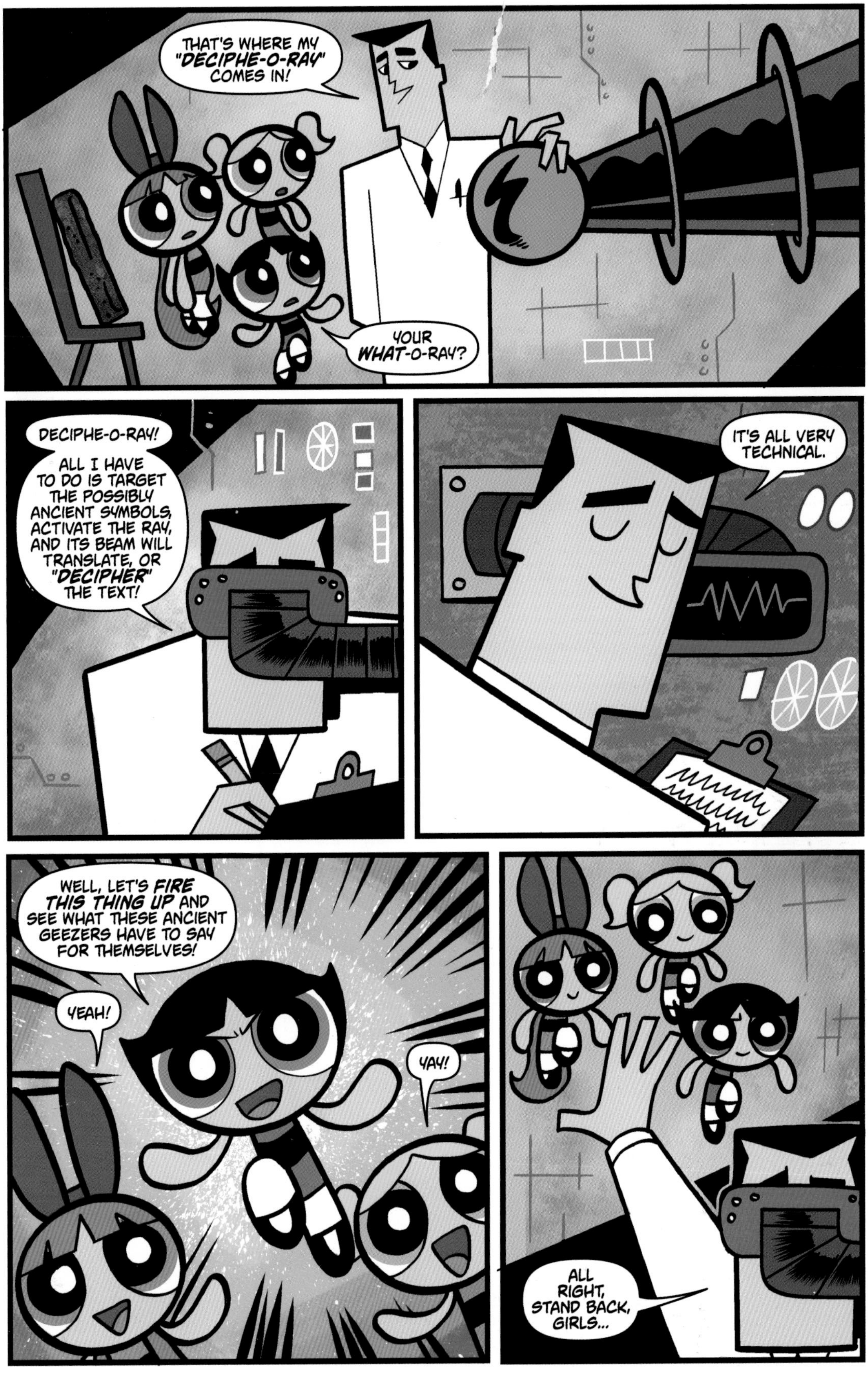
THAT'S WHERE MY "DECIPHE-O-RAY" COMES IN!
YOUR WHAT-O-RAY?
DECIPHE-O-RAY!
ALL I HAVE TO DO IS TARGET THE POSSIBLY ANCIENT SYMBOLS, ACTIVATE THE RAY, AND ITS BEAM WILL TRANSLATE, OR "DECIPHER" THE TEXT!
IT'S ALL VERY TECHNICAL.
WELL, LET'S FIRE THIS THING UP AND SEE WHAT THESE ANCIENT GEEZERS HAVE TO SAY FOR THEMSELVES!
YEAH!
YAY!
ALL RIGHT, STAND BACK, GIRLS...

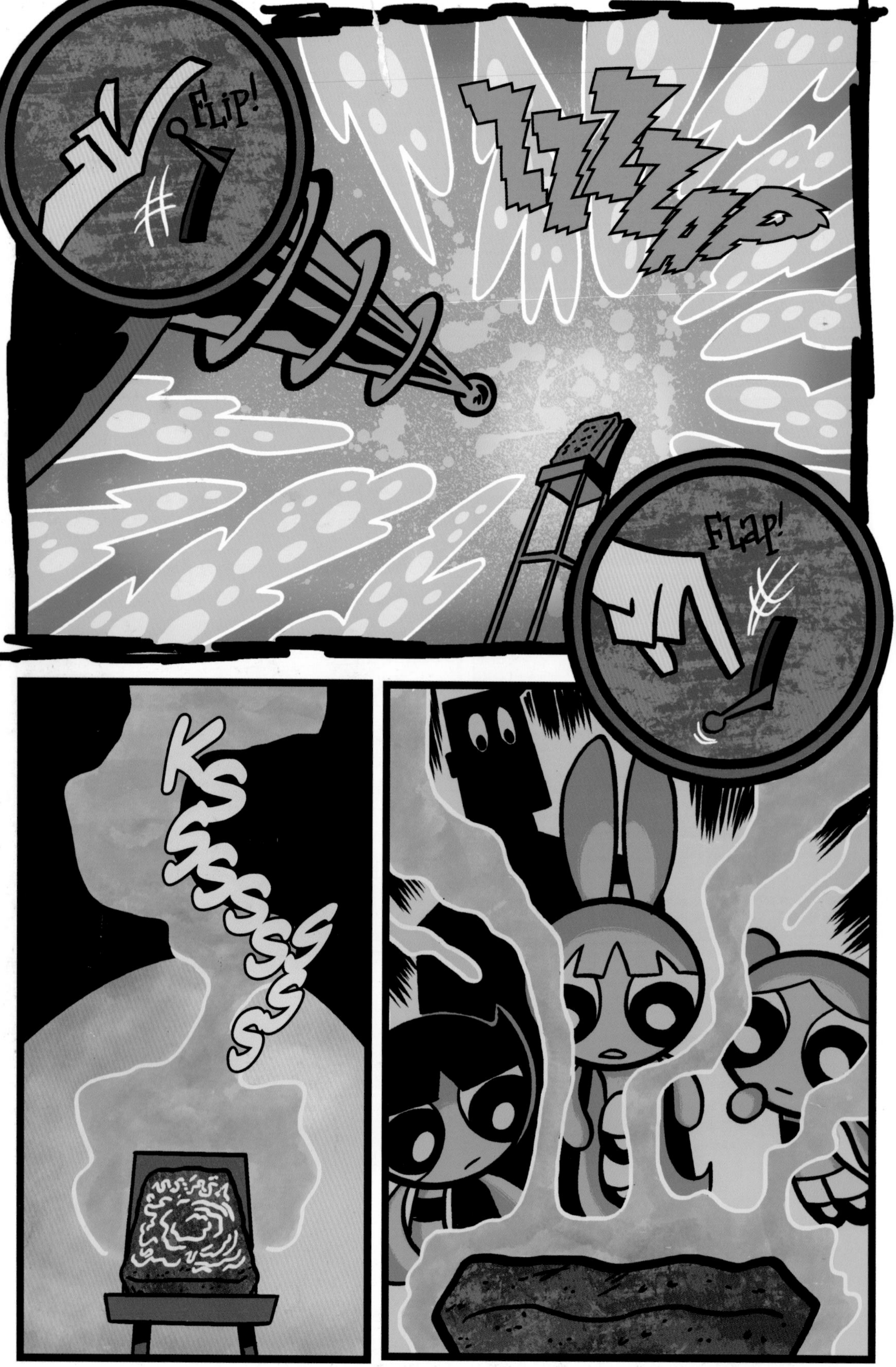
FLIP!
ZZZZZAP
FLAP!
KSSSSSSSS

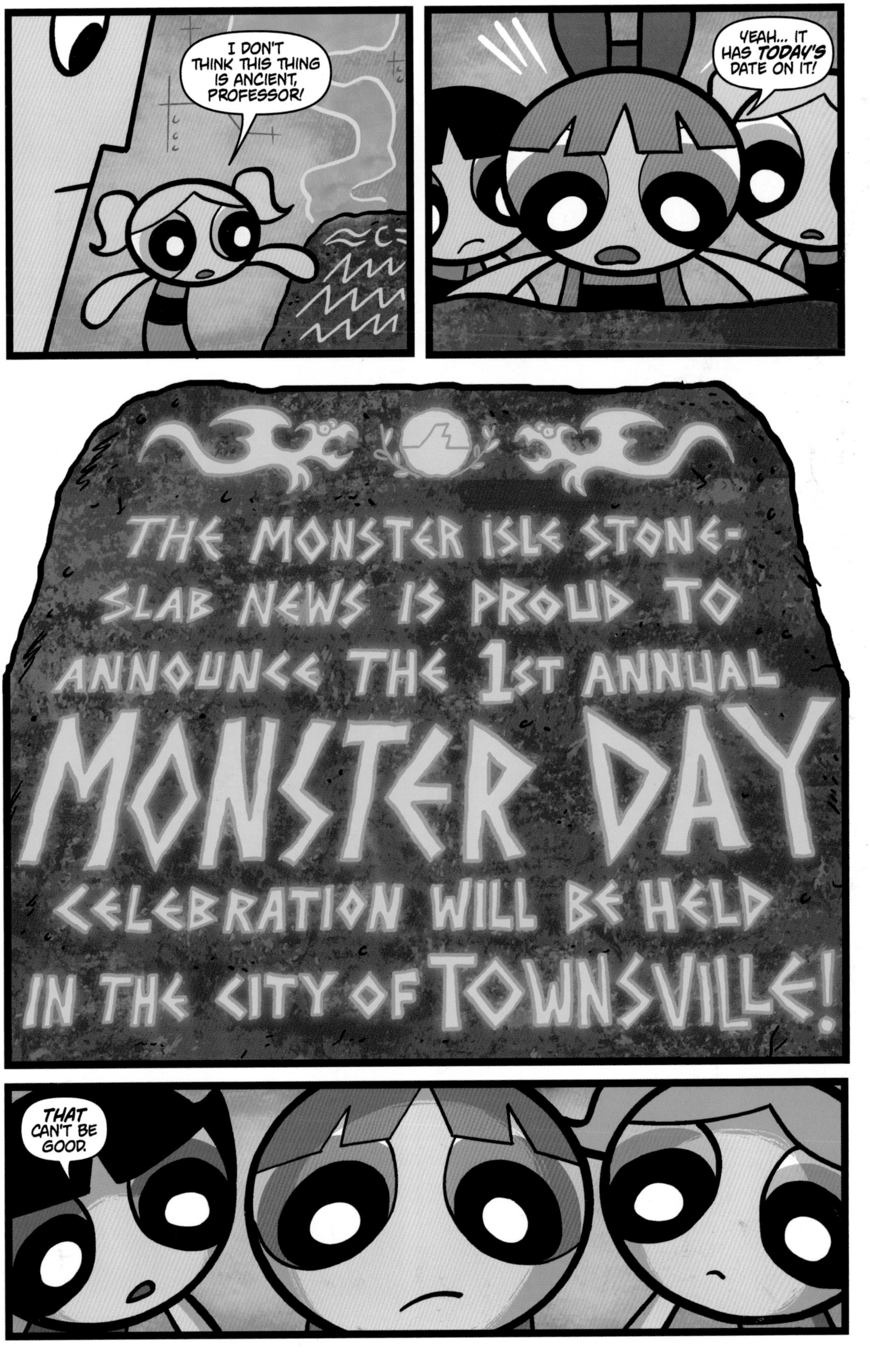
I DON'T THINK THIS THING IS ANCIENT, PROFESSOR!
YEAH... IT HAS TODAY'S DATE ON IT!
THE MONSTER ISLE STONE-SLAB NEWS IS PROUD TO ANNOUNCE THE 1ST ANNUAL MONSTER DAY CELEBRATION WILL BE HELD IN THE CITY OF TOWNSVILLE!
THAT CAN'T BE GOOD.

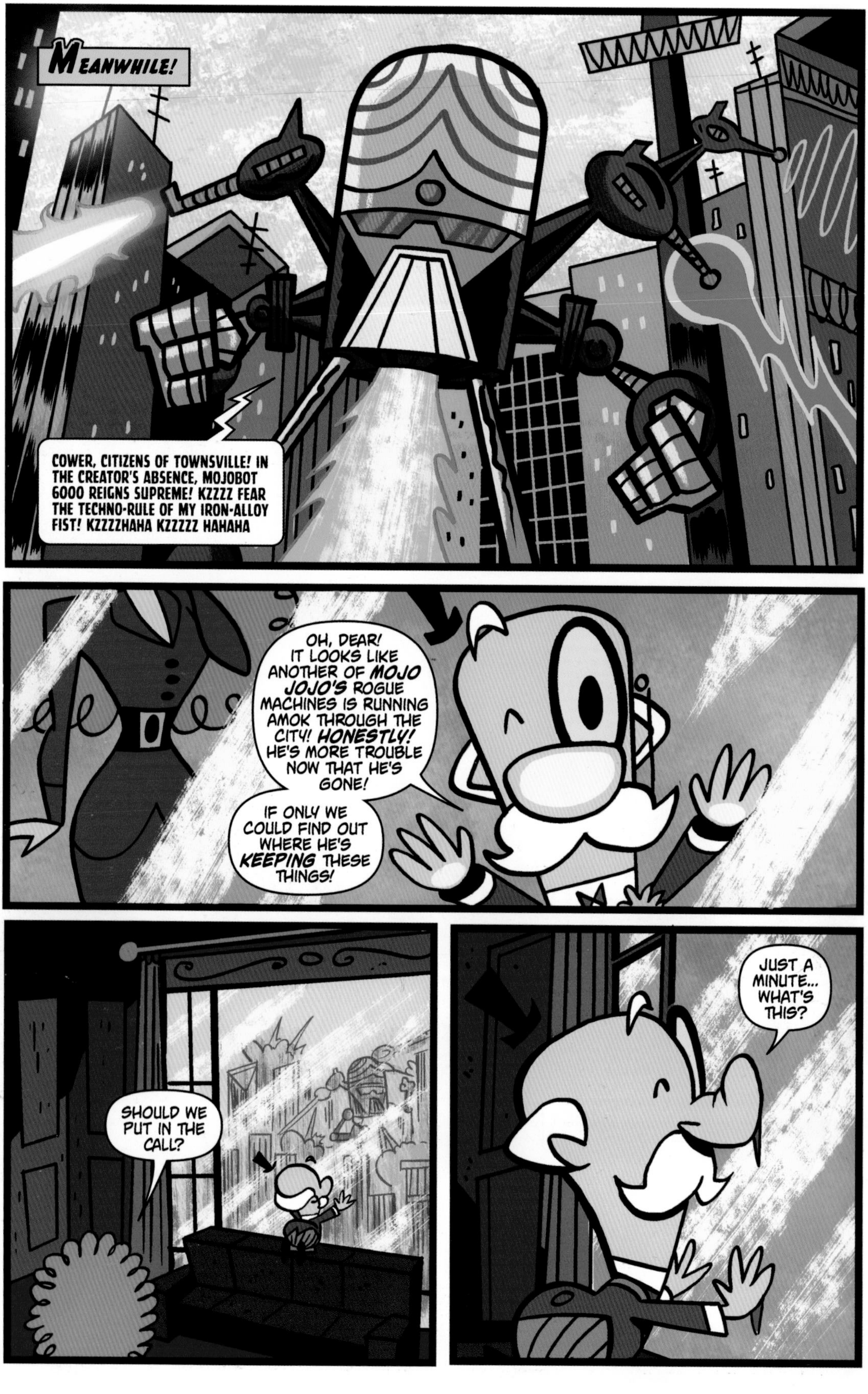
MEANWHILE!
COWER, CITIZENS OF TOWNSVILLE! IN THE CREATOR'S ABSENCE, MOJOBOT 6000 REIGNS SUPREME! KZZZZ FEAR THE TECHNO-RULE OF MY IRON-ALLOY FIST! KZZZZHAHA KZZZZZ HAHAHA
OH, DEAR! IT LOOKS LIKE ANOTHER OF MOJO JOJO'S ROGUE MACHINES IS RUNNING AMOK THROUGH THE CITY! HONESTLY! HE'S MORE TROUBLE NOW THAT HE'S GONE!
IF ONLY WE COULD FIND OUT WHERE HE'S KEEPING THESE THINGS!
SHOULD WE PUT IN THE CALL?
JUST A MINUTE... WHAT'S THIS?

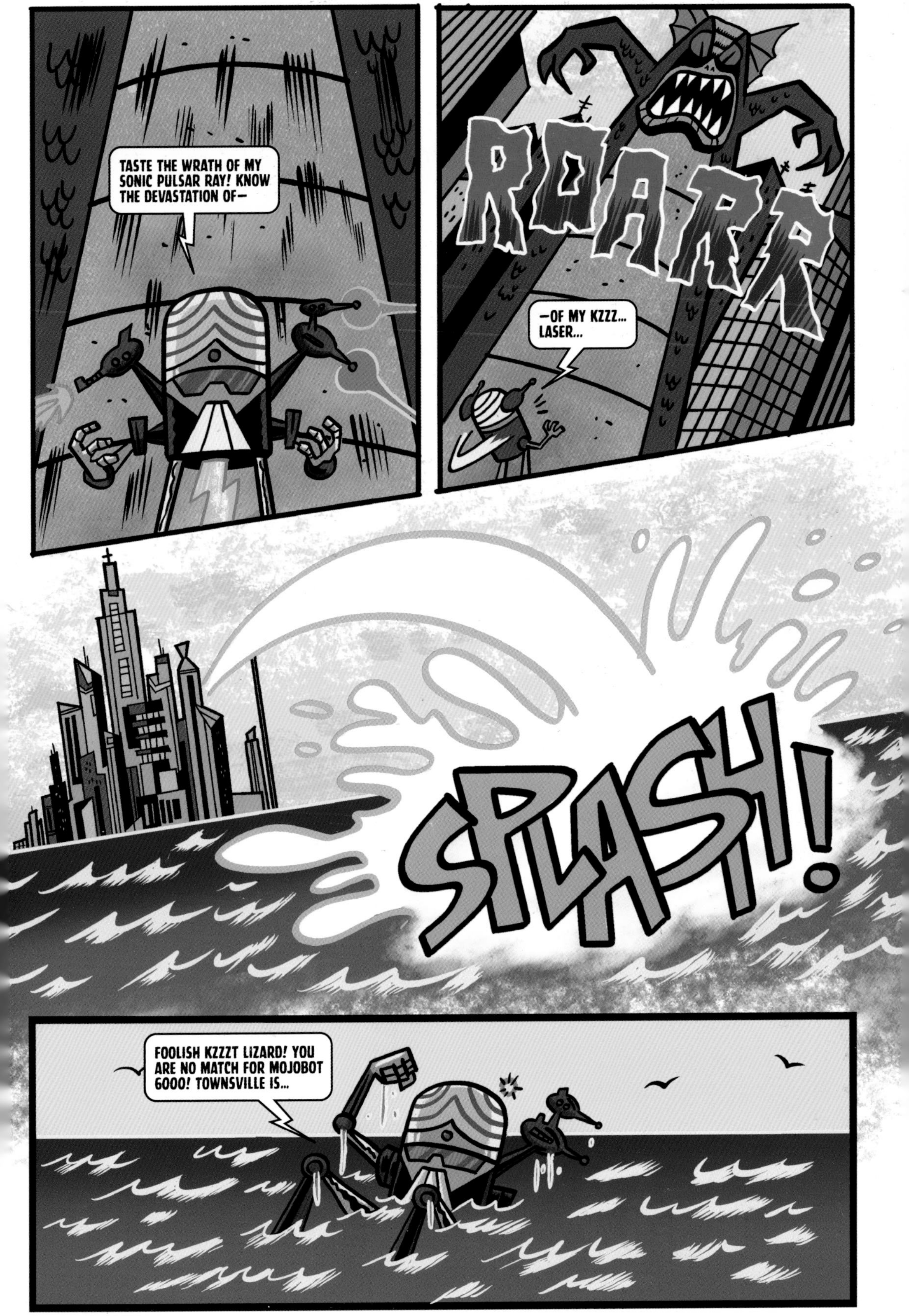
TASTE THE WRATH OF MY SONIC PULSAR RAY! KNOW THE DEVASTATION OF—
ROARR
—OF MY KZZZ... LASER...
SPLASH!
FOOLISH KZZZT LIZARD! YOU ARE NO MATCH FOR MOJOBOT 6000! TOWNSVILLE IS...

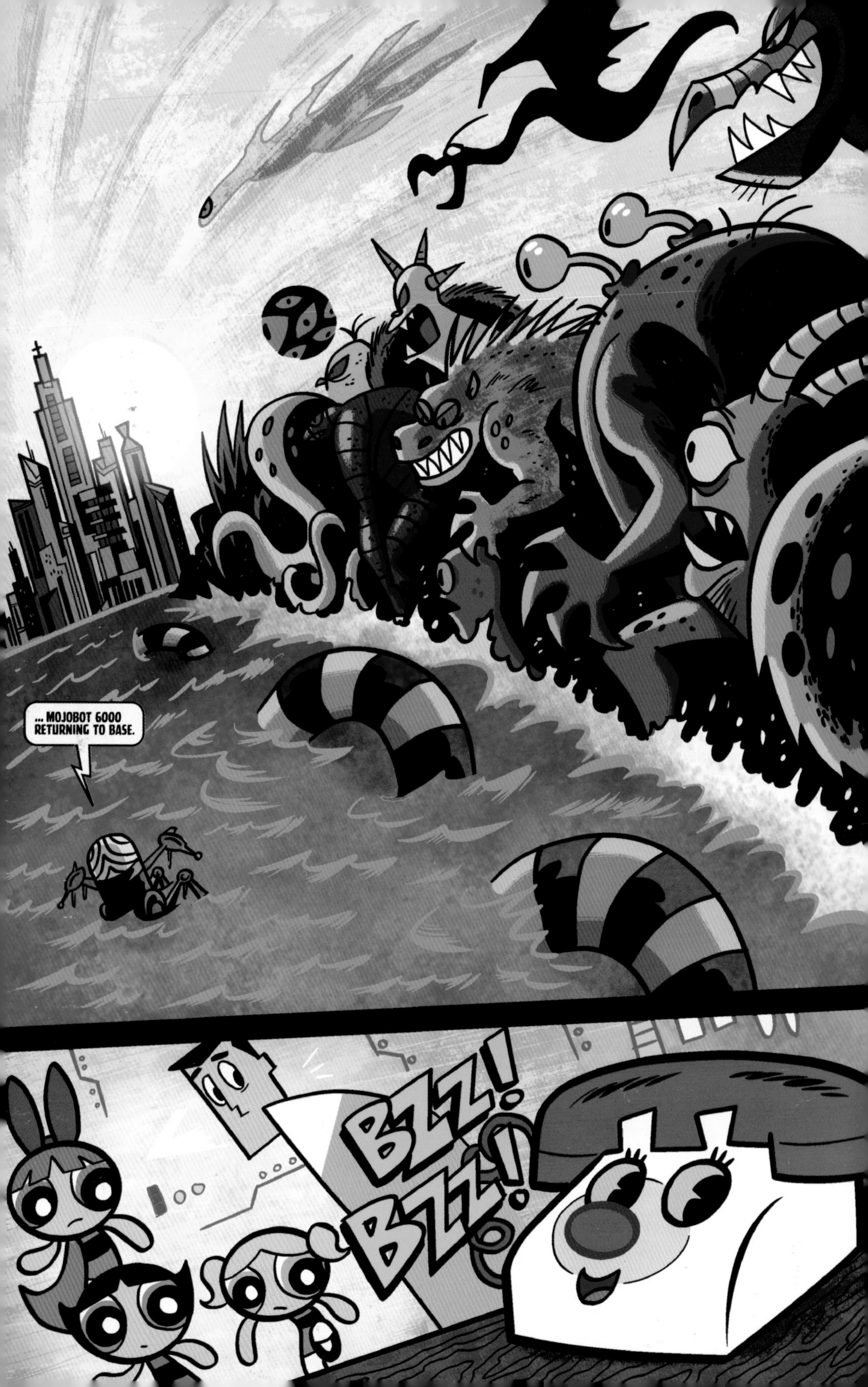

... MOJOBOT 6000 RETURNING TO BASE.
BZZ! BZZ!

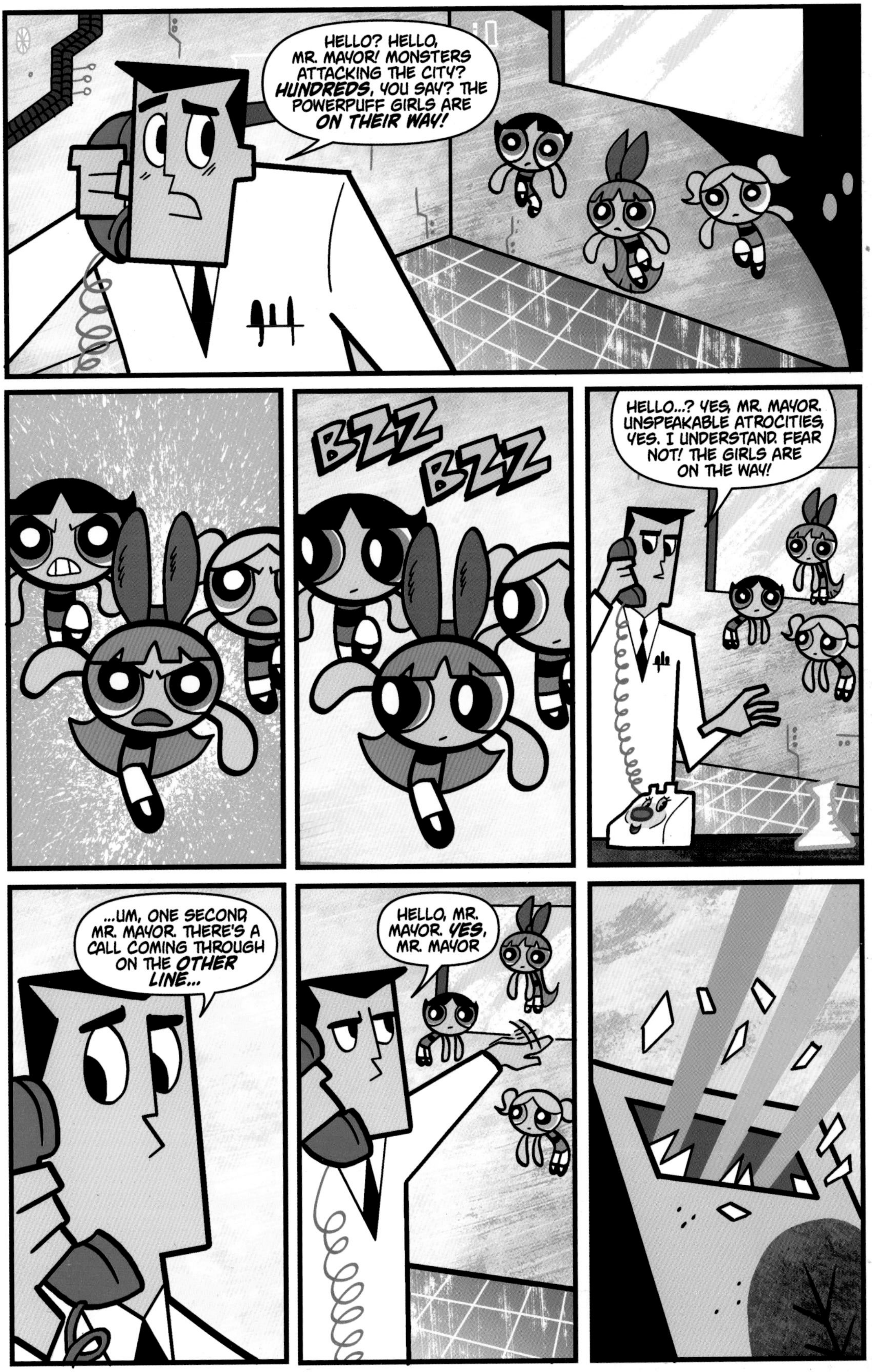
HELLO? HELLO, MR. MAYOR! MONSTERS ATTACKING THE CITY? HUNDREDS, YOU SAY? THE POWERPUFF GIRLS ARE ON THEIR WAY!
BZZ BZZ
HELLO...? YES, MR. MAYOR. UNSPEAKABLE ATROCITIES, YES. I UNDERSTAND. FEAR NOT! THE GIRLS ARE ON THE WAY!
...UM, ONE SECOND, MR. MAYOR. THERE'S A CALL COMING THROUGH ON THE OTHER LINE...
HELLO, MR. MAYOR. YES, MR. MAYOR

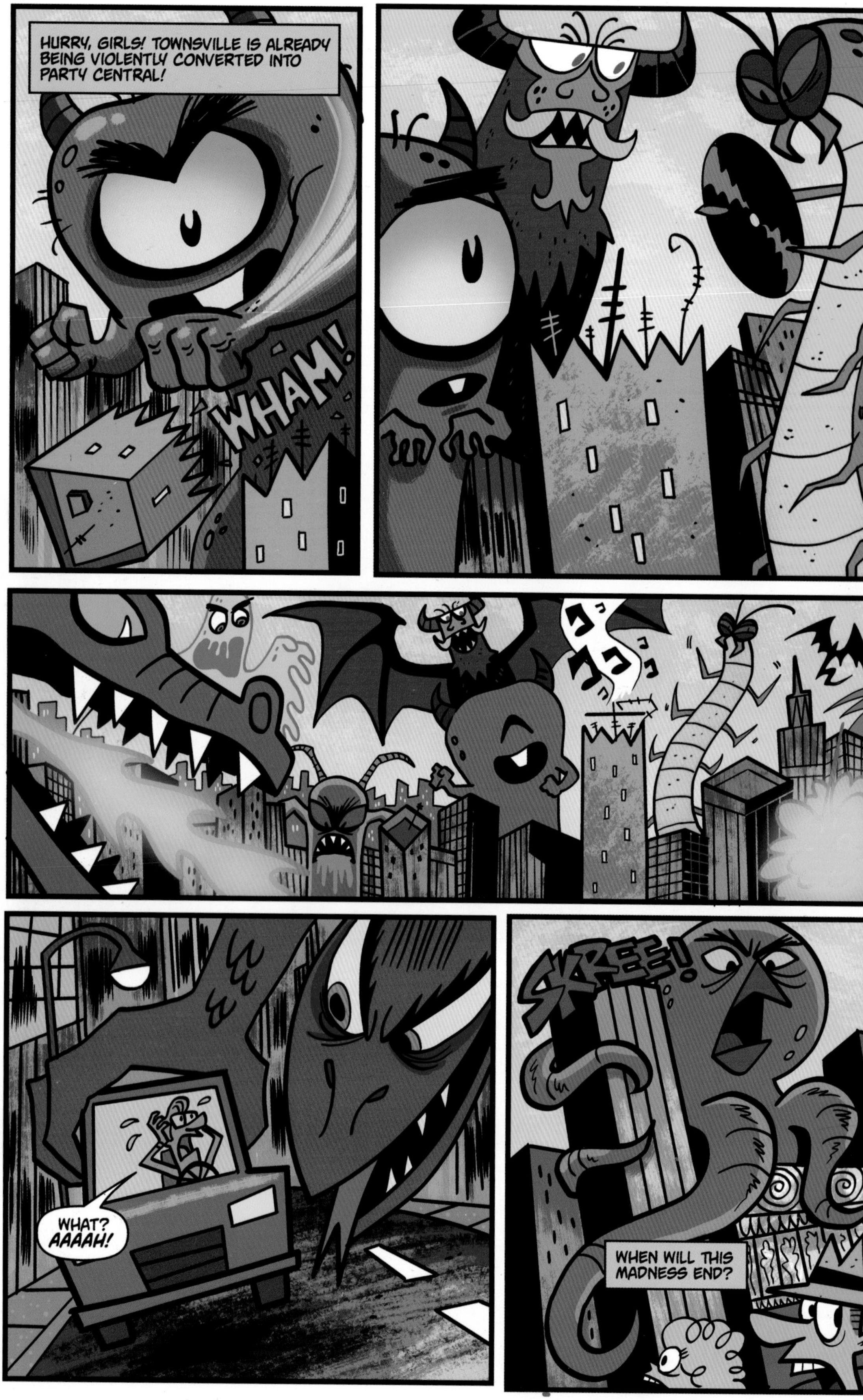
HURRY, GIRLS! TOWNSVILLE IS ALREADY BEING VIOLENTLY CONVERTED INTO PARTY CENTRAL!
WHAM!
WHAT? AAAAH!
SKREE!
WHEN WILL THIS MADNESS END?

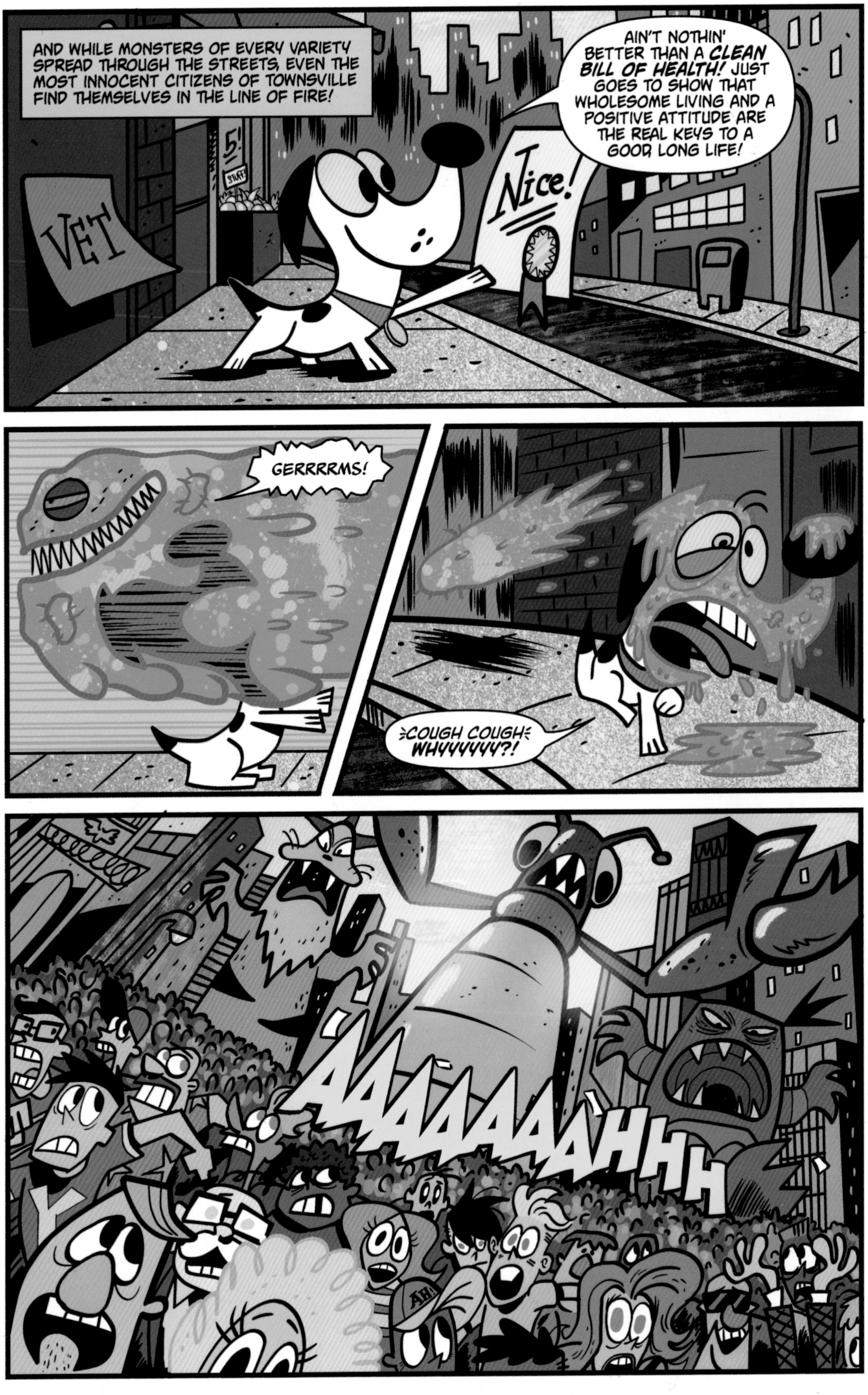
AND WHILE MONSTERS OF EVERY VARIETY SPREAD THROUGH THE STREETS, EVEN THE MOST INNOCENT CITIZENS OF TOWNSVILLE FIND THEMSELVES IN THE LINE OF FIRE!
AIN'T NOTHIN' BETTER THAN A CLEAN BILL OF HEALTH! JUST GOES TO SHOW THAT WHOLESOME LIVING AND A POSITIVE ATTITUDE ARE THE REAL KEYS TO A GOOD LONG LIFE!
VET
Nice!
GERRRRMS!
COUGH COUGH WHYYYYYY?!
AAAAAAAHHH

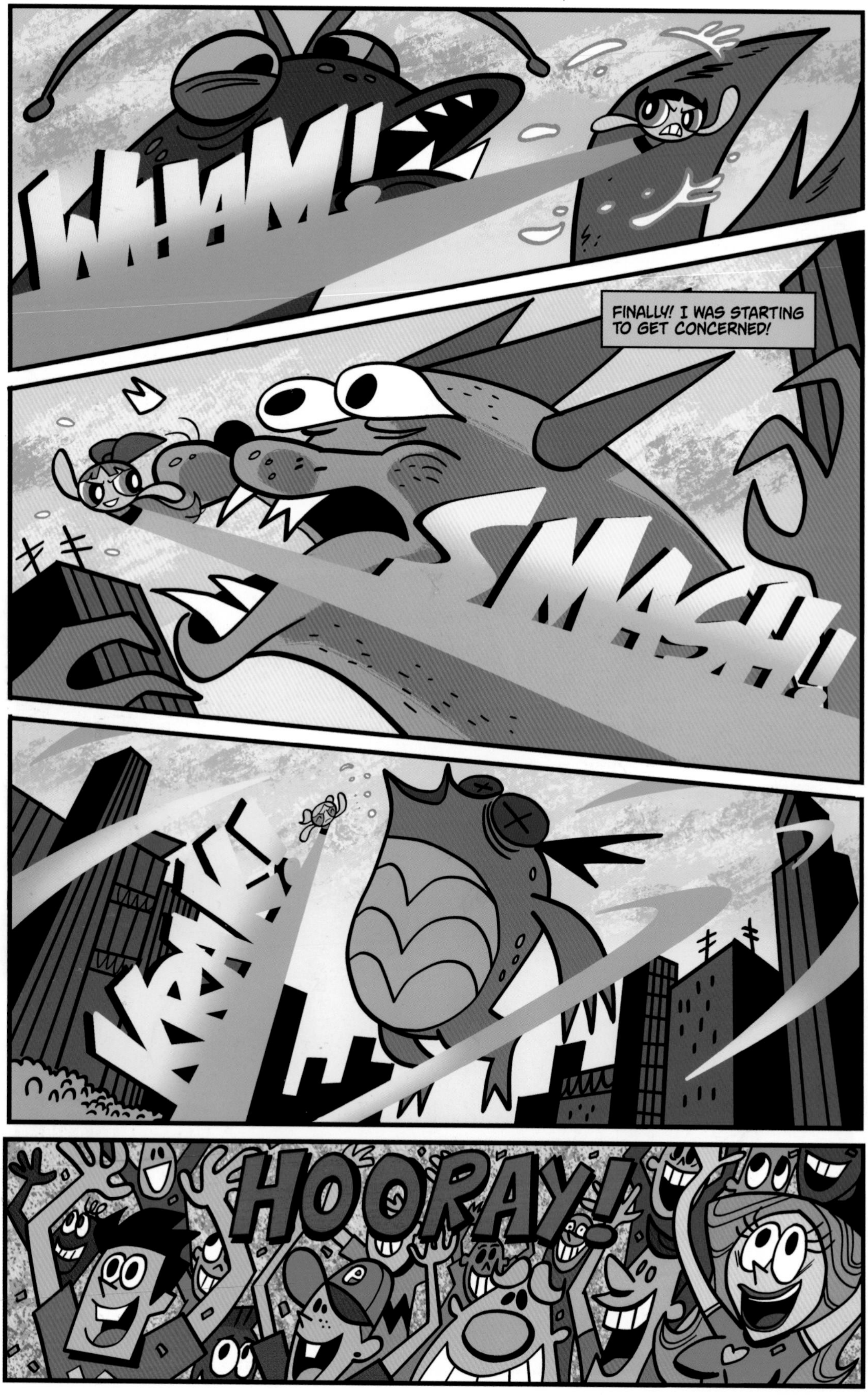
WHAM!
FINALLY! I WAS STARTING TO GET CONCERNED!
SMASH!
HOORAY!

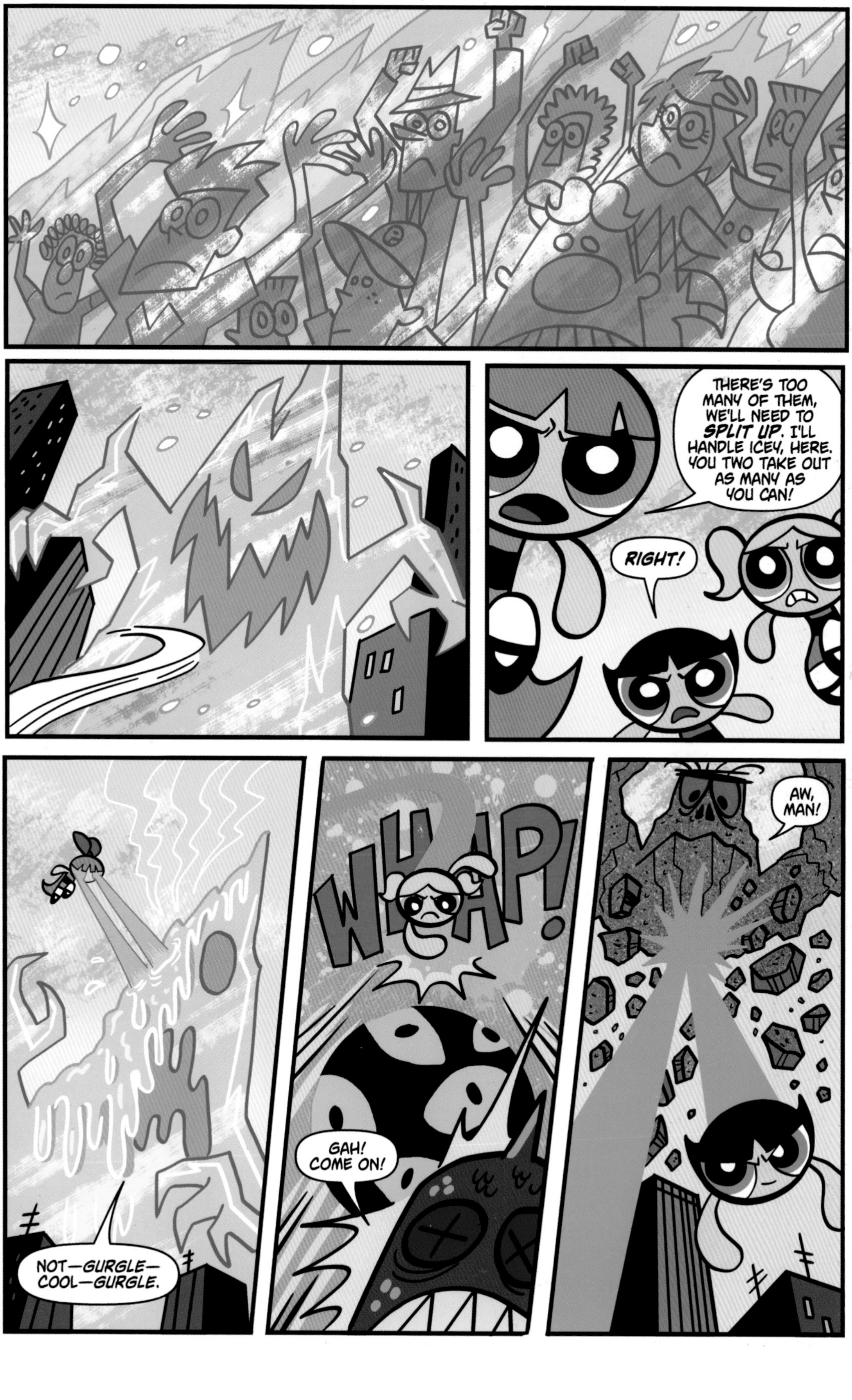
THERE'S TOO MANY OF THEM, WE'LL NEED TO SPLIT UP. I'LL HANDLE ICEY, HERE. YOU TWO TAKE OUT AS MANY AS YOU CAN!
RIGHT!
NOT—GURGLE—COOL—GURGLE.
WHAP!
GAH! COME ON!
AW, MAN!

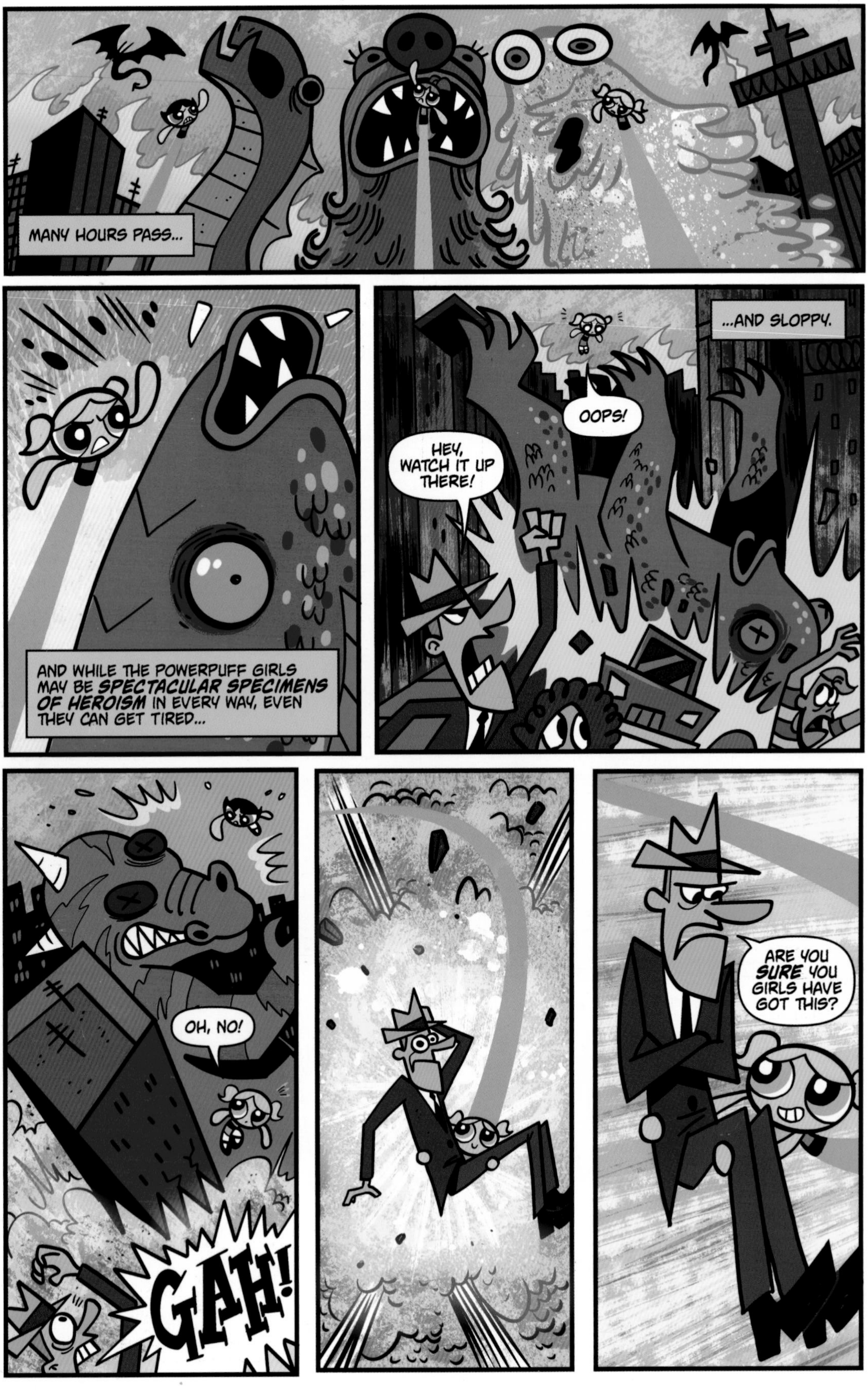
MANY HOURS PASS...
AND WHILE THE POWERPUFF GIRLS MAY BE SPECTACULAR SPECIMENS OF HEROISM IN EVERY WAY, EVEN THEY CAN GET TIRED...
...AND SLOPPY.
OOPS!
HEY, WATCH IT UP THERE!
OH, NO!
GAH!
ARE YOU SURE YOU GIRLS HAVE GOT THIS?

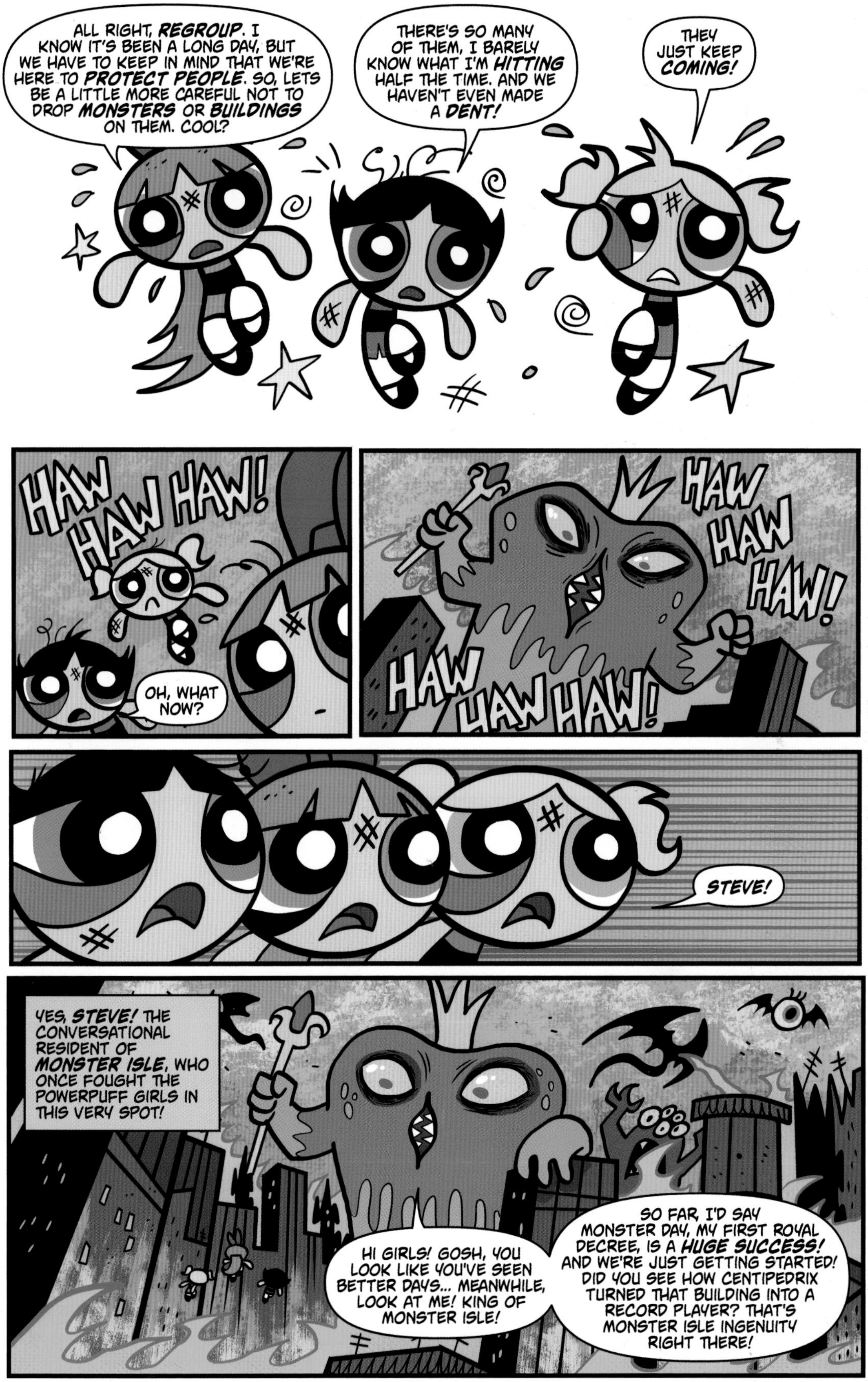
ALL RIGHT, REGROUP. I KNOW IT'S BEEN A LONG DAY, BUT WE HAVE TO KEEP IN MIND THAT WE'RE HERE TO PROTECT PEOPLE. SO, LETS BE A LITTLE MORE CAREFUL NOT TO DROP MONSTERS OR BUILDINGS ON THEM. COOL?
THERE'S SO MANY OF THEM, I BARELY KNOW WHAT I'M HITTING HALF THE TIME. AND WE HAVEN'T EVEN MADE A DENT!
THEY JUST KEEP COMING!
HAW HAW HAW!
OH, WHAT NOW?
HAW HAW HAW!
HAW HAW HAW!
STEVE!
YES, STEVE! THE CONVERSATIONAL RESIDENT OF MONSTER ISLE, WHO ONCE FOUGHT THE POWERPUFF GIRLS IN THIS VERY SPOT!
HI GIRLS! GOSH, YOU LOOK LIKE YOU'VE SEEN BETTER DAYS... MEANWHILE, LOOK AT ME! KING OF MONSTER ISLE!
SO FAR, I'D SAY MONSTER DAY, MY FIRST ROYAL DECREE, IS A HUGE SUCCESS! AND WE'RE JUST GETTING STARTED! DID YOU SEE HOW CENTIPEDRIX TURNED THAT BUILDING INTO A RECORD PLAYER? THAT'S MONSTER ISLE INGENUITY RIGHT THERE!

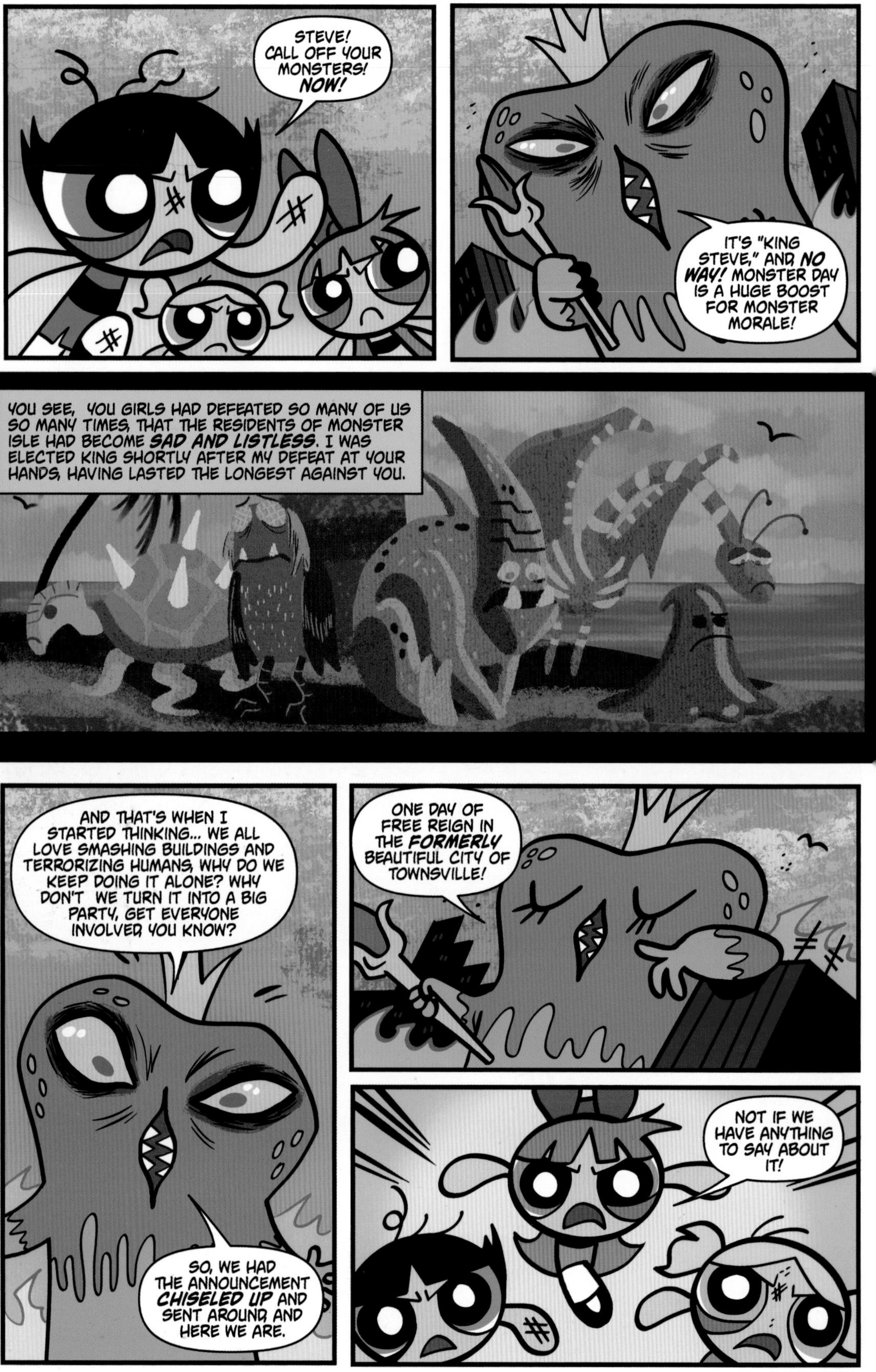
STEVE! CALL OFF YOUR MONSTERS! NOW!
IT'S "KING STEVE," AND NO WAY! MONSTER DAY IS A HUGE BOOST FOR MONSTER MORALE!
YOU SEE, YOU GIRLS HAD DEFEATED SO MANY OF US SO MANY TIMES, THAT THE RESIDENTS OF MONSTER ISLE HAD BECOME SAD AND LISTLESS. I WAS ELECTED KING SHORTLY AFTER MY DEFEAT AT YOUR HANDS, HAVING LASTED THE LONGEST AGAINST YOU.
AND THAT'S WHEN I STARTED THINKING... WE ALL LOVE SMASHING BUILDINGS AND TERRORIZING HUMANS, WHY DO WE KEEP DOING IT ALONE? WHY DON'T WE TURN IT INTO A BIG PARTY, GET EVERYONE INVOLVED YOU KNOW?
SO, WE HAD THE ANNOUNCEMENT CHISELED UP AND SENT AROUND AND HERE WE ARE.
ONE DAY OF FREE REIGN IN THE FORMERLY BEAUTIFUL CITY OF TOWNSVILLE!
NOT IF WE HAVE ANYTHING TO SAY ABOUT IT!

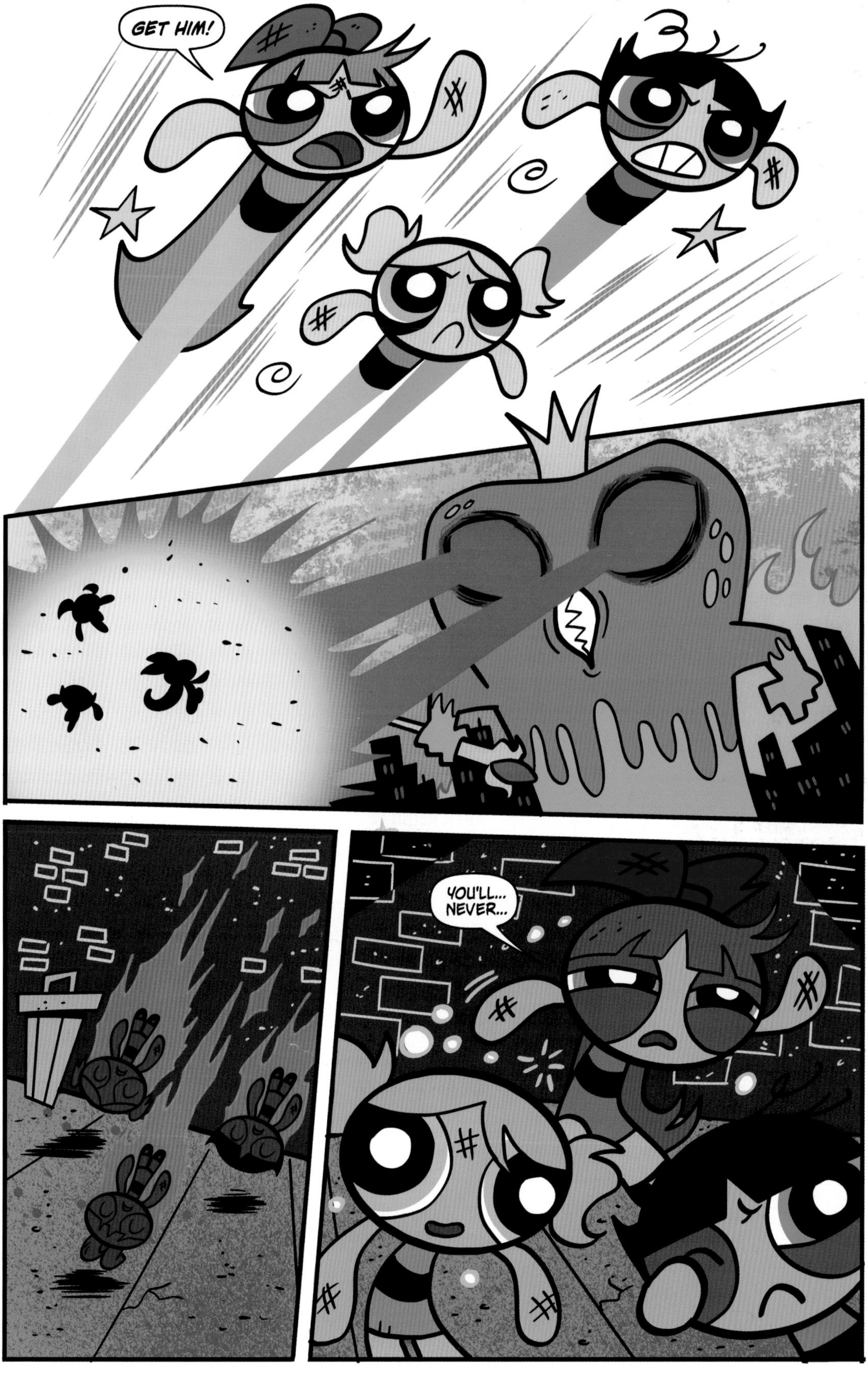
GET HIM!
YOU'LL... NEVER...

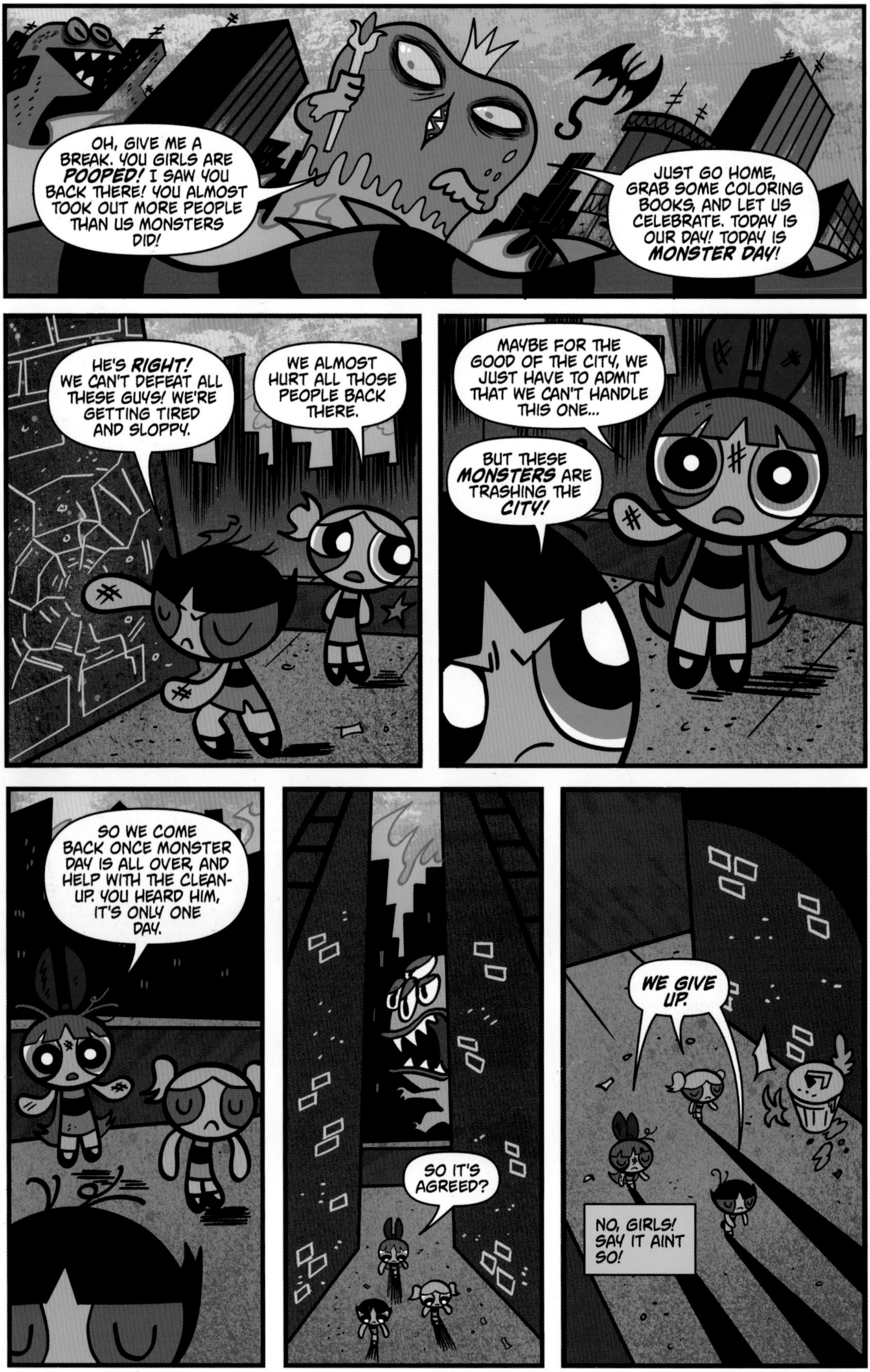
OH, GIVE ME A BREAK. YOU GIRLS ARE POOPED! I SAW YOU BACK THERE! YOU ALMOST TOOK OUT MORE PEOPLE THAN US MONSTERS DID!
JUST GO HOME, GRAB SOME COLORING BOOKS, AND LET US CELEBRATE. TODAY IS OUR DAY! TODAY IS MONSTER DAY!
HE'S RIGHT! WE CAN'T DEFEAT ALL THESE GUYS! WE'RE GETTING TIRED AND SLOPPY.
WE ALMOST HURT ALL THOSE PEOPLE BACK THERE.
MAYBE FOR THE GOOD OF THE CITY, WE JUST HAVE TO ADMIT THAT WE CAN'T HANDLE THIS ONE...
BUT THESE MONSTERS ARE TRASHING THE CITY!
SO WE COME BACK ONCE MONSTER DAY IS ALL OVER, AND HELP WITH THE CLEAN-UP. YOU HEARD HIM, IT'S ONLY ONE DAY.
SO IT'S AGREED?
WE GIVE UP.
NO, GIRLS! SAY IT AINT SO!

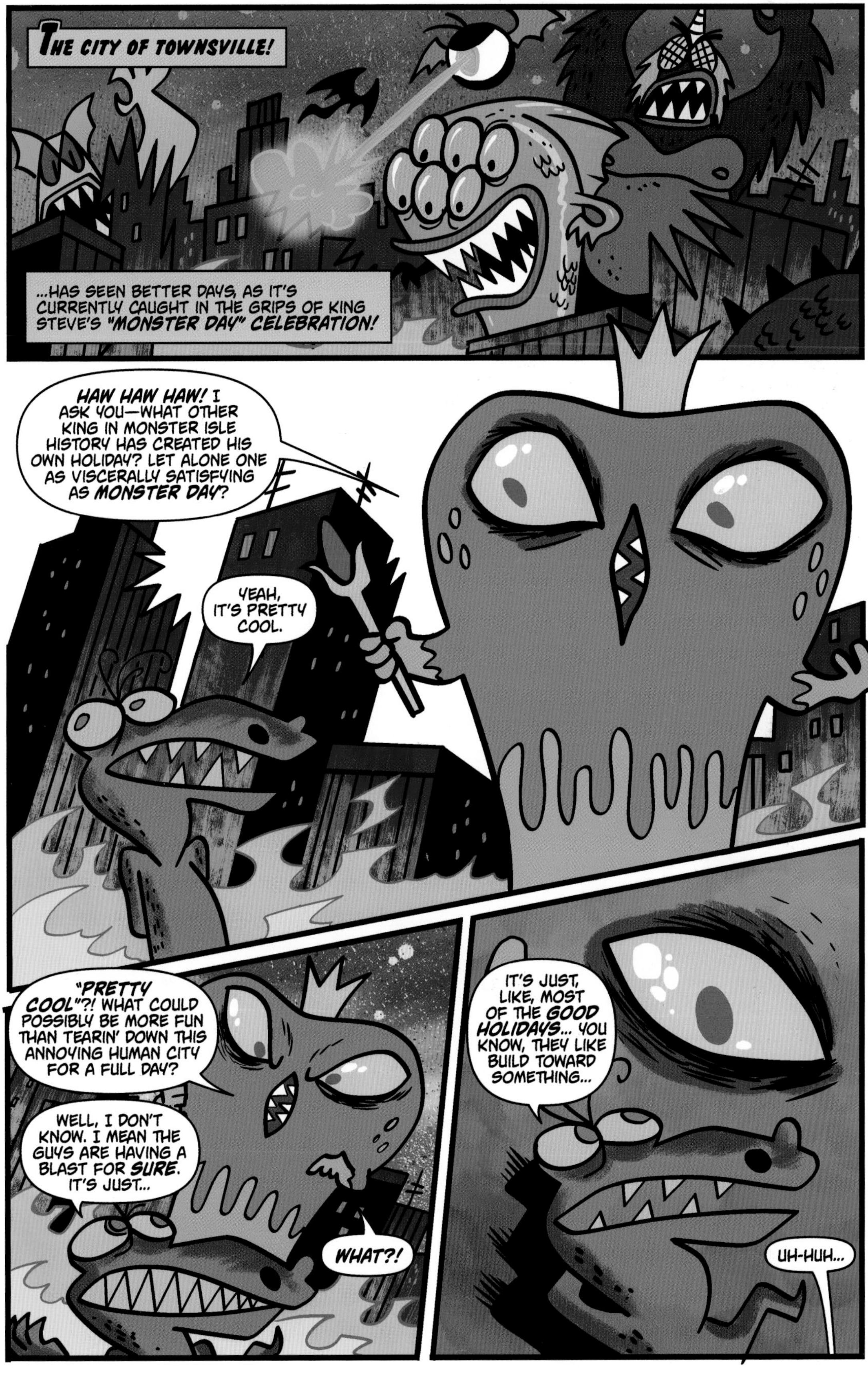
THE CITY OF TOWNSVILLE!
...HAS SEEN BETTER DAYS, AS IT'S CURRENTLY CAUGHT IN THE GRIPS OF KING STEVE'S "MONSTER DAY" CELEBRATION!
HAW HAW HAW! I ASK YOU—WHAT OTHER KING IN MONSTER ISLE HISTORY HAS CREATED HIS OWN HOLIDAY? LET ALONE ONE AS VISCERALLY SATISFYING AS MONSTER DAY?
YEAH, IT'S PRETTY COOL.
"PRETTY COOL"?! WHAT COULD POSSIBLY BE MORE FUN THAN TEARIN' DOWN THIS ANNOYING HUMAN CITY FOR A FULL DAY?
WELL, I DON'T KNOW. I MEAN THE GUYS ARE HAVING A BLAST FOR SURE. IT'S JUST...
WHAT?!
IT'S JUST, LIKE, MOST OF THE GOOD HOLIDAYS... YOU KNOW, THEY LIKE BUILD TOWARD SOMETHING...
UH-HUH...

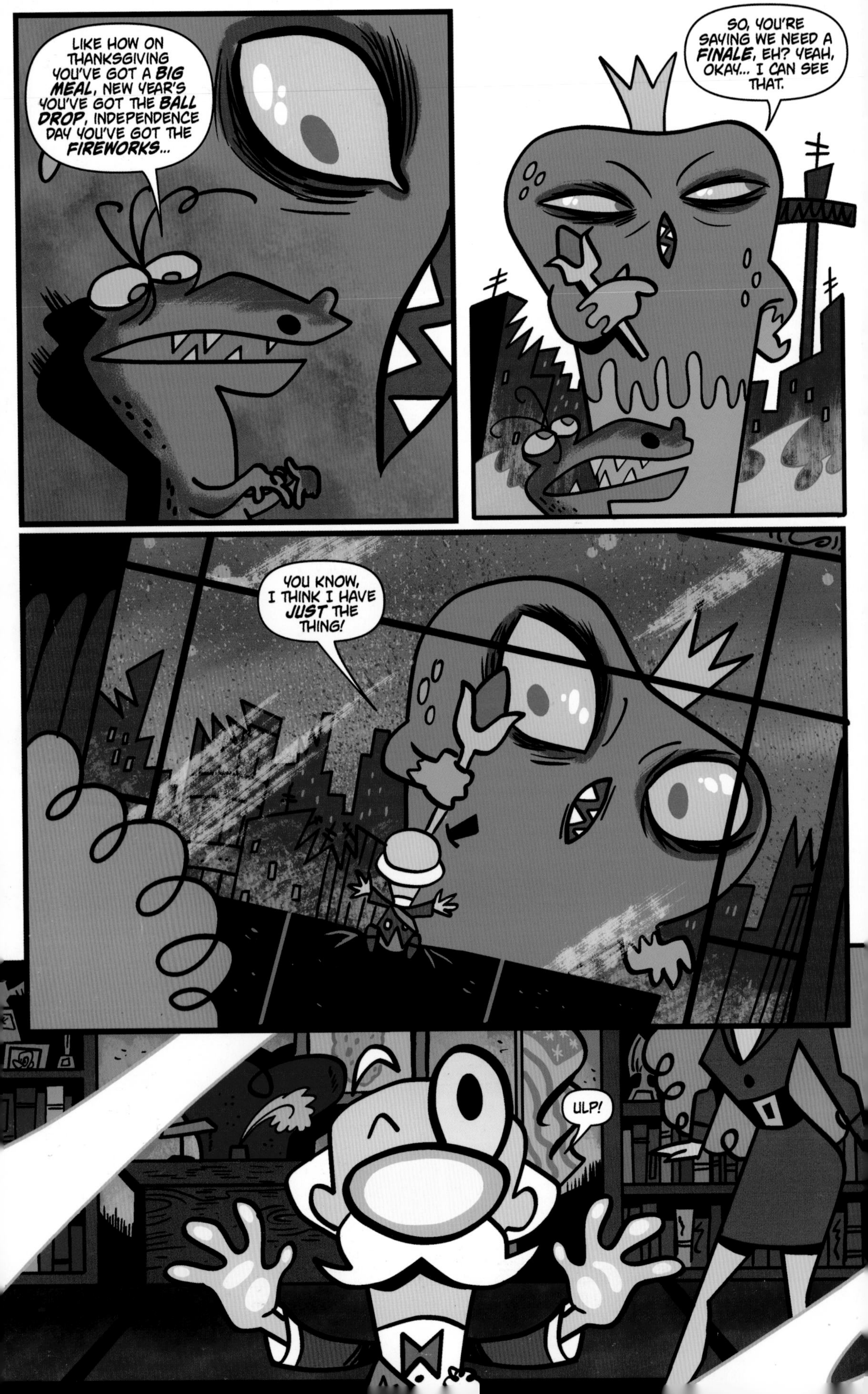
LIKE HOW ON THANKSGIVING YOU'VE GOT A BIG MEAL, NEW YEAR'S YOU'VE GOT THE BALL DROP, INDEPENDENCE DAY YOU'VE GOT THE FIREWORKS...
SO, YOU'RE SAYING WE NEED A FINALE, EH? YEAH, OKAY... I CAN SEE THAT.
YOU KNOW, I THINK I HAVE JUST THE THING!
ULP!

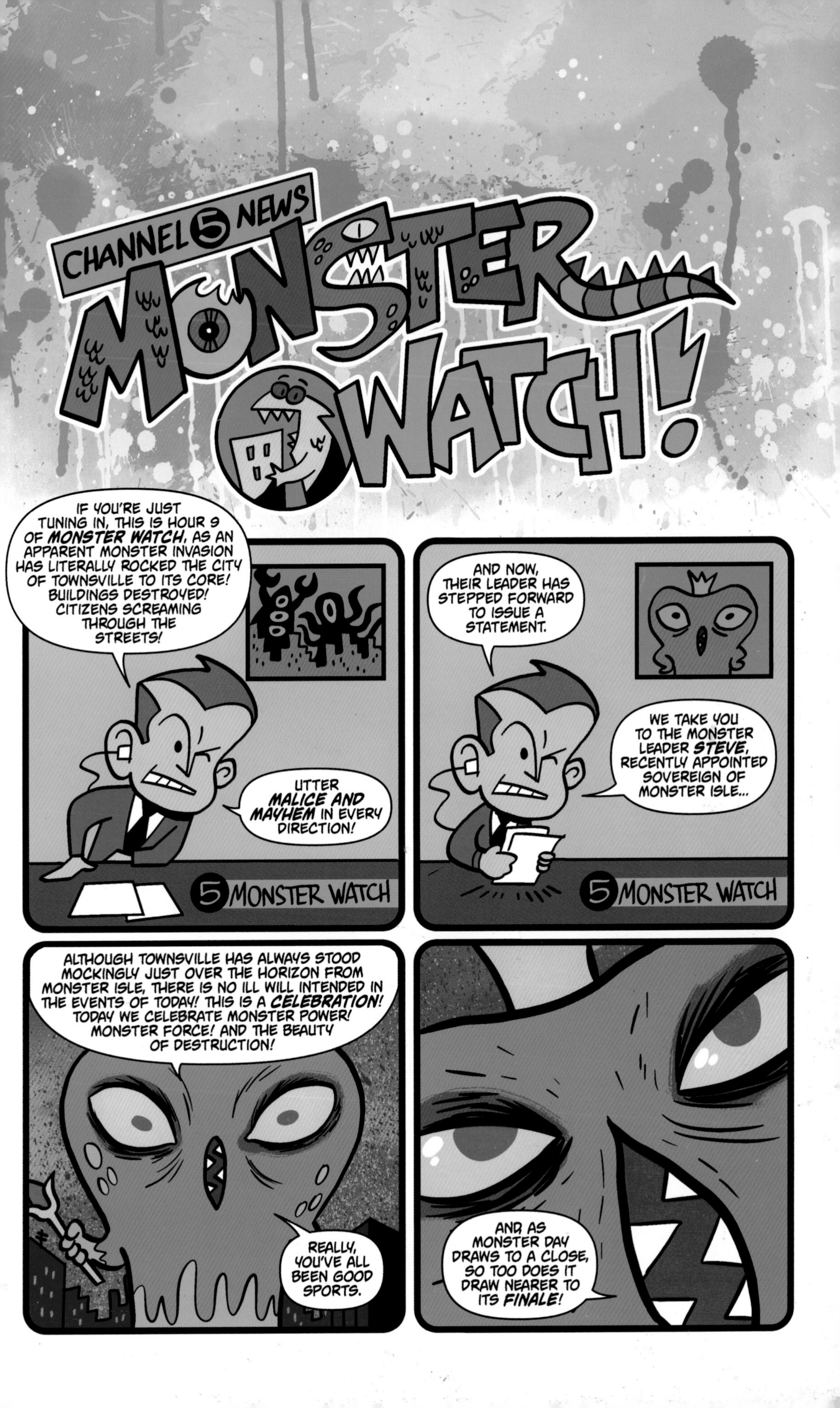
CHANNEL 5 NEWS
MONSTER WATCH!
IF YOU'RE JUST TUNING IN, THIS IS HOUR 9 OF *MONSTER WATCH*, AS AN APPARENT MONSTER INVASION HAS LITERALLY ROCKED THE CITY OF TOWNSVILLE TO ITS CORE! BUILDINGS DESTROYED! CITIZENS SCREAMING THROUGH THE STREETS!
UTTER *MALICE AND MAYHEM* IN EVERY DIRECTION!
5 MONSTER WATCH
AND NOW, THEIR LEADER HAS STEPPED FORWARD TO ISSUE A STATEMENT.
WE TAKE YOU TO THE MONSTER LEADER *STEVE*, RECENTLY APPOINTED SOVEREIGN OF MONSTER ISLE...
5 MONSTER WATCH
ALTHOUGH TOWNSVILLE HAS ALWAYS STOOD MOCKINGLY JUST OVER THE HORIZON FROM MONSTER ISLE, THERE IS NO ILL WILL INTENDED IN THE EVENTS OF TODAY! THIS IS A *CELEBRATION*! TODAY WE CELEBRATE MONSTER POWER! MONSTER FORCE! AND THE BEAUTY OF DESTRUCTION!
REALLY, YOU'VE ALL BEEN GOOD SPORTS.
AND AS MONSTER DAY DRAWS TO A CLOSE, SO TOO DOES IT DRAW NEARER TO ITS *FINALE*!

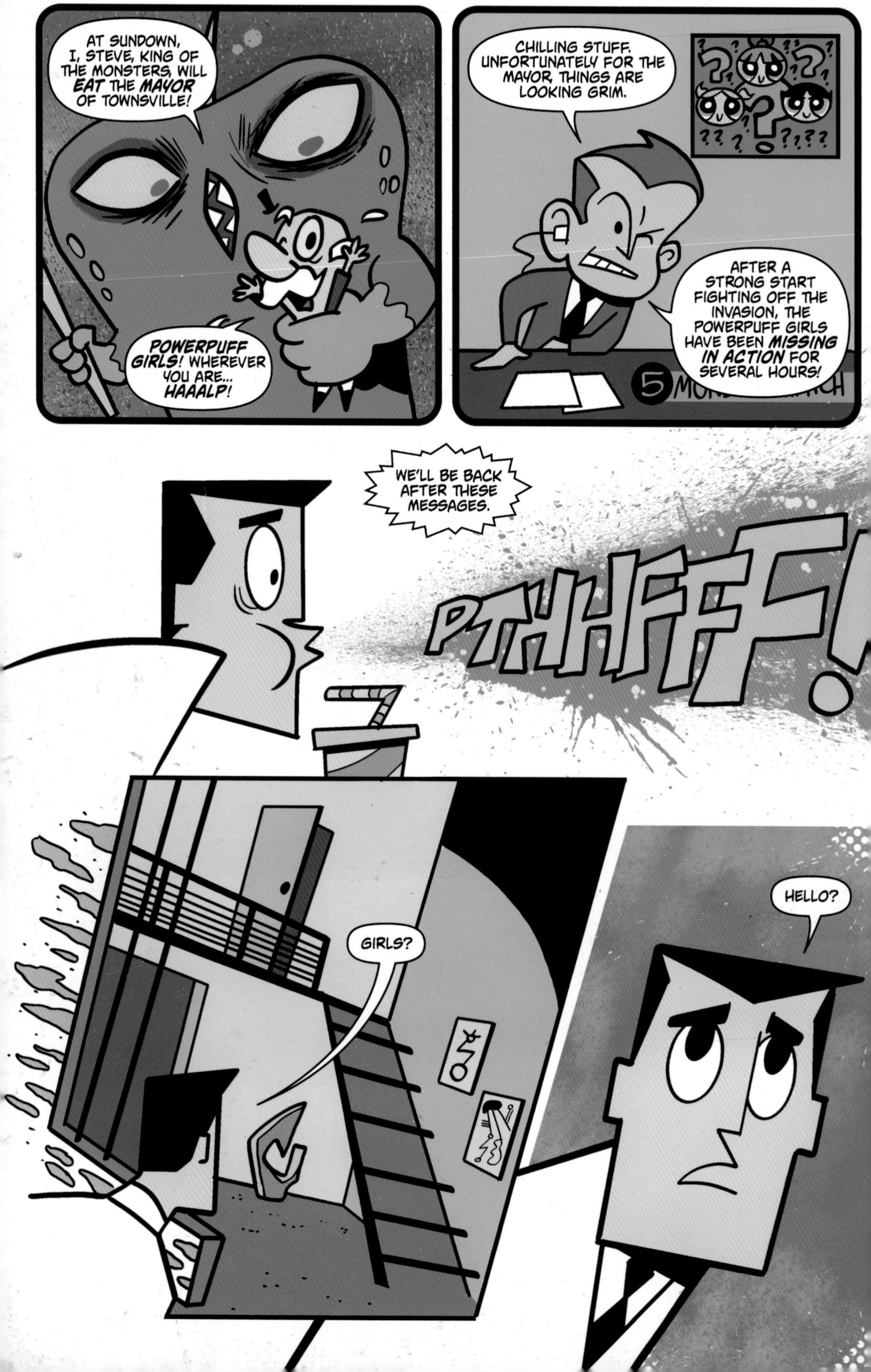
AT SUNDOWN, I, STEVE, KING OF THE MONSTERS, WILL EAT THE MAYOR OF TOWNSVILLE!
POWERPUFF GIRLS! WHEREVER YOU ARE... HAAALP!
CHILLING STUFF. UNFORTUNATELY FOR THE MAYOR, THINGS ARE LOOKING GRIM.
AFTER A STRONG START FIGHTING OFF THE INVASION, THE POWERPUFF GIRLS HAVE BEEN MISSING IN ACTION FOR SEVERAL HOURS!
WE'LL BE BACK AFTER THESE MESSAGES.
PTHHFFF!
GIRLS?
HELLO?

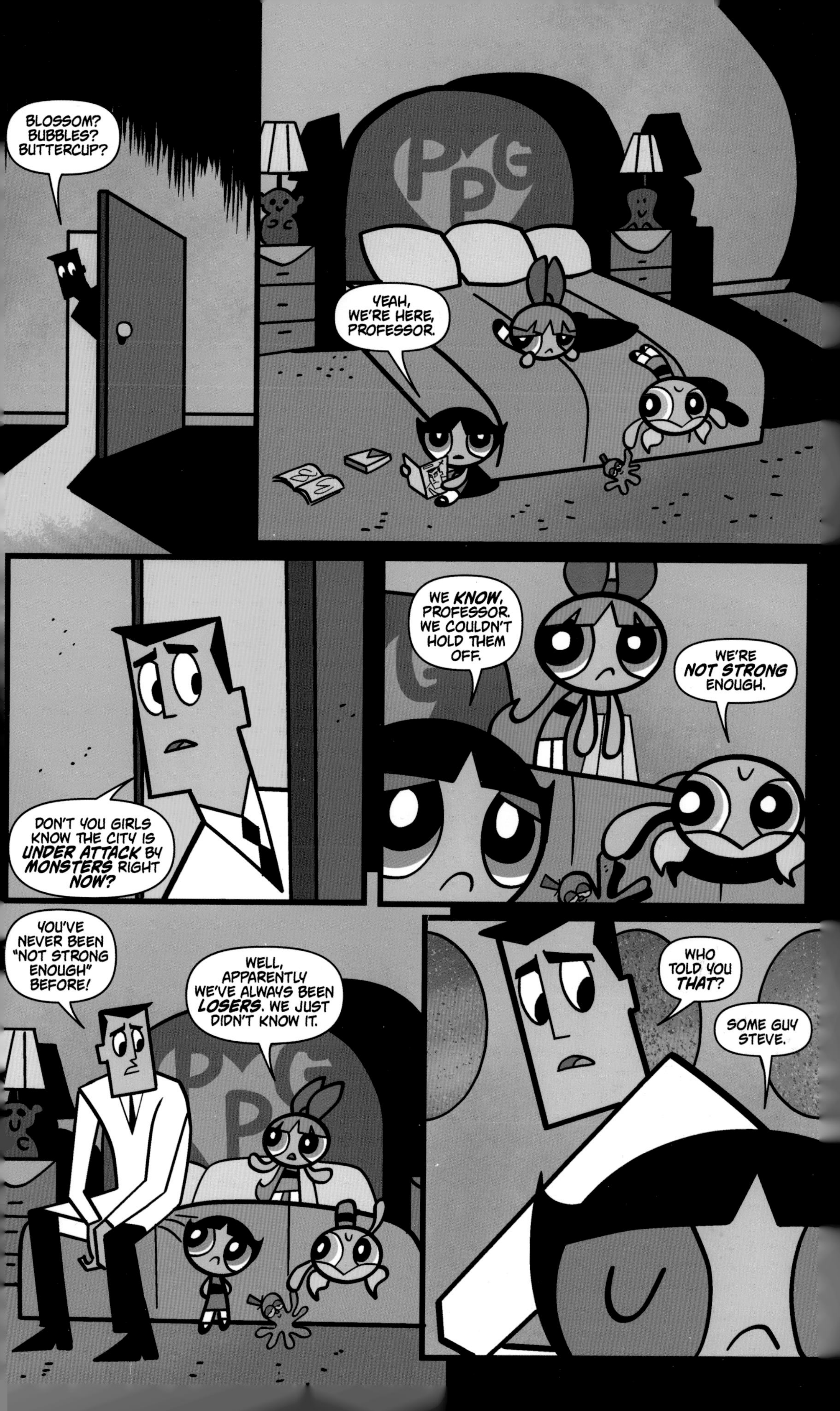
BLOSSOM? BUBBLES? BUTTERCUP?
YEAH, WE'RE HERE, PROFESSOR.
DON'T YOU GIRLS KNOW THE CITY IS UNDER ATTACK BY MONSTERS RIGHT NOW?
WE KNOW, PROFESSOR. WE COULDN'T HOLD THEM OFF.
WE'RE NOT STRONG ENOUGH.
YOU'VE NEVER BEEN "NOT STRONG ENOUGH" BEFORE!
WELL, APPARENTLY WE'VE ALWAYS BEEN LOSERS. WE JUST DIDN'T KNOW IT.
WHO TOLD YOU THAT?
SOME GUY STEVE.

WELL, I DON'T WANT YOU LISTENING TO "SOME GUY STEVE." YOU'RE THE POWERPUFF GIRLS! YOU'RE SUPERHEROES!

IT WAS A MESS OUT THERE, PROFESSOR. IT'S BETTER FOR EVERYONE IF WE JUST LAY LOW UNTIL THIS WHOLE THING IS OVER.

WELL! THE GIRLS I KNOW WOULD NEVER GIVE UP ON TOWNSVILLE JUST BECAUSE "SOME GUY STEVE" SAID SO!

THE GIRLS I KNOW CAN SOLVE ANY PROBLEM USING THEIR BRAINS... AND THEIR HEARTS.

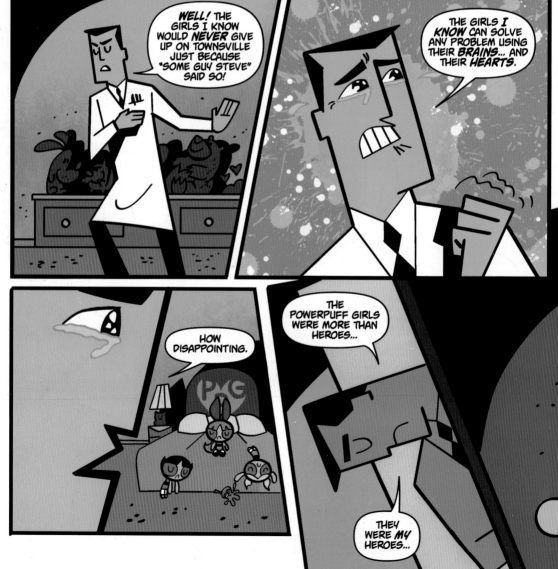

HOW DISAPPOINTING.

THE POWERPUFF GIRLS WERE MORE THAN HEROES...

THEY WERE MY HEROES...

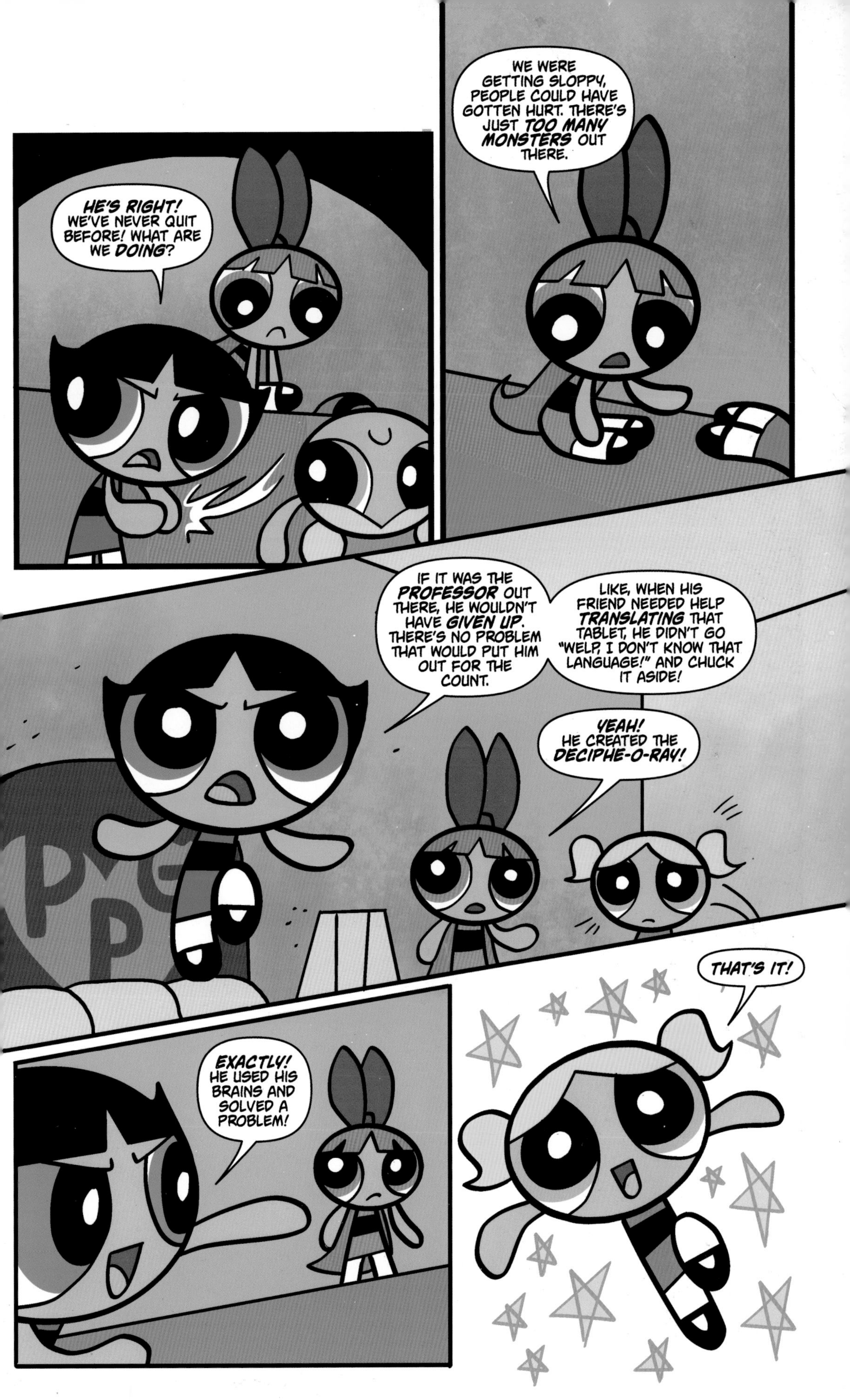
HE'S RIGHT! WE'VE NEVER QUIT BEFORE! WHAT ARE WE DOING?
WE WERE GETTING SLOPPY, PEOPLE COULD HAVE GOTTEN HURT. THERE'S JUST TOO MANY MONSTERS OUT THERE.
IF IT WAS THE PROFESSOR OUT THERE, HE WOULDN'T HAVE GIVEN UP. THERE'S NO PROBLEM THAT WOULD PUT HIM OUT FOR THE COUNT.
LIKE, WHEN HIS FRIEND NEEDED HELP TRANSLATING THAT TABLET, HE DIDN'T GO "WELP, I DON'T KNOW THAT LANGUAGE!" AND CHUCK IT ASIDE!
YEAH! HE CREATED THE DECIPHE-O-RAY!
EXACTLY! HE USED HIS BRAINS AND SOLVED A PROBLEM!
THAT'S IT!

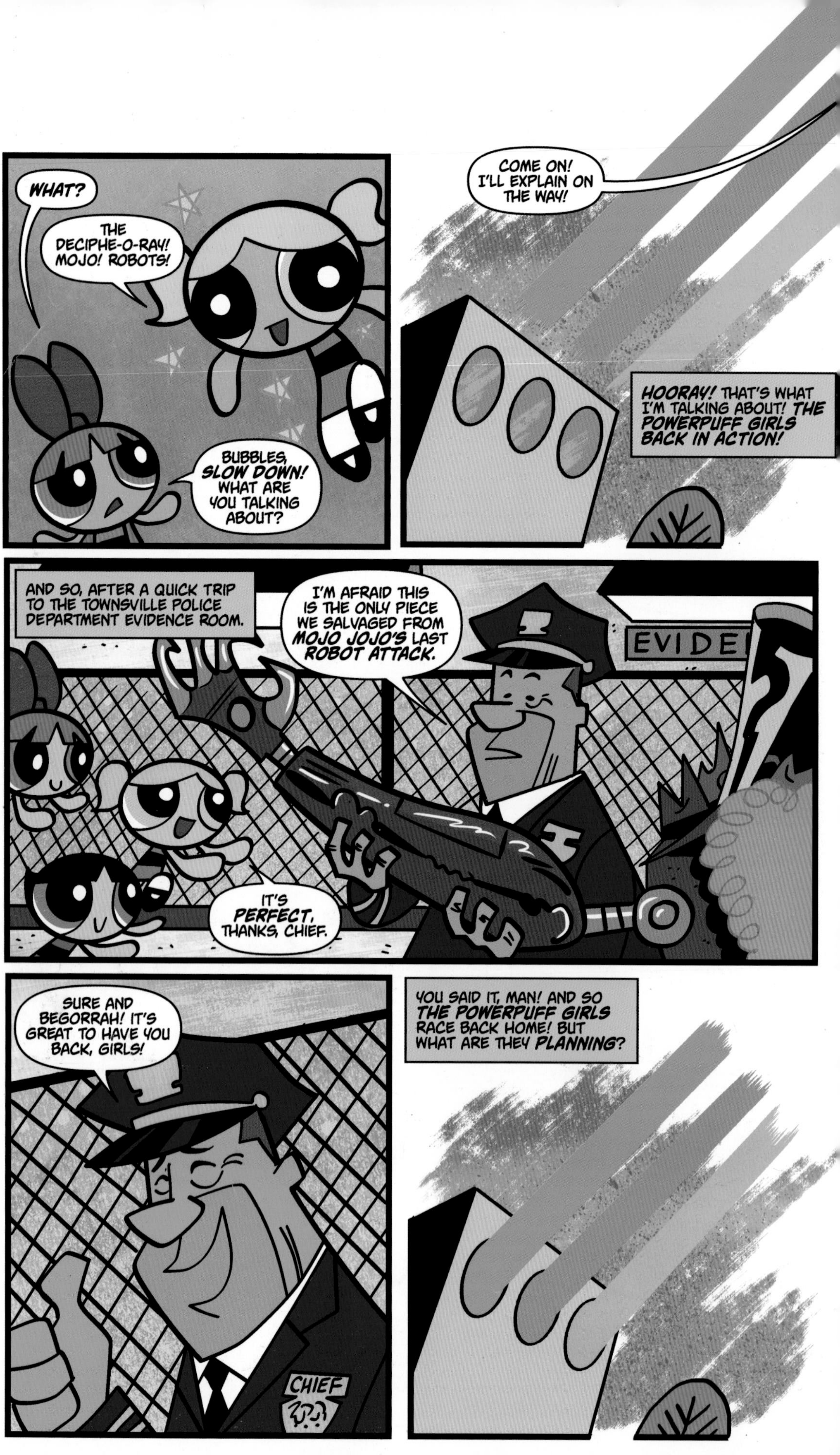
WHAT?
THE DECIPHE-O-RAY! MOJO! ROBOTS!
BUBBLES, SLOW DOWN! WHAT ARE YOU TALKING ABOUT?
COME ON! I'LL EXPLAIN ON THE WAY!
HOORAY! THAT'S WHAT I'M TALKING ABOUT! THE POWERPUFF GIRLS BACK IN ACTION!
AND SO, AFTER A QUICK TRIP TO THE TOWNSVILLE POLICE DEPARTMENT EVIDENCE ROOM.
I'M AFRAID THIS IS THE ONLY PIECE WE SALVAGED FROM MOJO JOJO'S LAST ROBOT ATTACK.
EVIDE
IT'S PERFECT, THANKS, CHIEF.
SURE AND BEGORRAH! IT'S GREAT TO HAVE YOU BACK, GIRLS!
CHIEF
YOU SAID IT, MAN! AND SO THE POWERPUFF GIRLS RACE BACK HOME! BUT WHAT ARE THEY PLANNING?

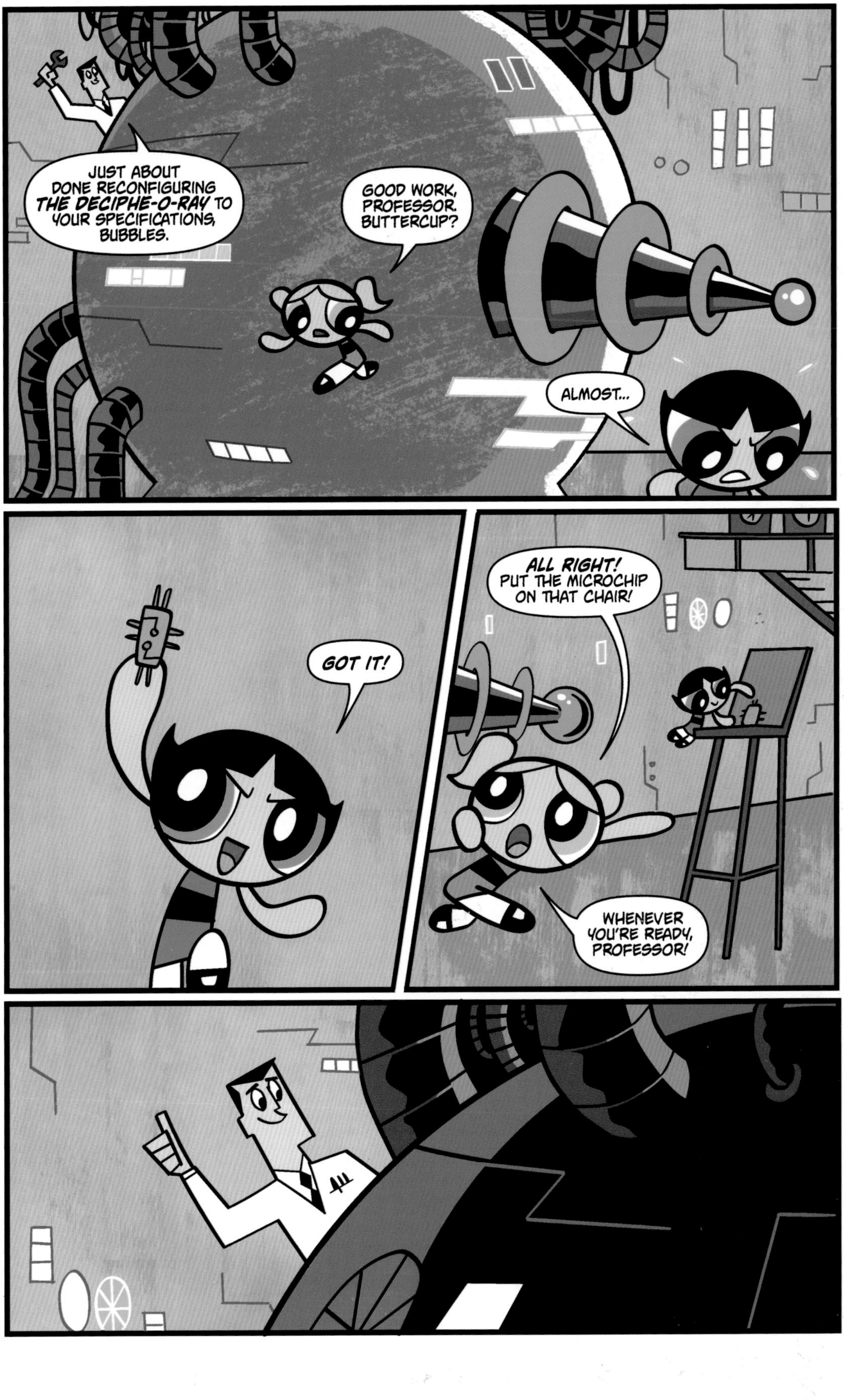
JUST ABOUT DONE RECONFIGURING THE DECIPHE-O-RAY TO YOUR SPECIFICATIONS, BUBBLES.
GOOD WORK, PROFESSOR. BUTTERCUP?
ALMOST...
GOT IT!
ALL RIGHT! PUT THE MICROCHIP ON THAT CHAIR!
WHENEVER YOU'RE READY, PROFESSOR!

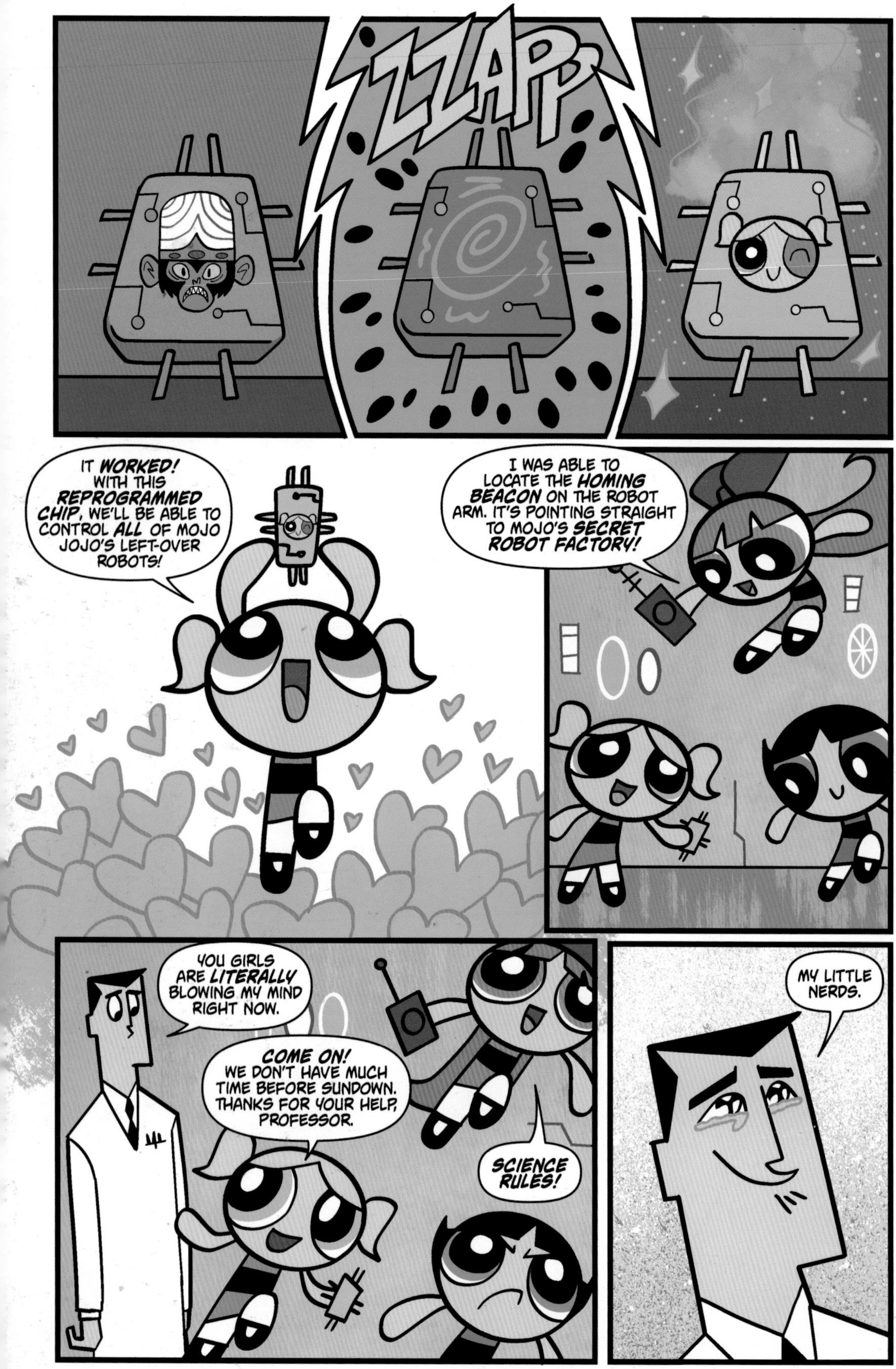
ZZAPP
IT WORKED! WITH THIS REPROGRAMMED CHIP, WE'LL BE ABLE TO CONTROL ALL OF MOJO JOJO'S LEFT-OVER ROBOTS!
I WAS ABLE TO LOCATE THE HOMING BEACON ON THE ROBOT ARM. IT'S POINTING STRAIGHT TO MOJO'S SECRET ROBOT FACTORY!
YOU GIRLS ARE LITERALLY BLOWING MY MIND RIGHT NOW.
COME ON! WE DON'T HAVE MUCH TIME BEFORE SUNDOWN. THANKS FOR YOUR HELP, PROFESSOR.
SCIENCE RULES!
MY LITTLE NERDS.

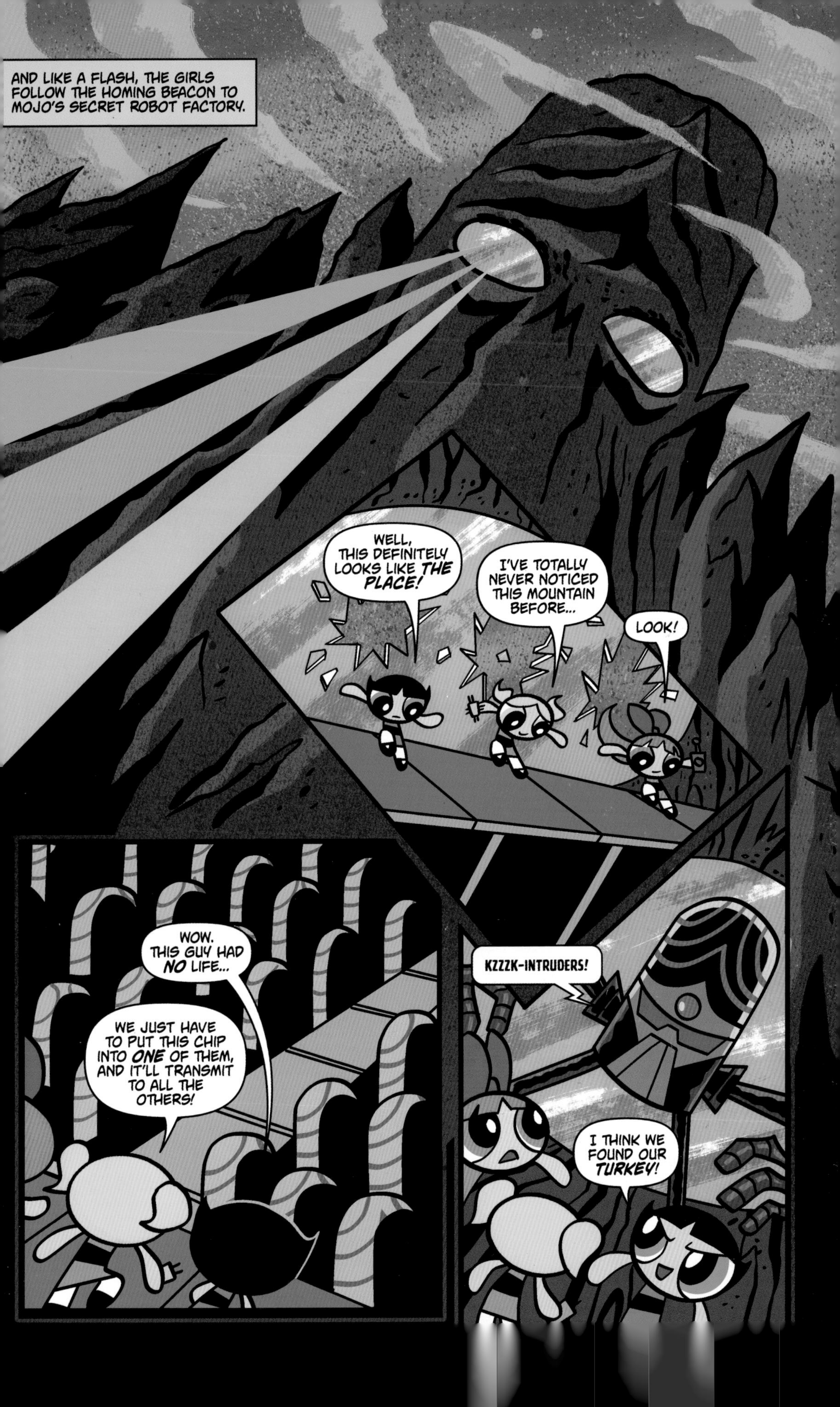
AND LIKE A FLASH, THE GIRLS FOLLOW THE HOMING BEACON TO MOJO'S SECRET ROBOT FACTORY.
WELL, THIS DEFINITELY LOOKS LIKE THE PLACE!
I'VE TOTALLY NEVER NOTICED THIS MOUNTAIN BEFORE...
LOOK!
WOW. THIS GUY HAD NO LIFE...
WE JUST HAVE TO PUT THIS CHIP INTO ONE OF THEM, AND IT'LL TRANSMIT TO ALL THE OTHERS!
KZZZK-INTRUDERS!
I THINK WE FOUND OUR TURKEY!

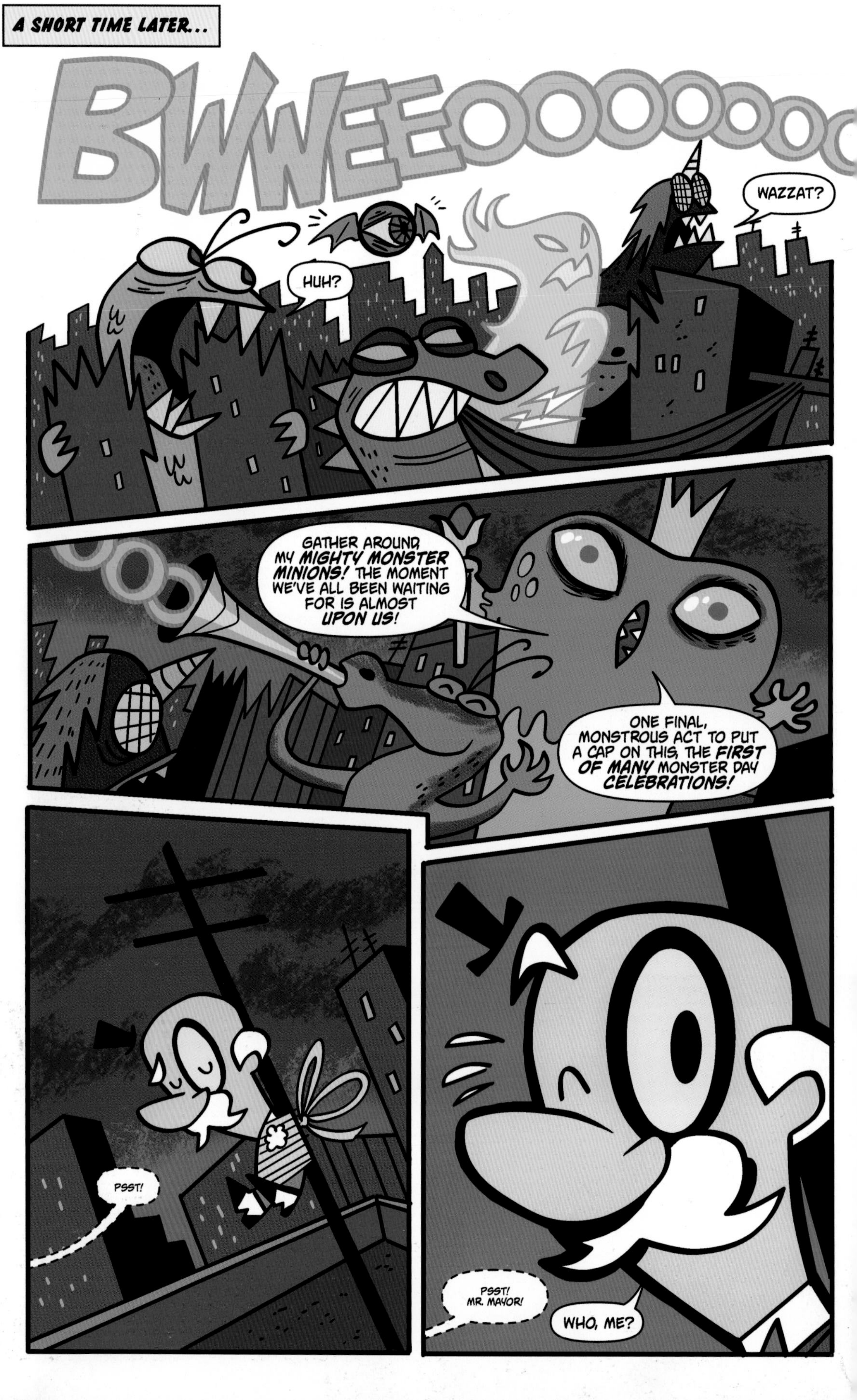
A SHORT TIME LATER...
BWWEEOOOOOOO
HUH?
WAZZAT?
GATHER AROUND, MY MIGHTY MONSTER MINIONS! THE MOMENT WE'VE ALL BEEN WAITING FOR IS ALMOST UPON US!
ONE FINAL, MONSTROUS ACT TO PUT A CAP ON THIS, THE FIRST OF MANY MONSTER DAY CELEBRATIONS!
PSST!
PSST! MR. MAYOR!
WHO, ME?

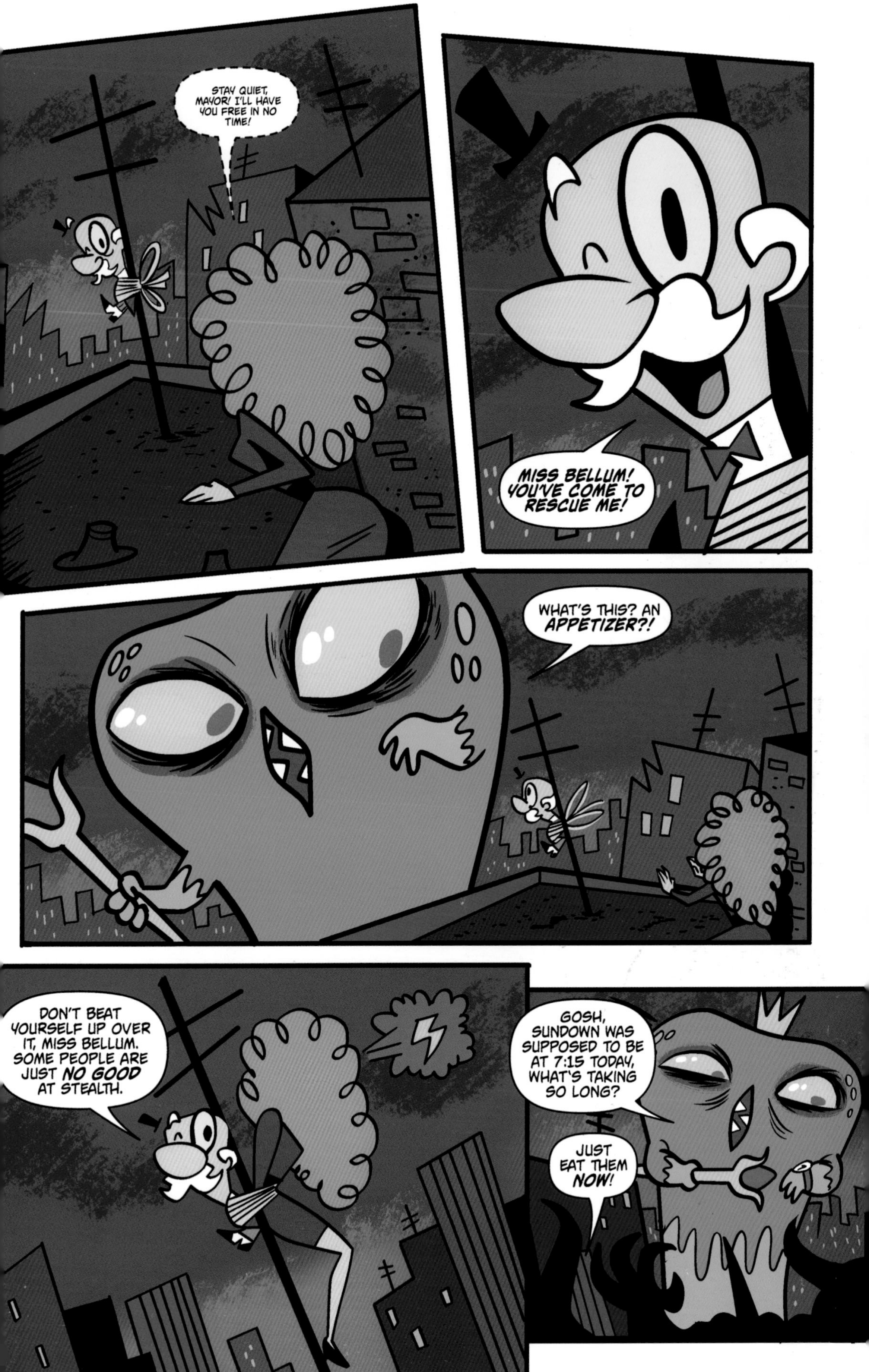
STAY QUIET, MAYOR! I'LL HAVE YOU FREE IN NO TIME!
MISS BELLUM! YOU'VE COME TO RESCUE ME!
WHAT'S THIS? AN APPETIZER?!
DON'T BEAT YOURSELF UP OVER IT, MISS BELLUM. SOME PEOPLE ARE JUST NO GOOD AT STEALTH.
GOSH, SUNDOWN WAS SUPPOSED TO BE AT 7:15 TODAY, WHAT'S TAKING SO LONG?
JUST EAT THEM NOW!

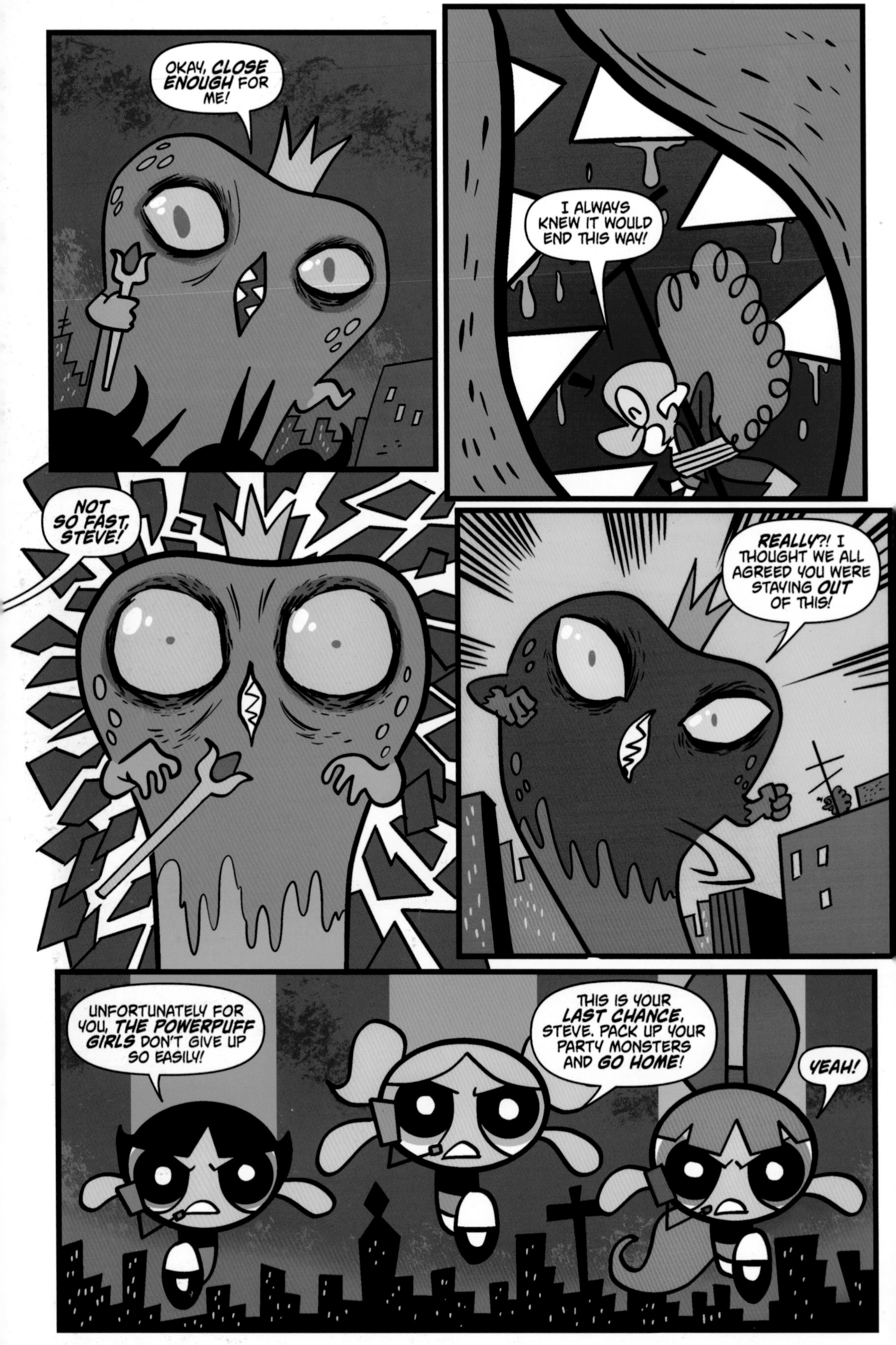
OKAY, CLOSE ENOUGH FOR ME!
I ALWAYS KNEW IT WOULD END THIS WAY!
NOT SO FAST, STEVE!
REALLY?! I THOUGHT WE ALL AGREED YOU WERE STAYING OUT OF THIS!
UNFORTUNATELY FOR YOU, THE POWERPUFF GIRLS DON'T GIVE UP SO EASILY!
THIS IS YOUR LAST CHANCE, STEVE. PACK UP YOUR PARTY MONSTERS AND GO HOME!
YEAH!

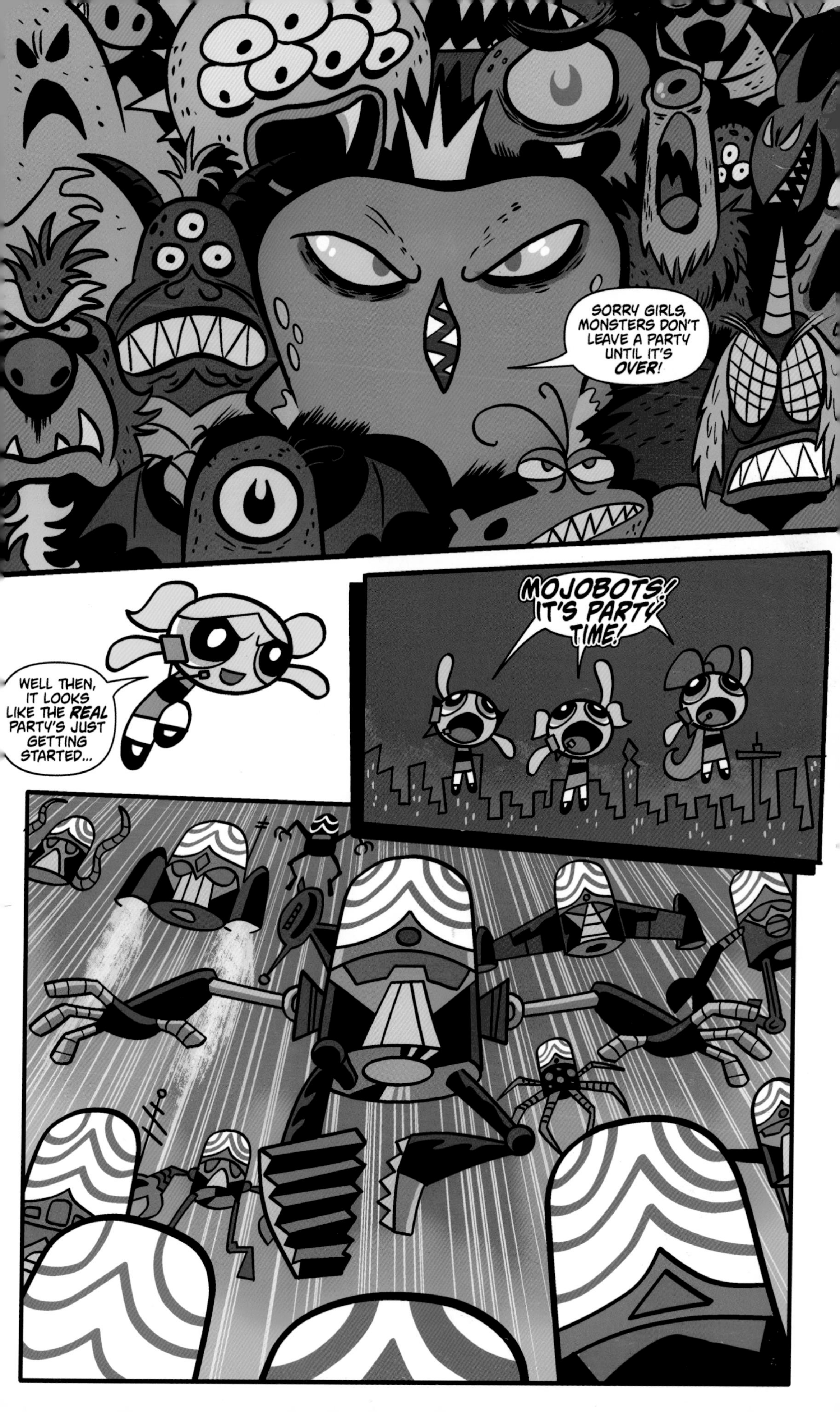
SORRY GIRLS, MONSTERS DON'T LEAVE A PARTY UNTIL IT'S OVER!
WELL THEN, IT LOOKS LIKE THE REAL PARTY'S JUST GETTING STARTED...
MOJOBOTS! IT'S PARTY TIME!

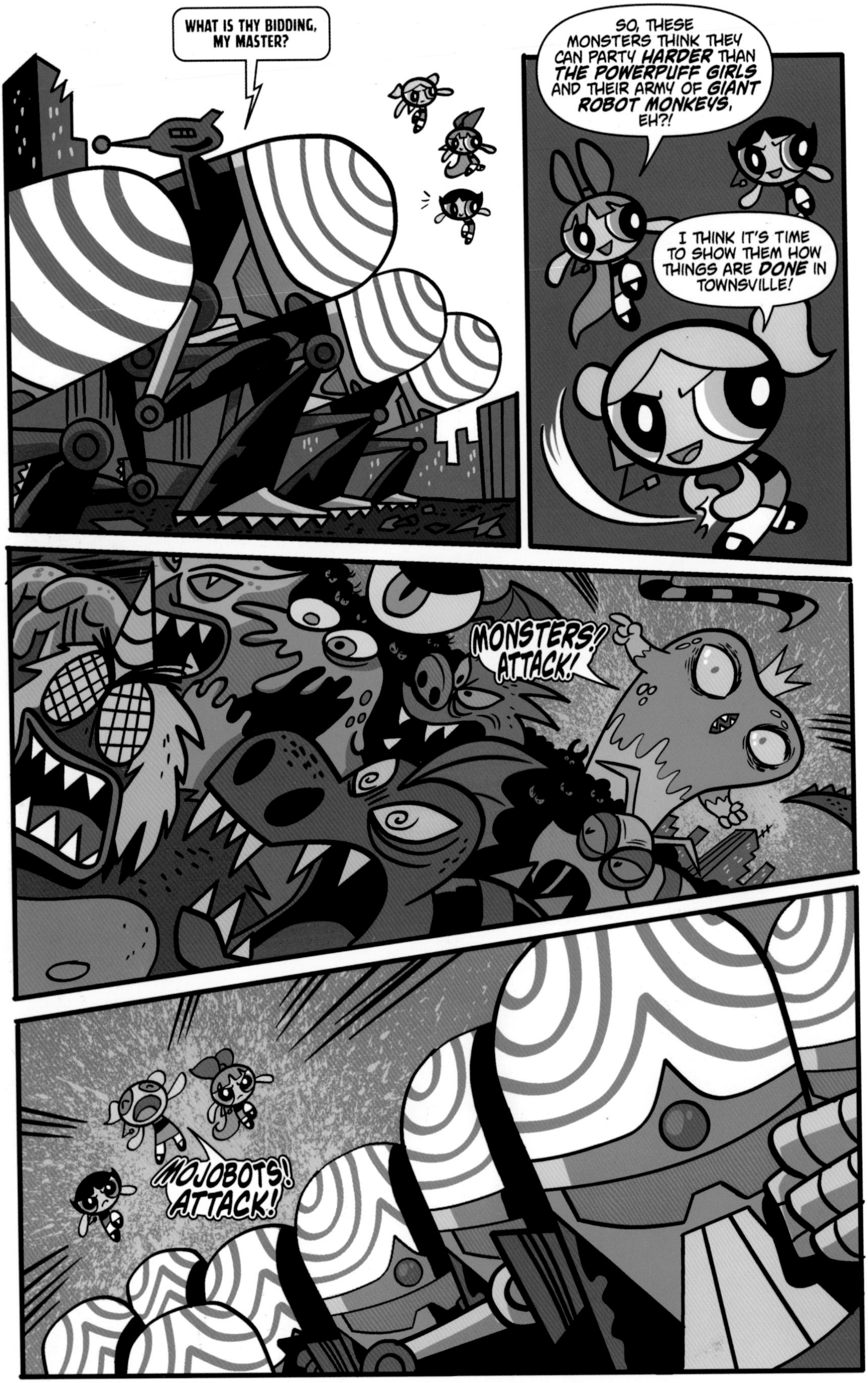
WHAT IS THY BIDDING, MY MASTER?
SO, THESE MONSTERS THINK THEY CAN PARTY HARDER THAN THE POWERPUFF GIRLS AND THEIR ARMY OF GIANT ROBOT MONKEYS, EH?!
I THINK IT'S TIME TO SHOW THEM HOW THINGS ARE DONE IN TOWNSVILLE!
MONSTERS! ATTACK!
MOJOBOTS! ATTACK!

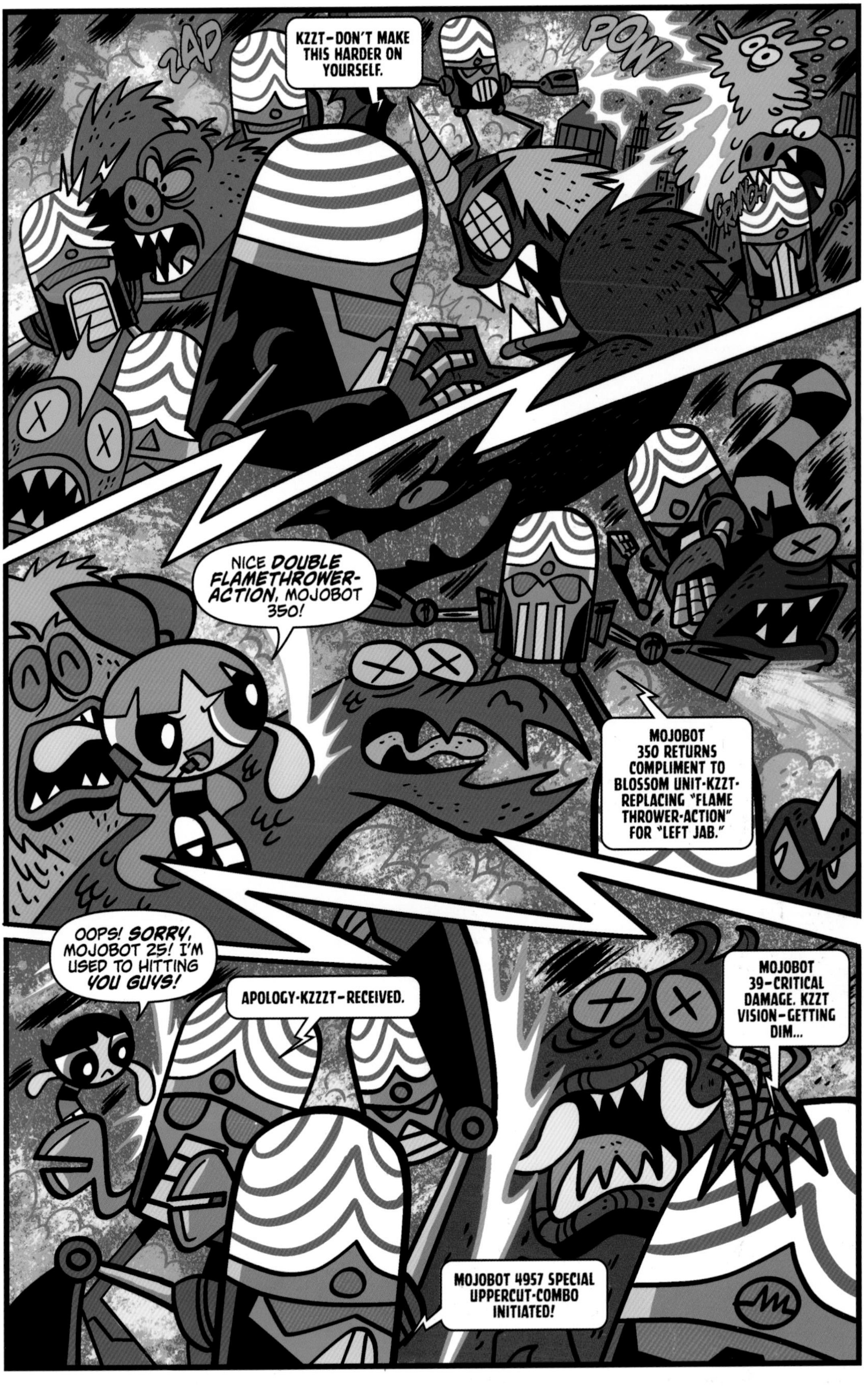
ZAP
KZZT–DON'T MAKE THIS HARDER ON YOURSELF.
POW
CRUNCH
NICE DOUBLE FLAMETHROWER-ACTION, MOJOBOT 350!
MOJOBOT 350 RETURNS COMPLIMENT TO BLOSSOM UNIT-KZZT-REPLACING "FLAME THROWER-ACTION" FOR "LEFT JAB."
OOPS! SORRY, MOJOBOT 25! I'M USED TO HITTING YOU GUYS!
APOLOGY-KZZZT–RECEIVED.
MOJOBOT 39–CRITICAL DAMAGE. KZZT VISION–GETTING DIM...
MOJOBOT 4957 SPECIAL UPPERCUT-COMBO INITIATED!

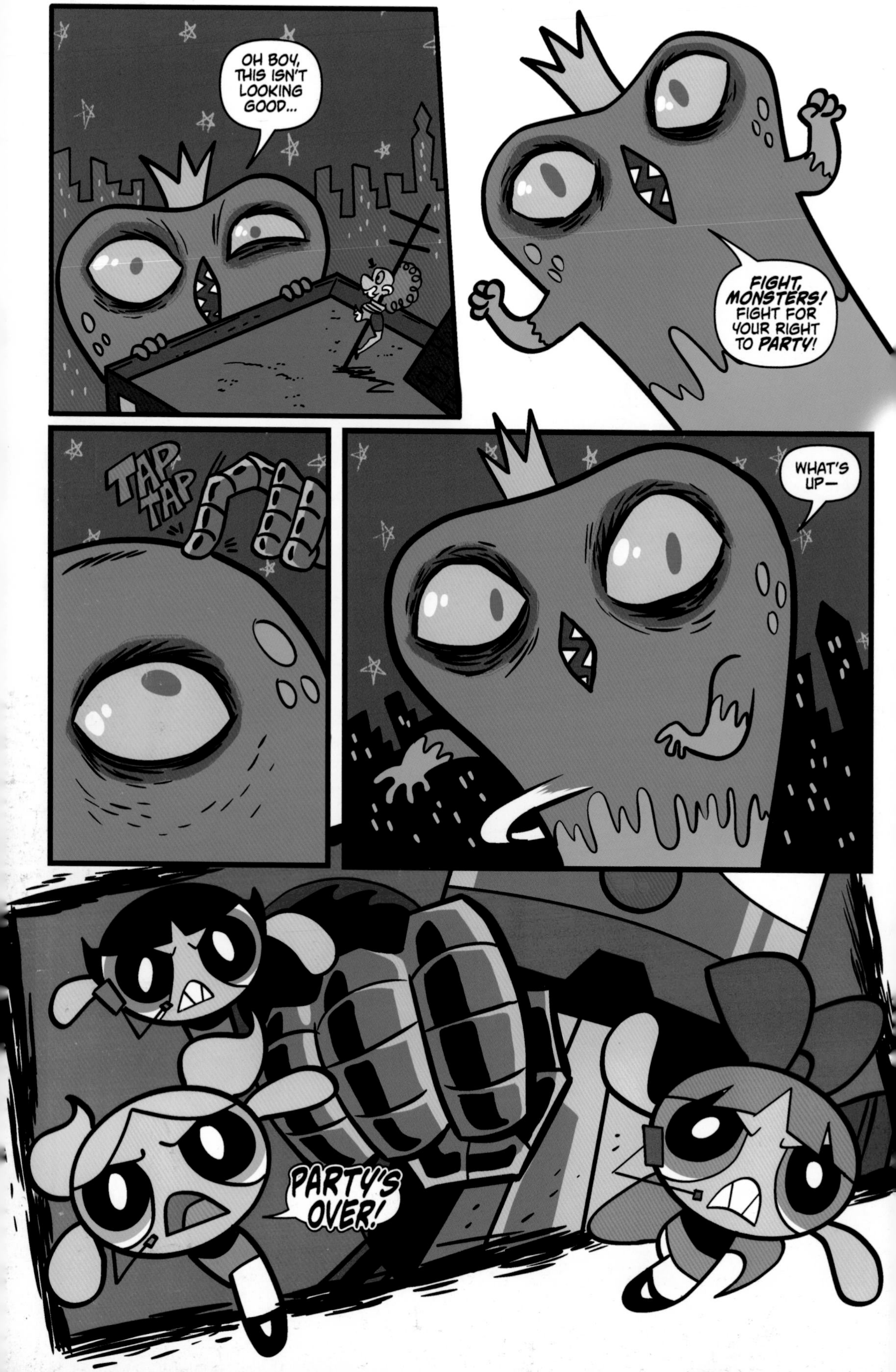
OH BOY, THIS ISN'T LOOKING GOOD...
FIGHT, MONSTERS! FIGHT FOR YOUR RIGHT TO PARTY!
TAP TAP
WHAT'S UP—
PARTY'S OVER!

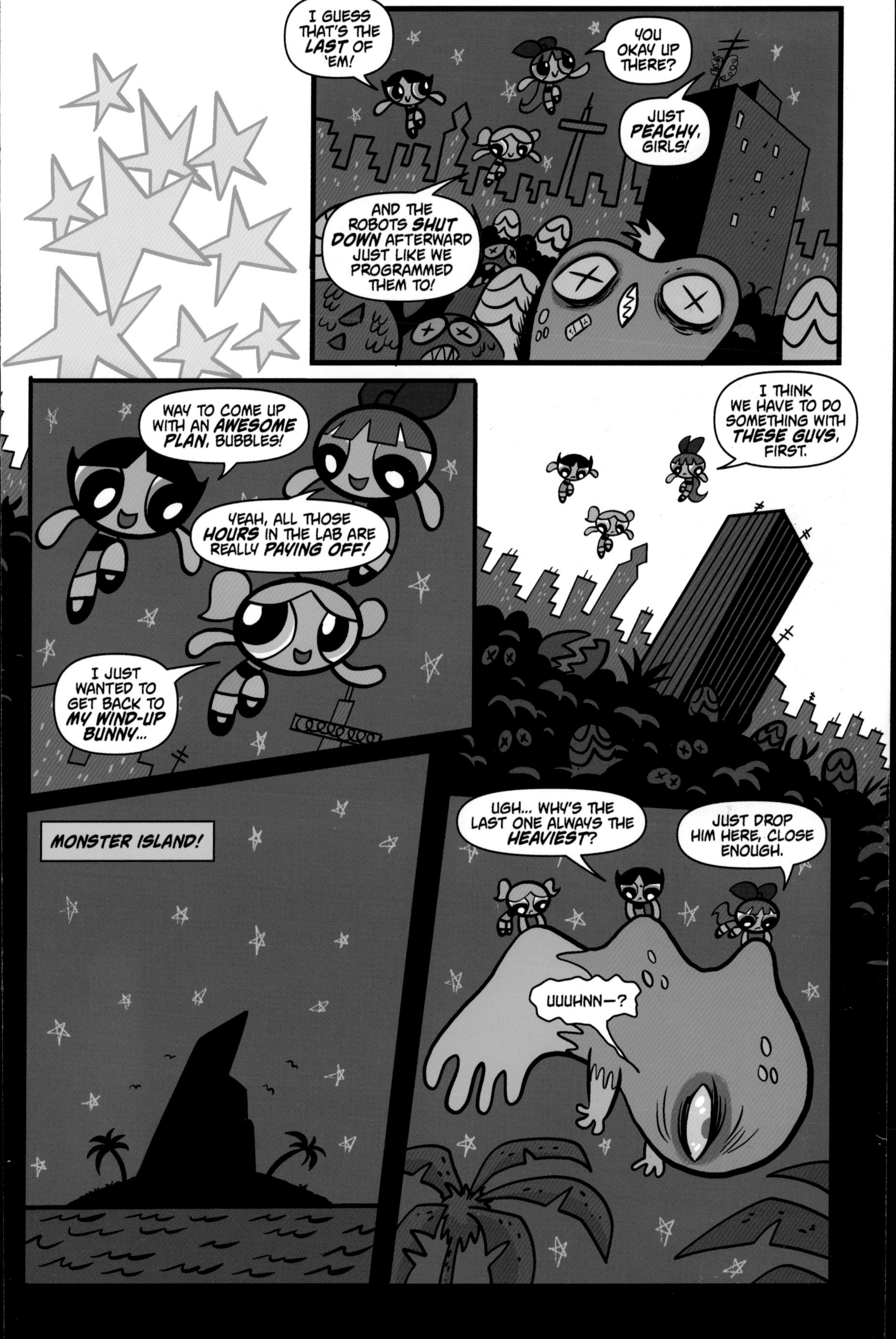
I GUESS THAT'S THE LAST OF 'EM!
YOU OKAY UP THERE?
JUST PEACHY, GIRLS!
AND THE ROBOTS SHUT DOWN AFTERWARD JUST LIKE WE PROGRAMMED THEM TO!
WAY TO COME UP WITH AN AWESOME PLAN, BUBBLES!
YEAH, ALL THOSE HOURS IN THE LAB ARE REALLY PAYING OFF!
I JUST WANTED TO GET BACK TO MY WIND-UP BUNNY...
I THINK WE HAVE TO DO SOMETHING WITH THESE GUYS, FIRST.
MONSTER ISLAND!
UGH... WHY'S THE LAST ONE ALWAYS THE HEAVIEST?
JUST DROP HIM HERE, CLOSE ENOUGH.
UUUHNN—?

OOF!

WAPP!

NOW FELLAS, I KNOW IT ALL KIND OF *FELL APART* AT THE END THERE...

GRRRRRRR

ALL RIGHT, GUYS! DON'T LOSE YOUR COOL! I *SAID I WAS SORRY!*

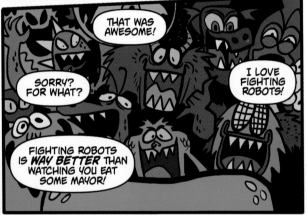

THAT WAS AWESOME!

SORRY? FOR WHAT?

I LOVE FIGHTING ROBOTS!

FIGHTING ROBOTS IS *WAY BETTER* THAN WATCHING YOU EAT SOME MAYOR!

OH... HAHA...

I GUESS WE'D BETTER *START PLANNING* FOR *NEXT YEAR!*

STEVE!!

STEVE!!

STEVE!!

STEVE!!

AND THUS THE DAY IS *SAVED!*

...FOR NOW...

BY *THE POWERPUFF GIRLS!*

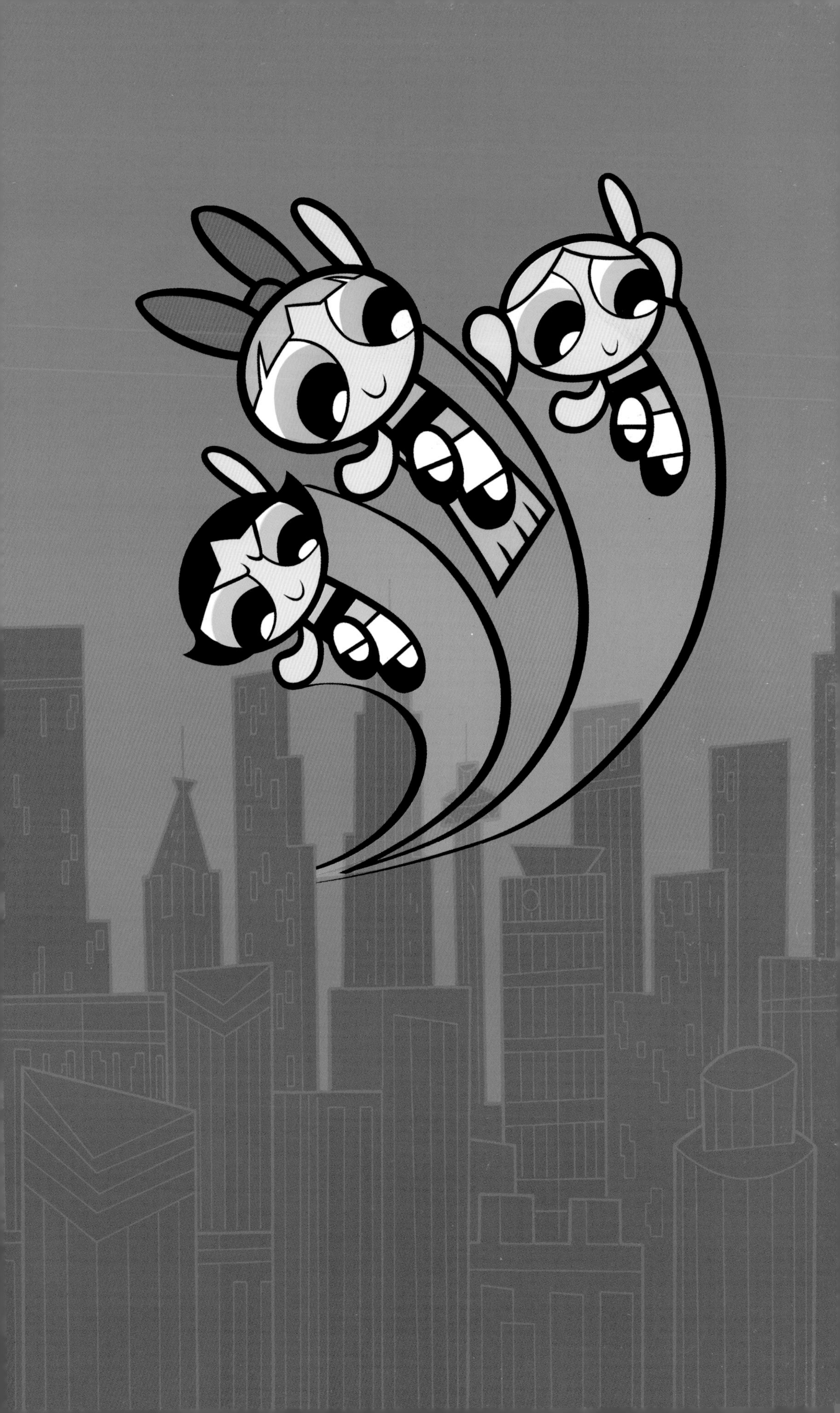

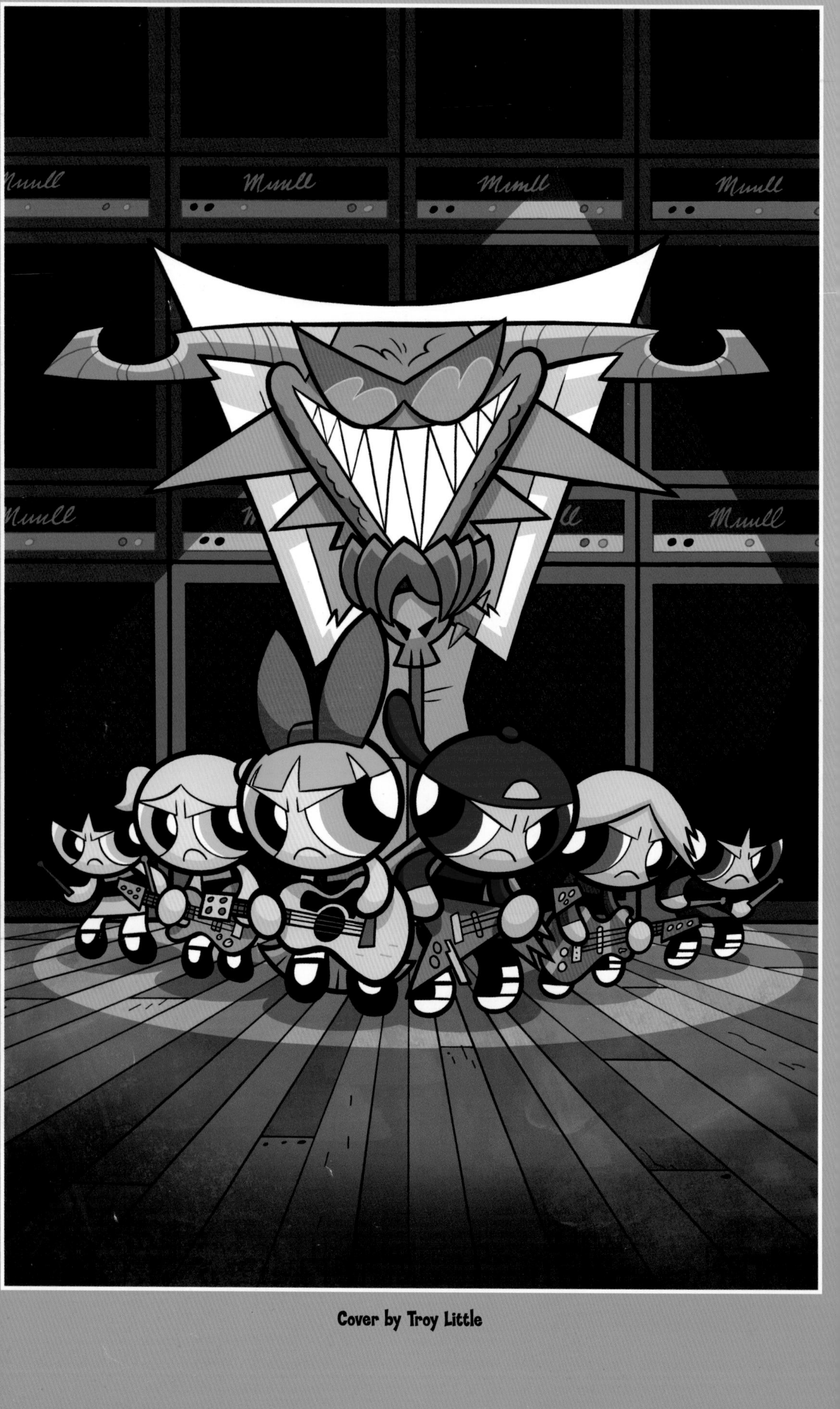
Marshall
Marshall
Marshall
Marshall
Marshall
Marshall

Cover by Troy Little

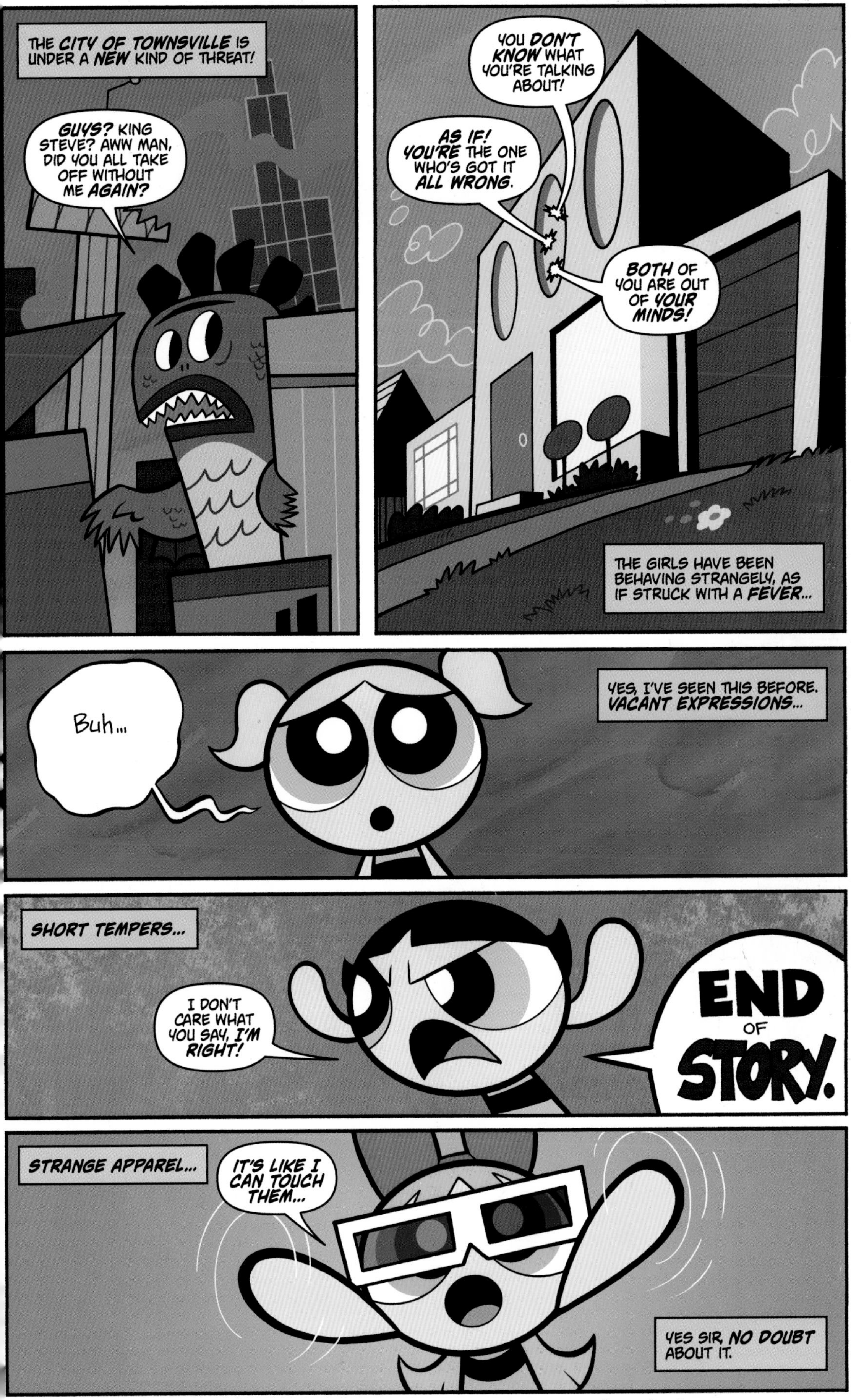
THE CITY OF TOWNSVILLE IS UNDER A NEW KIND OF THREAT!
GUYS? KING STEVE? AWW MAN, DID YOU ALL TAKE OFF WITHOUT ME AGAIN?
YOU DON'T KNOW WHAT YOU'RE TALKING ABOUT!
AS IF! YOU'RE THE ONE WHO'S GOT IT ALL WRONG.
BOTH OF YOU ARE OUT OF YOUR MINDS!
THE GIRLS HAVE BEEN BEHAVING STRANGELY, AS IF STRUCK WITH A FEVER...
Buh...
YES, I'VE SEEN THIS BEFORE. VACANT EXPRESSIONS...
SHORT TEMPERS...
I DON'T CARE WHAT YOU SAY, I'M RIGHT!
END OF STORY.
STRANGE APPAREL...
IT'S LIKE I CAN TOUCH THEM...
YES SIR, NO DOUBT ABOUT IT.

Story and Art by Troy Little · Lettering by Neil Uyetake and Troy Little

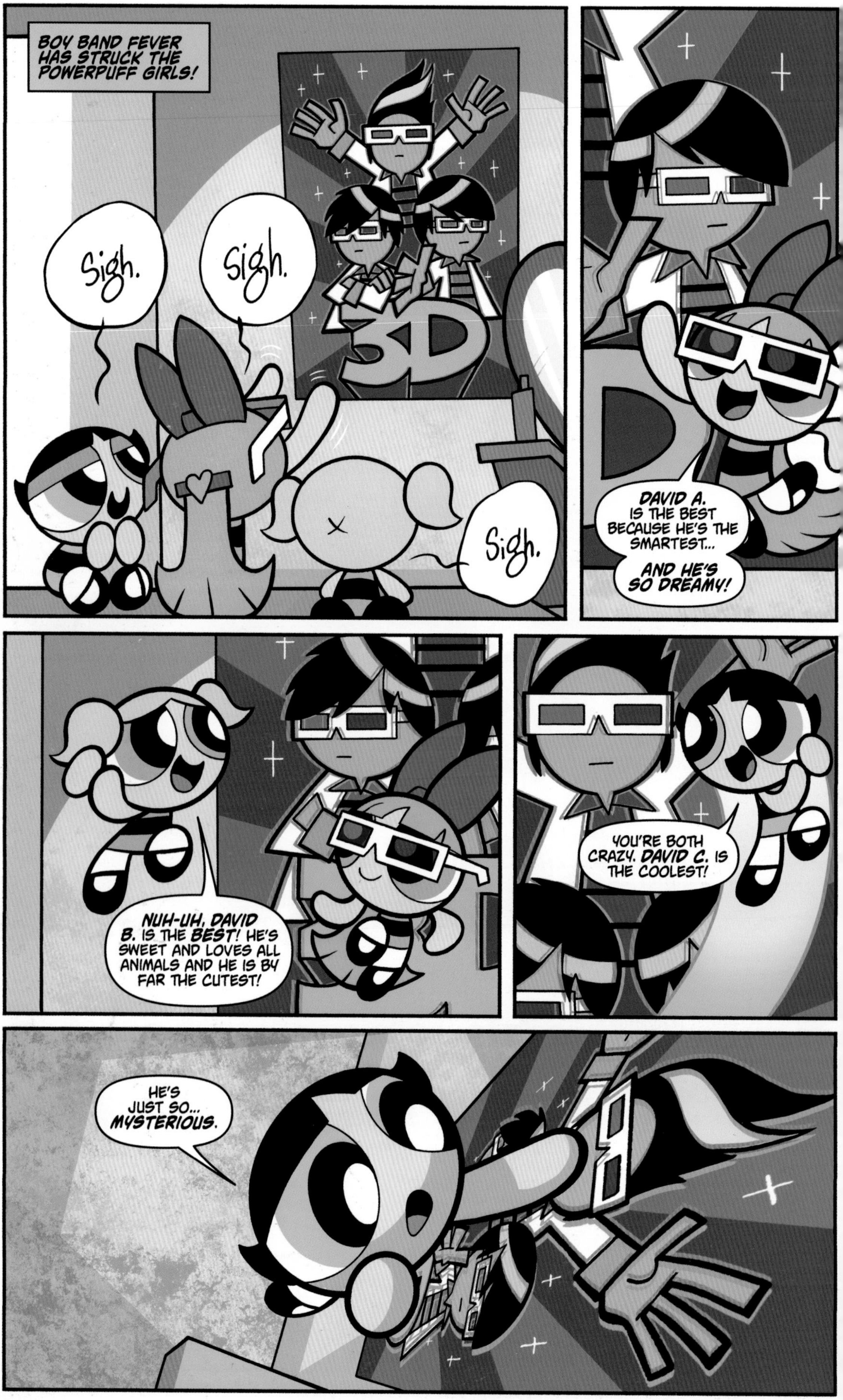
BOY BAND FEVER HAS STRUCK THE POWERPUFF GIRLS!
Sigh.
Sigh.
3D
Sigh.
DAVID A. IS THE BEST BECAUSE HE'S THE SMARTEST...
AND HE'S SO DREAMY!
NUH-UH, DAVID B. IS THE BEST! HE'S SWEET AND LOVES ALL ANIMALS AND HE IS BY FAR THE CUTEST!
YOU'RE BOTH CRAZY. DAVID C. IS THE COOLEST!
HE'S JUST SO... MYSTERIOUS.

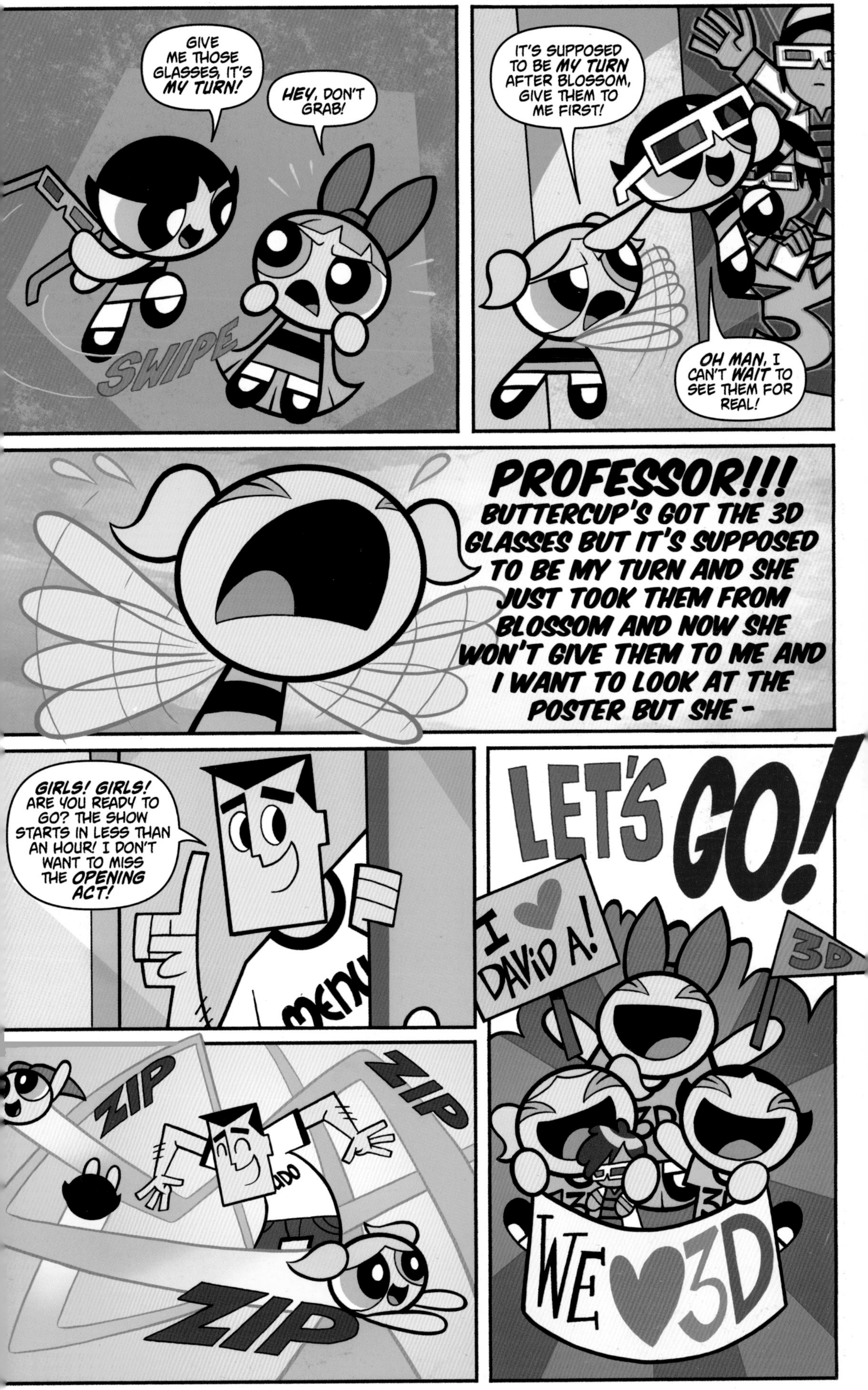
GIVE ME THOSE GLASSES, IT'S MY TURN!
HEY, DON'T GRAB!
SWIPE
IT'S SUPPOSED TO BE MY TURN AFTER BLOSSOM, GIVE THEM TO ME FIRST!
OH MAN, I CAN'T WAIT TO SEE THEM FOR REAL!
PROFESSOR!!! BUTTERCUP'S GOT THE 3D GLASSES BUT IT'S SUPPOSED TO BE MY TURN AND SHE JUST TOOK THEM FROM BLOSSOM AND NOW SHE WON'T GIVE THEM TO ME AND I WANT TO LOOK AT THE POSTER BUT SHE -
GIRLS! GIRLS! ARE YOU READY TO GO? THE SHOW STARTS IN LESS THAN AN HOUR! I DON'T WANT TO MISS THE OPENING ACT!
ZIP
ZIP
ZIP
LET'S GO!
I ♥ DAVID A!
3D
WE ♥ 3D

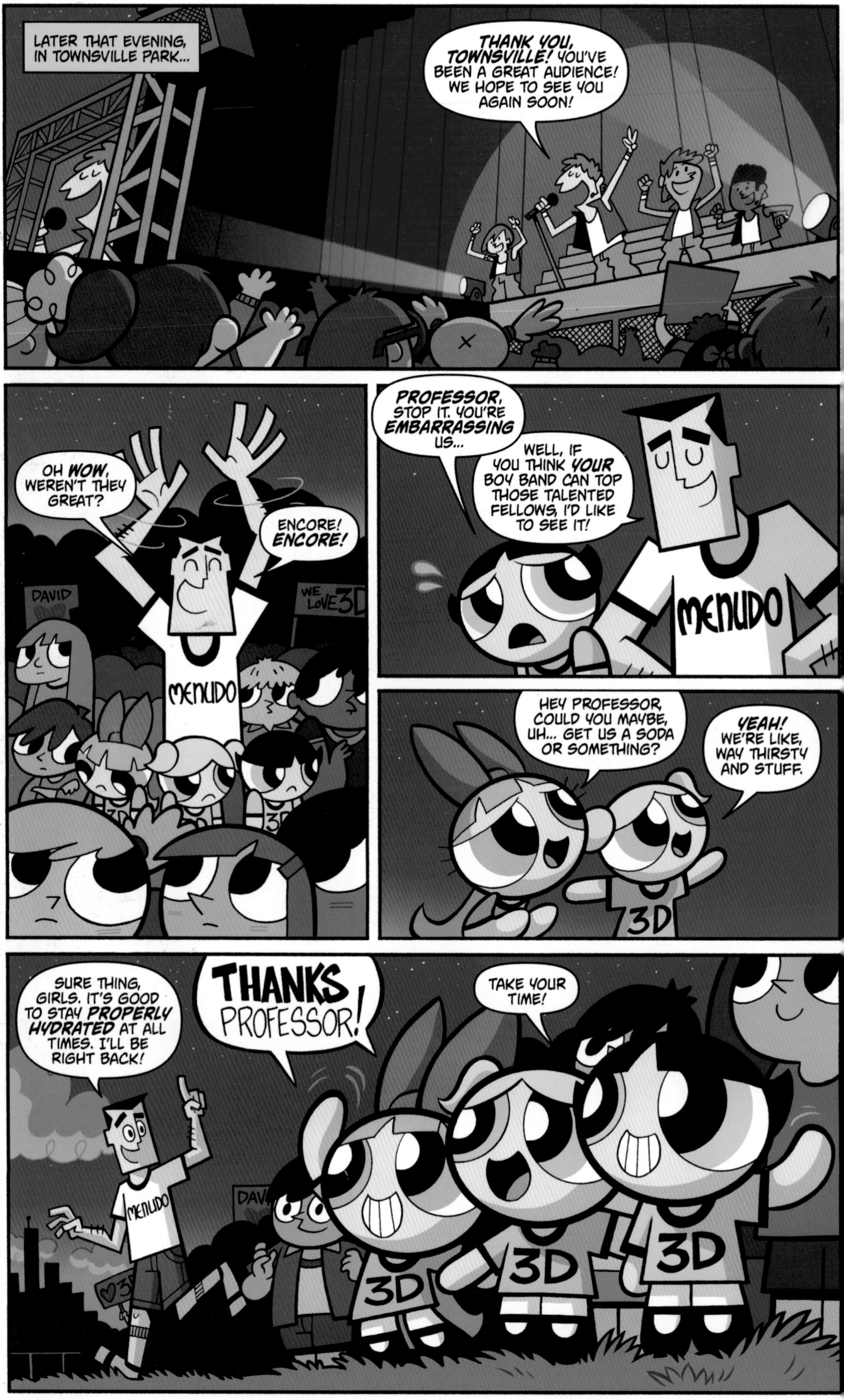
LATER THAT EVENING, IN TOWNSVILLE PARK...
THANK YOU, TOWNSVILLE! YOU'VE BEEN A GREAT AUDIENCE! WE HOPE TO SEE YOU AGAIN SOON!
OH WOW, WEREN'T THEY GREAT?
ENCORE! ENCORE!
DAVID
WE LOVE 3D
MENUDO
PROFESSOR, STOP IT. YOU'RE EMBARRASSING US...
WELL, IF YOU THINK YOUR BOY BAND CAN TOP THOSE TALENTED FELLOWS, I'D LIKE TO SEE IT!
MENUDO
HEY PROFESSOR, COULD YOU MAYBE, UH... GET US A SODA OR SOMETHING?
YEAH! WE'RE LIKE, WAY THIRSTY AND STUFF.
3D
SURE THING, GIRLS. IT'S GOOD TO STAY PROPERLY HYDRATED AT ALL TIMES. I'LL BE RIGHT BACK!
THANKS PROFESSOR!
TAKE YOUR TIME!
MENUDO
3D
3D
3D

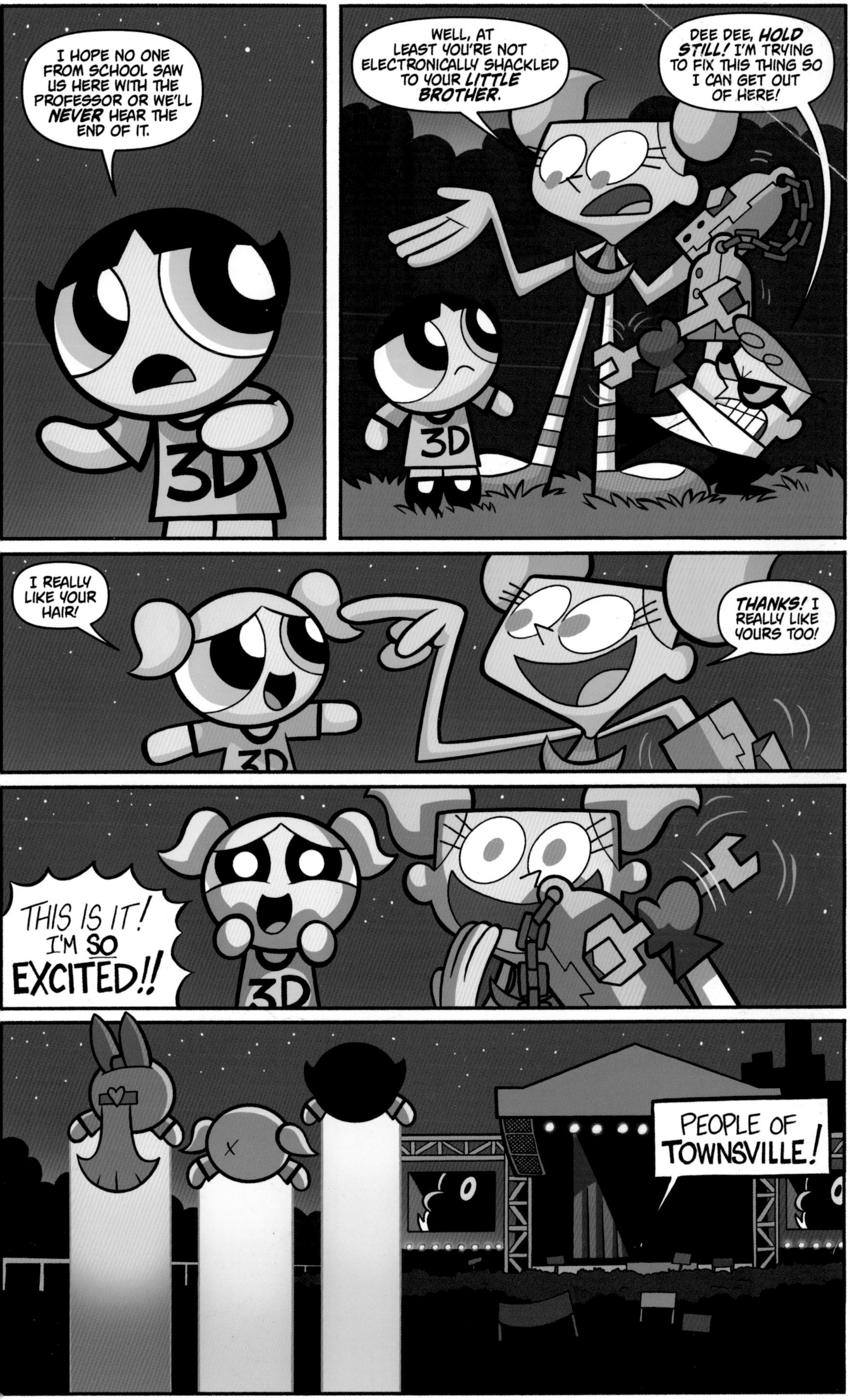
I HOPE NO ONE FROM SCHOOL SAW US HERE WITH THE PROFESSOR OR WE'LL NEVER HEAR THE END OF IT.
WELL, AT LEAST YOU'RE NOT ELECTRONICALLY SHACKLED TO YOUR LITTLE BROTHER.
DEE DEE, HOLD STILL! I'M TRYING TO FIX THIS THING SO I CAN GET OUT OF HERE!
I REALLY LIKE YOUR HAIR!
THANKS! I REALLY LIKE YOURS TOO!
THIS IS IT! I'M SO EXCITED!!
PEOPLE OF TOWNSVILLE!

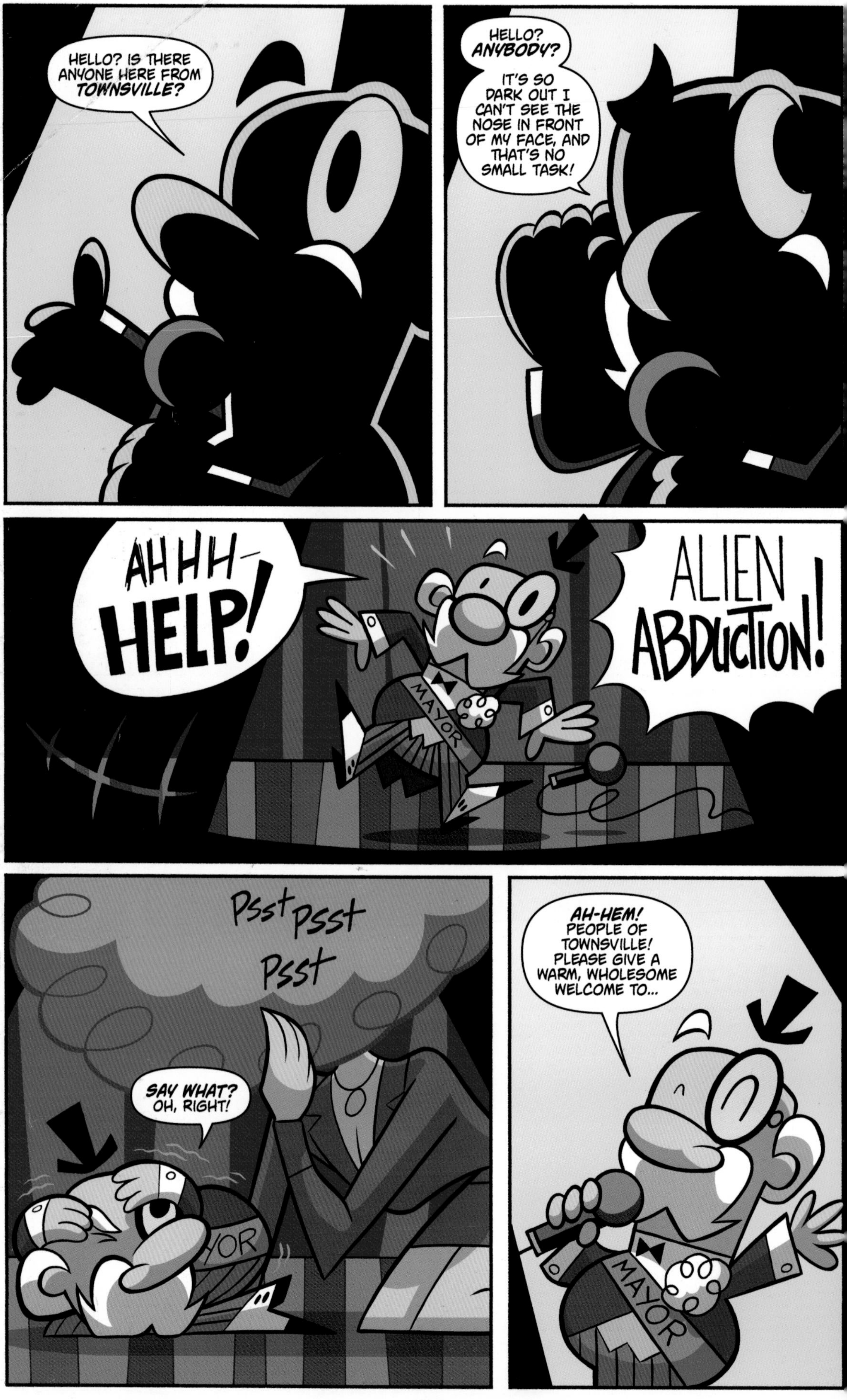
HELLO? IS THERE ANYONE HERE FROM TOWNSVILLE?
HELLO? ANYBODY?
IT'S SO DARK OUT I CAN'T SEE THE NOSE IN FRONT OF MY FACE, AND THAT'S NO SMALL TASK!
AHHH-HELP!
ALIEN ABDUCTION!
MAYOR
Psst Psst Psst
SAY WHAT? OH, RIGHT!
AH-HEM! PEOPLE OF TOWNSVILLE! PLEASE GIVE A WARM, WHOLESOME WELCOME TO...
MAYOR

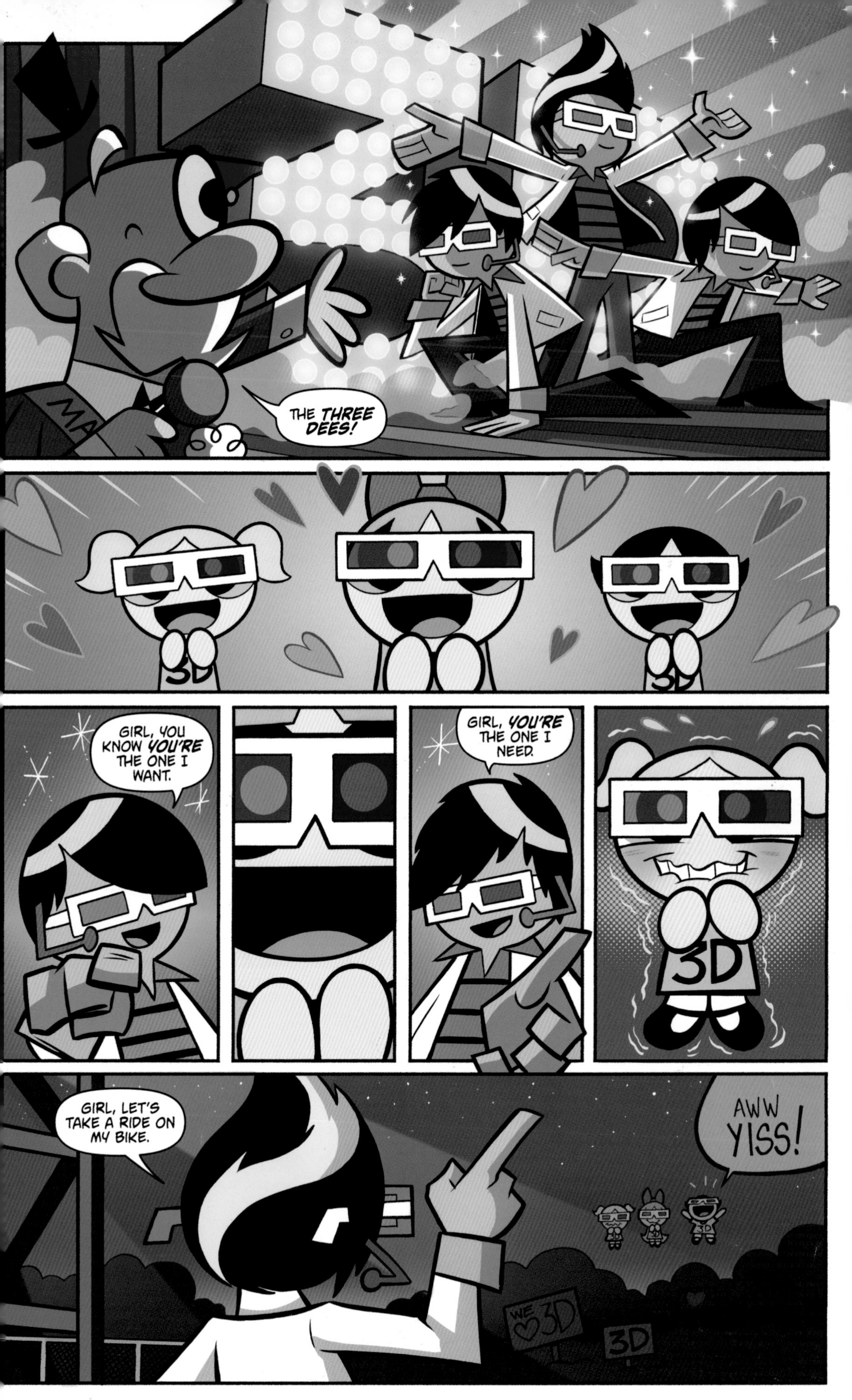
THE THREE DEES!
GIRL, YOU KNOW YOU'RE THE ONE I WANT.
GIRL, YOU'RE THE ONE I NEED.
GIRL, LET'S TAKE A RIDE ON MY BIKE.
AWW YISS!
WE ♡ 3D
3D

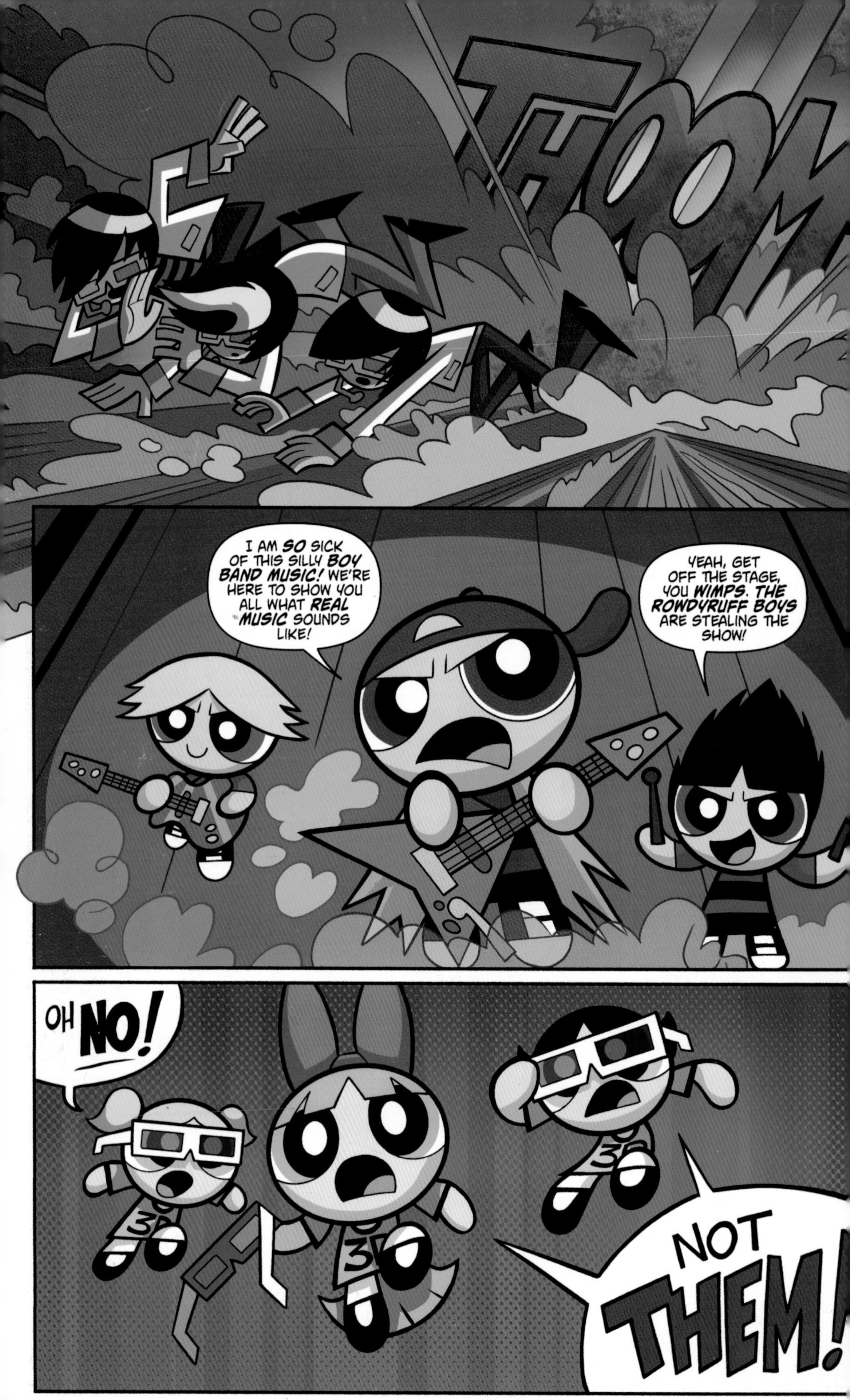
THOOM!
I AM SO SICK OF THIS SILLY BOY BAND MUSIC! WE'RE HERE TO SHOW YOU ALL WHAT REAL MUSIC SOUNDS LIKE!
YEAH, GET OFF THE STAGE, YOU WIMPS. THE ROWDYRUFF BOYS ARE STEALING THE SHOW!
OH NO!
NOT THEM!

BOOMER, KNOCK THESE KIDS OFF THE BLOCK.
WITH PLEASURE!
ZAK
YEOW!
BOOM
WOW, NICE CATCH!
THANKS, GIRLS!
HEY, YOU LIKE MOTORCYCLES?
TEE HE HEE HEE TEE TEHEE
THANKS, POWERPUFF GIRLS!

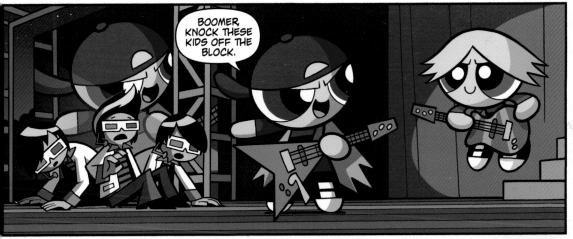

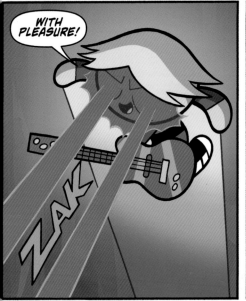

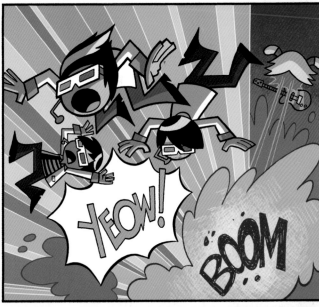

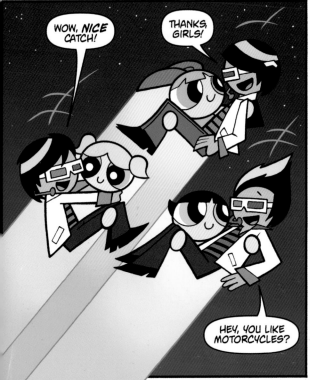

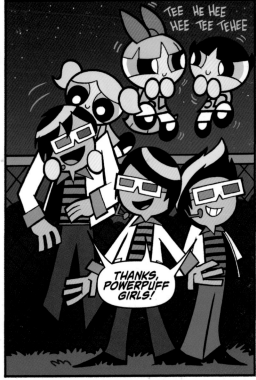

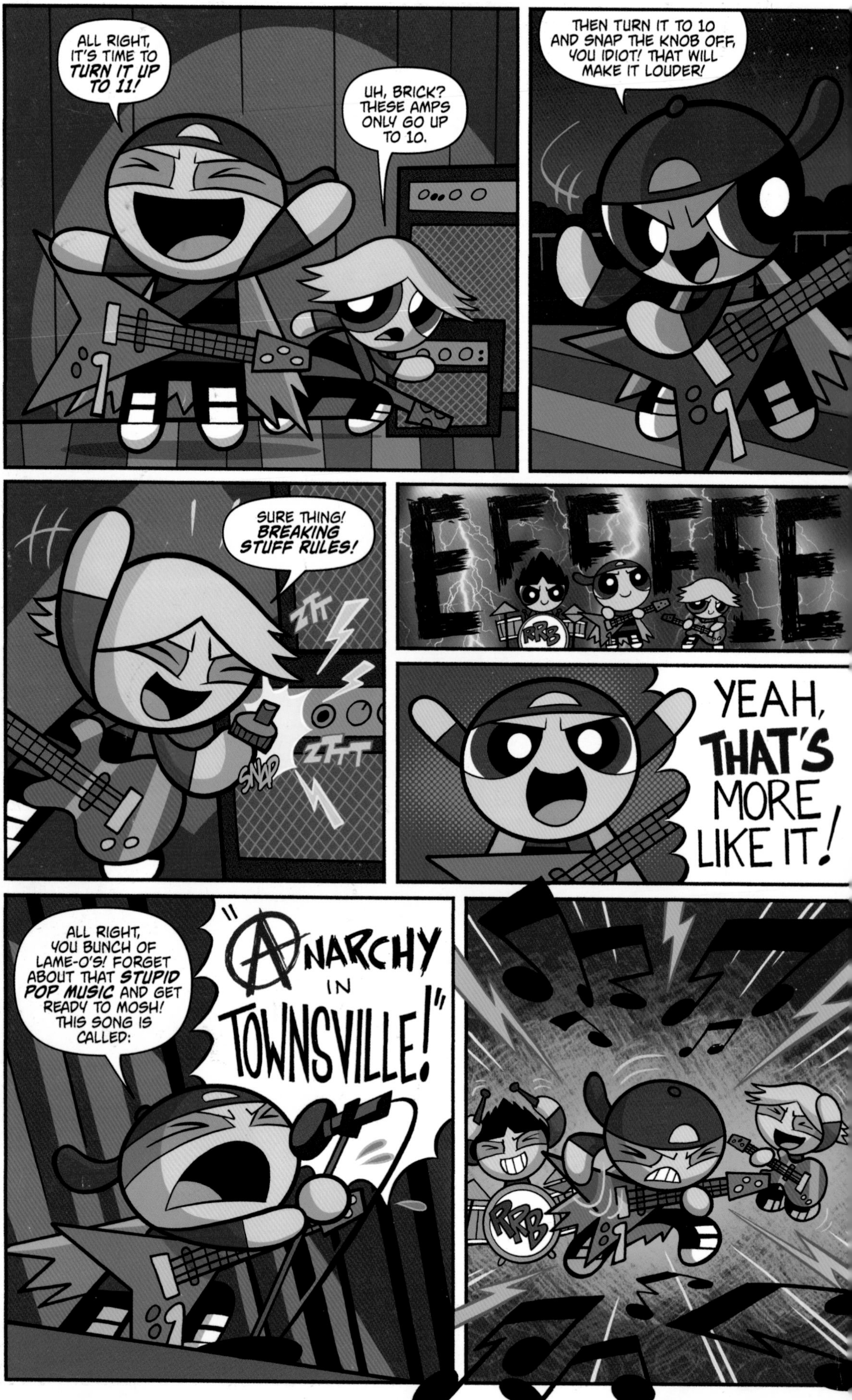

ALL RIGHT, IT'S TIME TO TURN IT UP TO 11!
UH, BRICK? THESE AMPS ONLY GO UP TO 10.
THEN TURN IT TO 10 AND SNAP THE KNOB OFF, YOU IDIOT! THAT WILL MAKE IT LOUDER!
SURE THING! BREAKING STUFF RULES!
ZTT
SNAP
ZTTT
EEEEE
RRB
YEAH, THAT'S MORE LIKE IT!
ALL RIGHT, YOU BUNCH OF LAME-O'S! FORGET ABOUT THAT STUPID POP MUSIC AND GET READY TO MOSH! THIS SONG IS CALLED:
"ANARCHY IN TOWNSVILLE!"
RRB

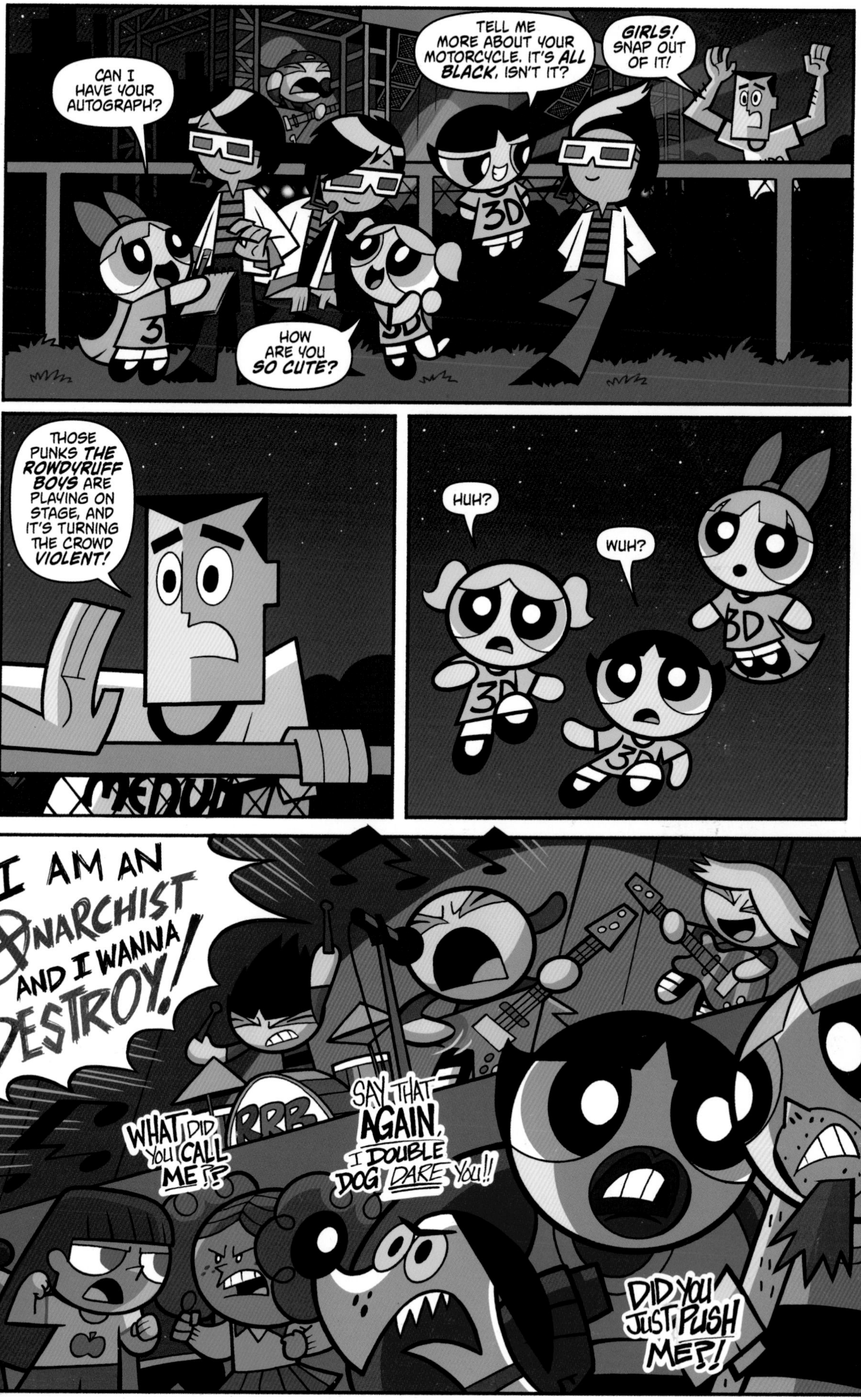
CAN I HAVE YOUR AUTOGRAPH?
TELL ME MORE ABOUT YOUR MOTORCYCLE. IT'S ALL BLACK, ISN'T IT?
GIRLS! SNAP OUT OF IT!
HOW ARE YOU SO CUTE?
3D
THOSE PUNKS THE ROWDYRUFF BOYS ARE PLAYING ON STAGE, AND IT'S TURNING THE CROWD VIOLENT!
HUH?
WUH?
I AM AN ANARCHIST AND I WANNA DESTROY!
RRB
WHAT DID YOU CALL ME?!
SAY THAT AGAIN, I DOUBLE DOG DARE YOU!!
DID YOU JUST PUSH ME?!

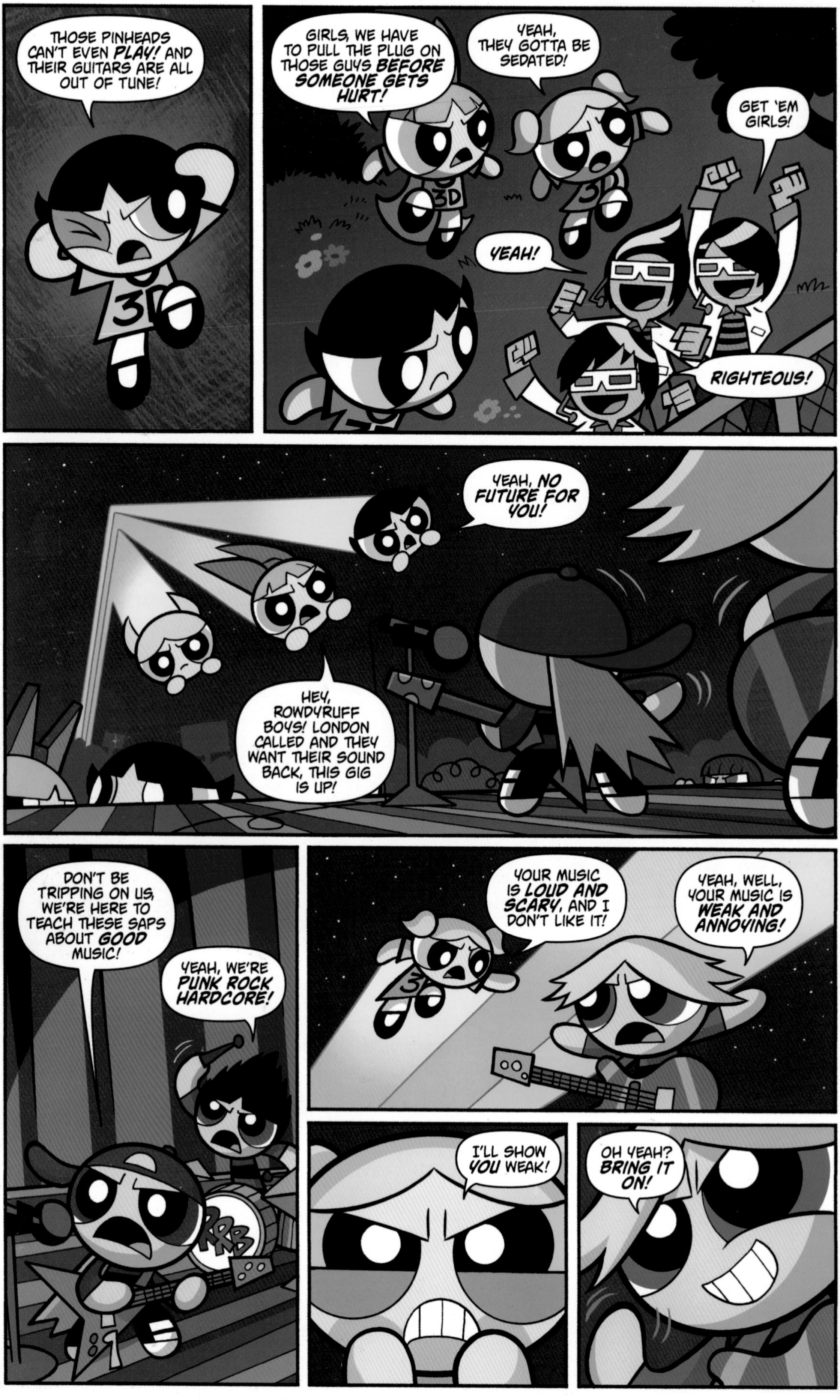
THOSE PINHEADS CAN'T EVEN PLAY! AND THEIR GUITARS ARE ALL OUT OF TUNE!
GIRLS, WE HAVE TO PULL THE PLUG ON THOSE GUYS BEFORE SOMEONE GETS HURT!
YEAH, THEY GOTTA BE SEDATED!
GET 'EM GIRLS!
YEAH!
RIGHTEOUS!
YEAH, NO FUTURE FOR YOU!
HEY, ROWDYRUFF BOYS! LONDON CALLED AND THEY WANT THEIR SOUND BACK, THIS GIG IS UP!
DON'T BE TRIPPING ON US, WE'RE HERE TO TEACH THESE SAPS ABOUT GOOD MUSIC!
YEAH, WE'RE PUNK ROCK HARDCORE!
YOUR MUSIC IS LOUD AND SCARY, AND I DON'T LIKE IT!
YEAH, WELL, YOUR MUSIC IS WEAK AND ANNOYING!
I'LL SHOW YOU WEAK!
OH YEAH? BRING IT ON!

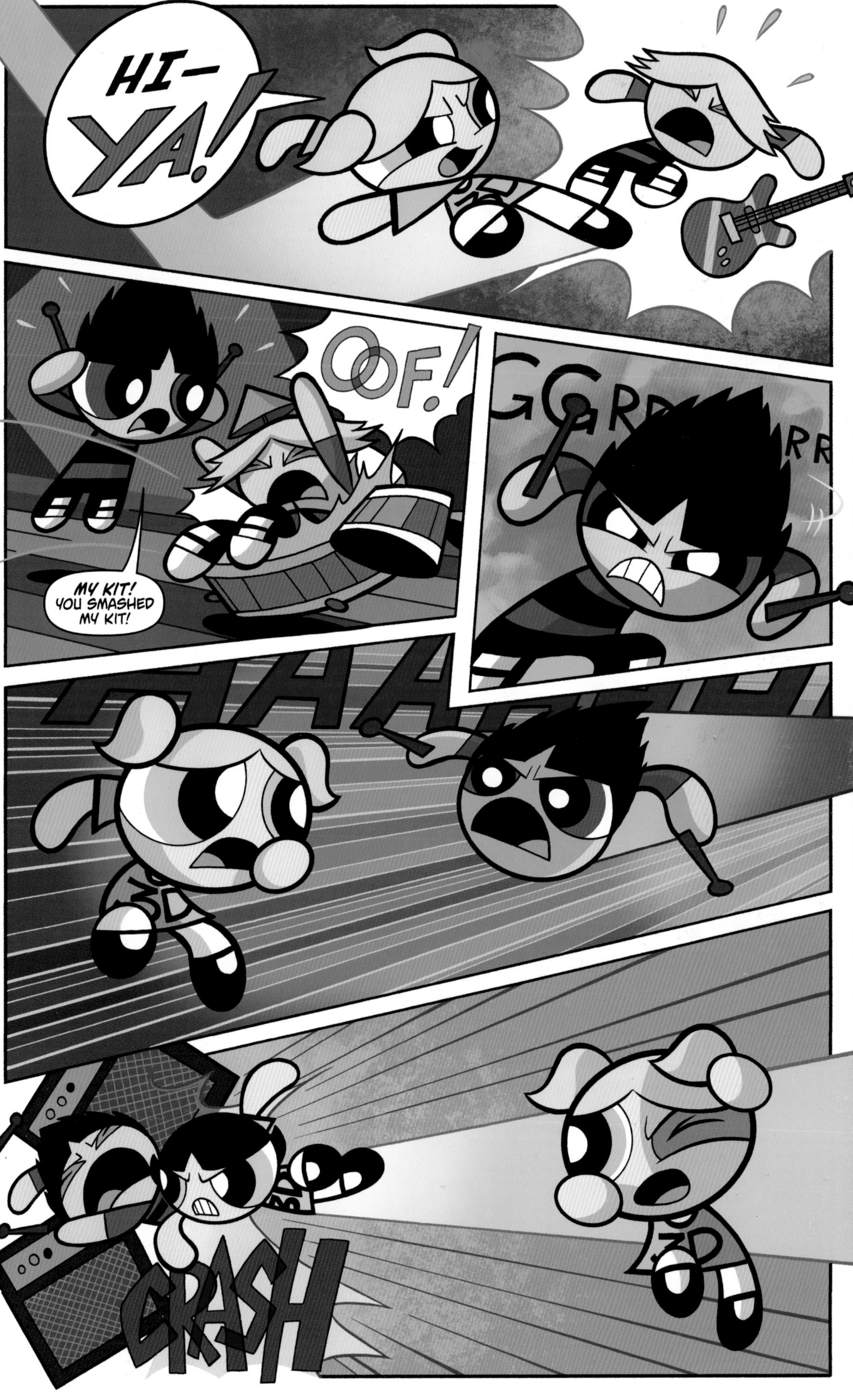
HI-YA!
OOF!
MY KIT! YOU SMASHED MY KIT!
GGRR
CRASH

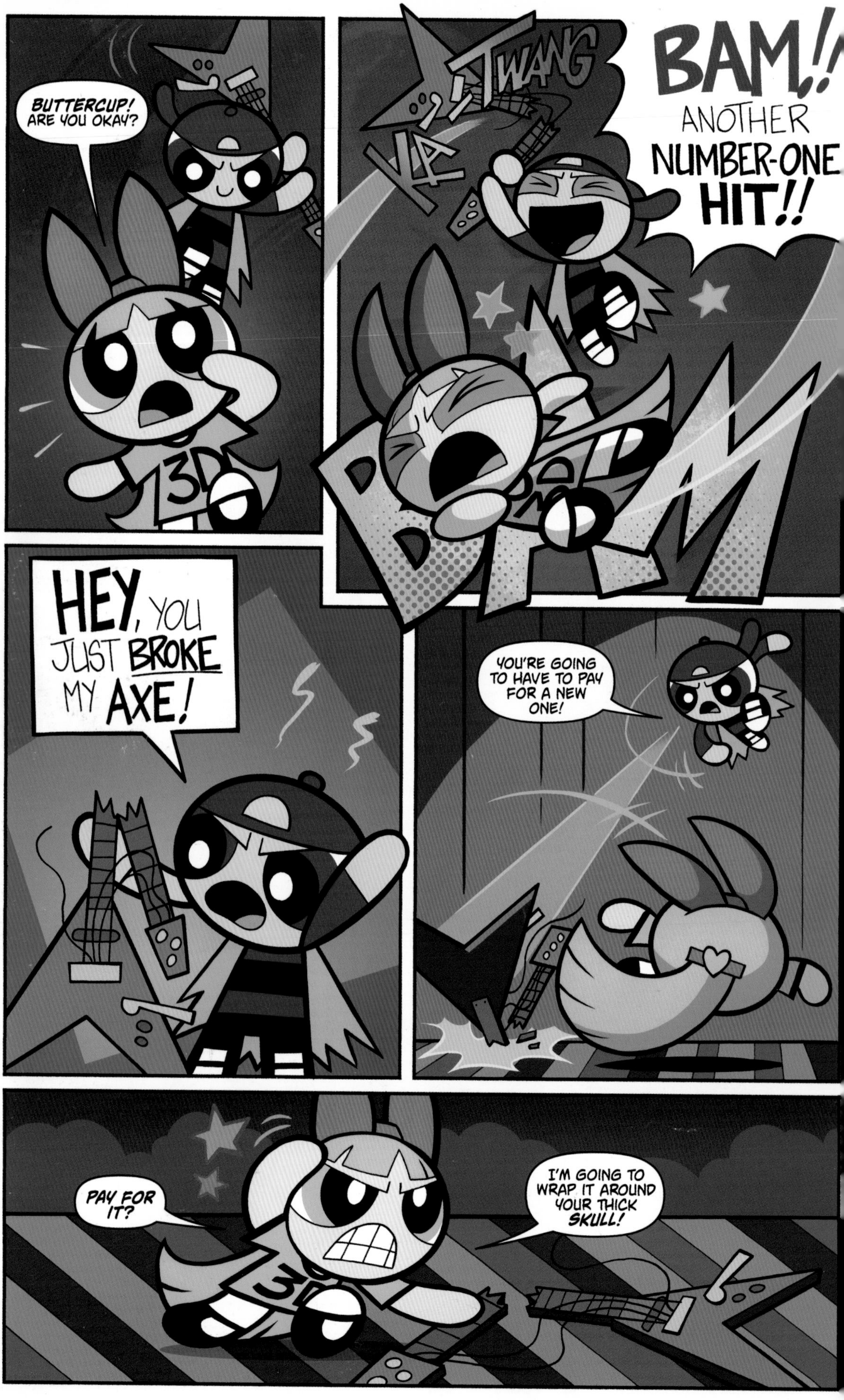
BUTTERCUP! ARE YOU OKAY?
TWANG
YA
BAM!! ANOTHER NUMBER-ONE HIT!!
HEY, YOU JUST BROKE MY AXE!
YOU'RE GOING TO HAVE TO PAY FOR A NEW ONE!
PAY FOR IT?
I'M GOING TO WRAP IT AROUND YOUR THICK SKULL!

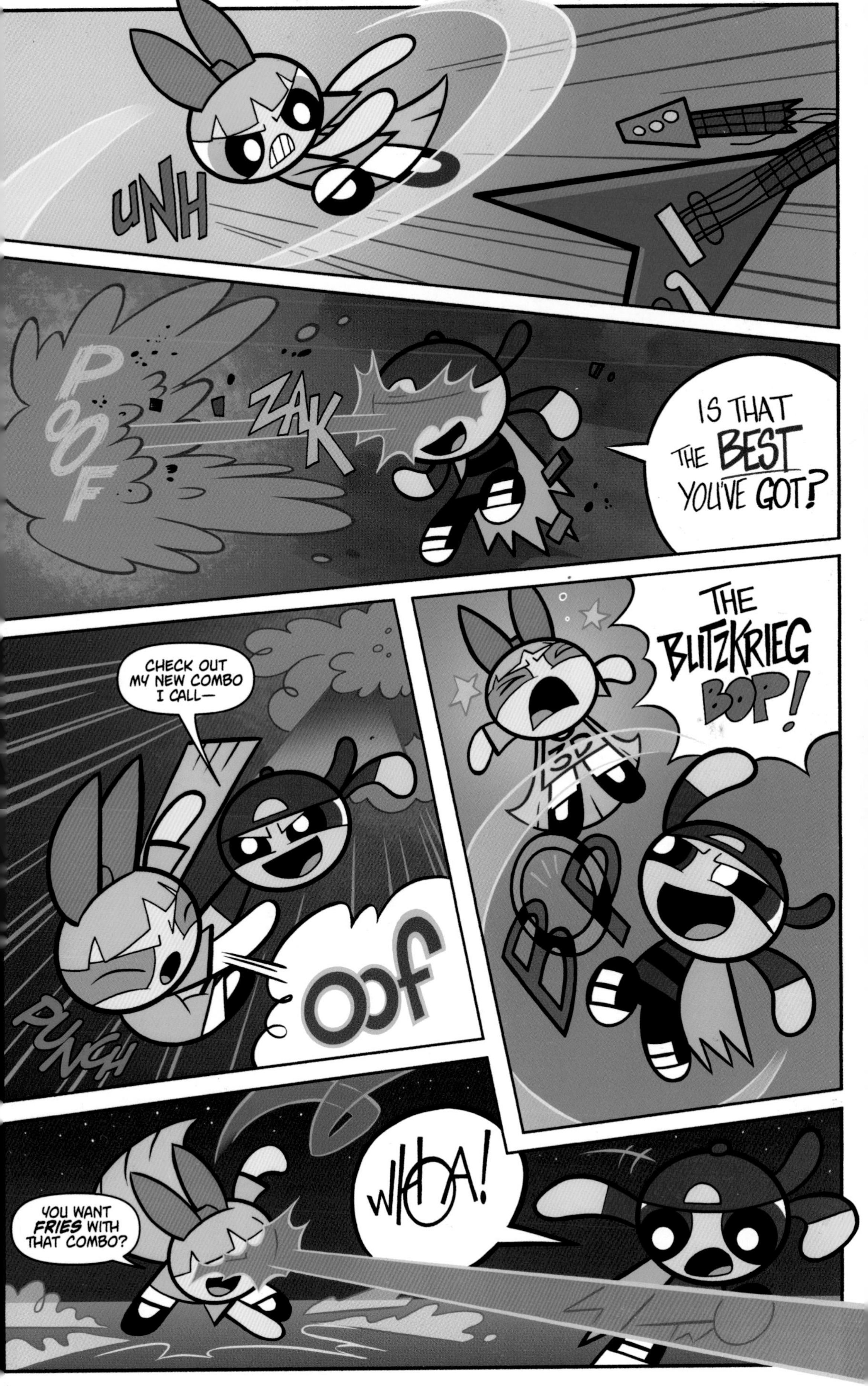
UNH
POOF
ZAK
IS THAT THE BEST YOU'VE GOT?
CHECK OUT MY NEW COMBO I CALL—
PUNCH
OOF
THE BLITZKRIEG BOP!
YOU WANT FRIES WITH THAT COMBO?
WHOA!

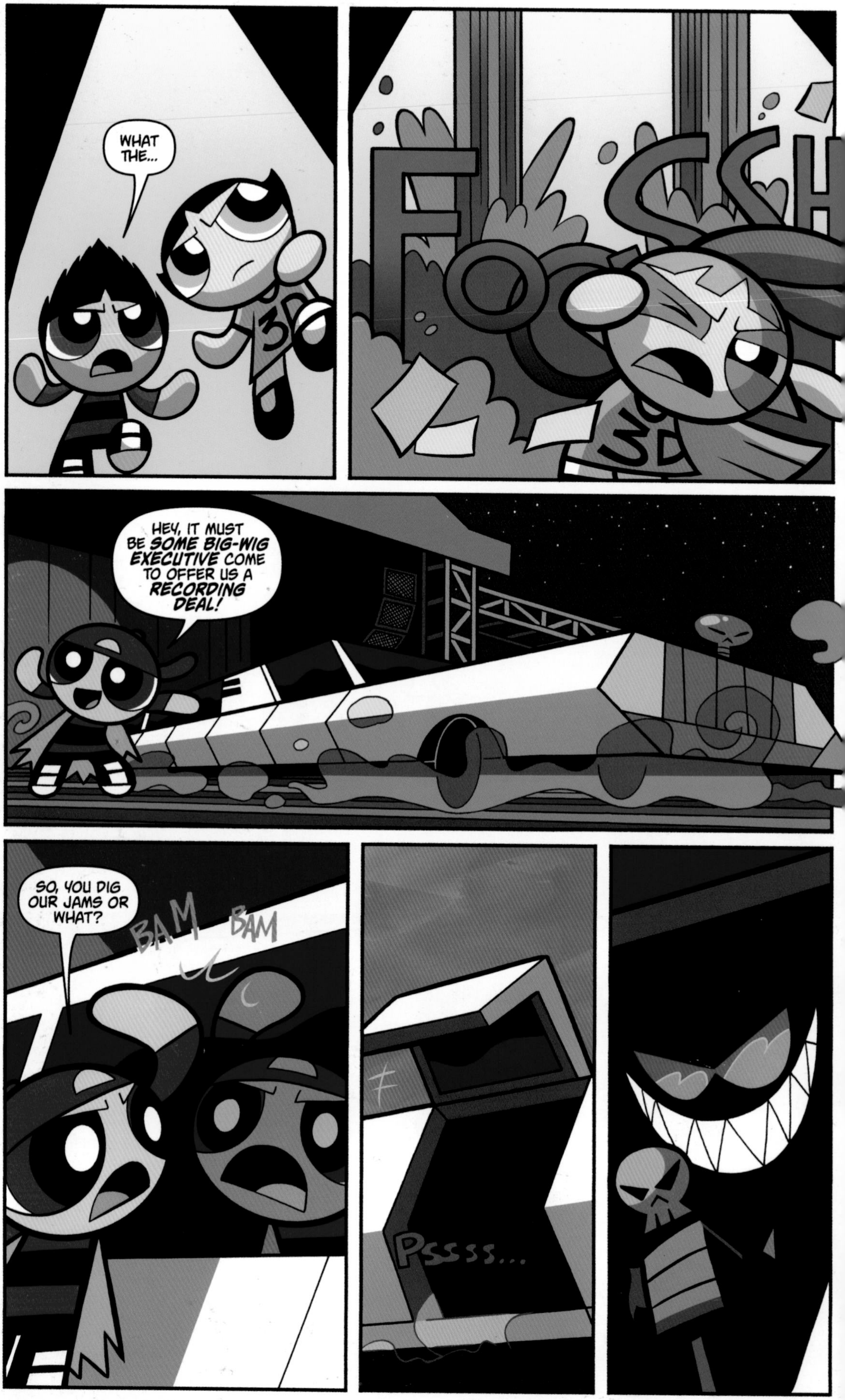
WHAT THE...
FOOSCH
HEY, IT MUST BE SOME BIG-WIG EXECUTIVE COME TO OFFER US A RECORDING DEAL!
SO, YOU DIG OUR JAMS OR WHAT?
BAM
BAM
PSSSS...

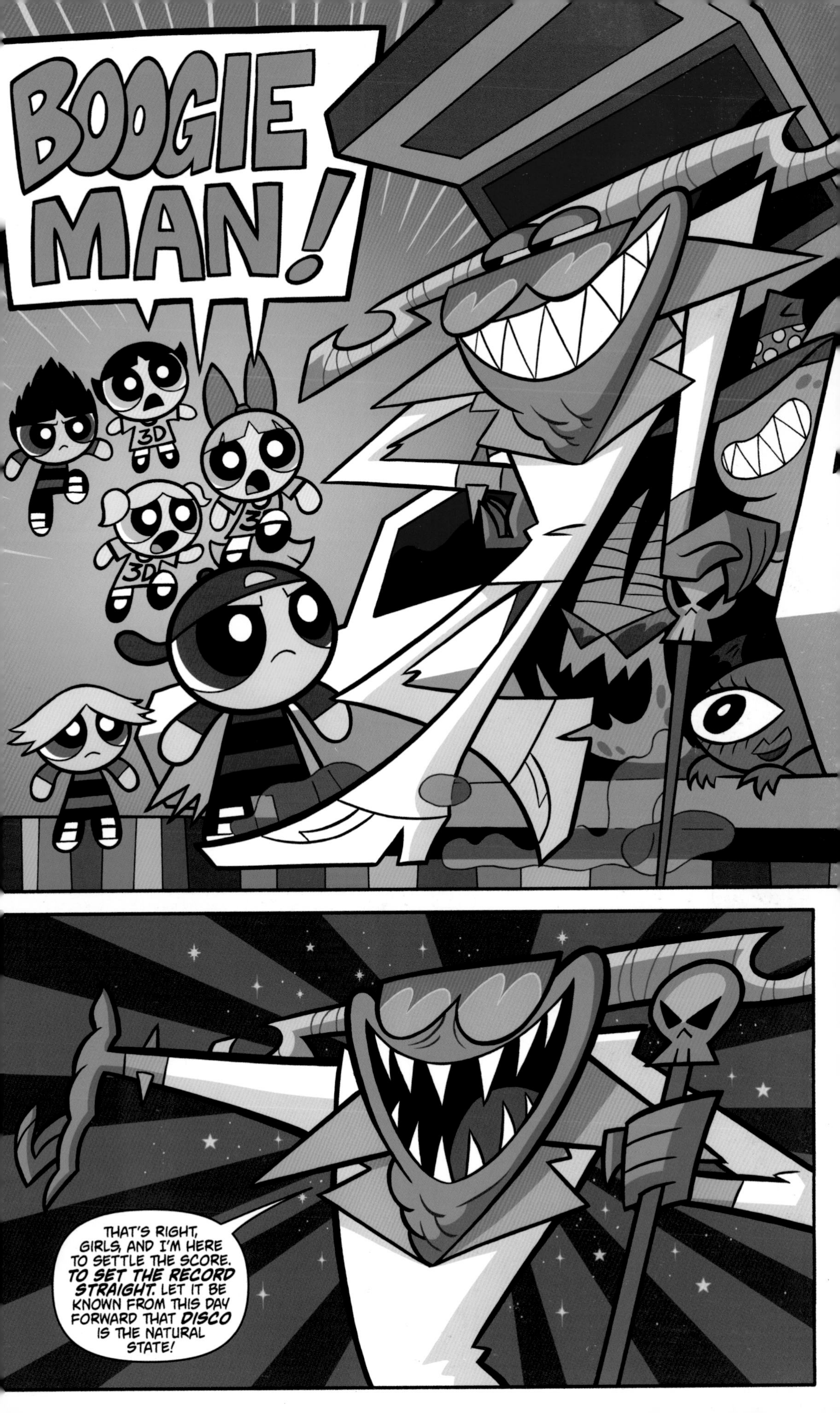
BOOGIE MAN!
THAT'S RIGHT, GIRLS, AND I'M HERE TO SETTLE THE SCORE. TO SET THE RECORD STRAIGHT. LET IT BE KNOWN FROM THIS DAY FORWARD THAT DISCO IS THE NATURAL STATE!

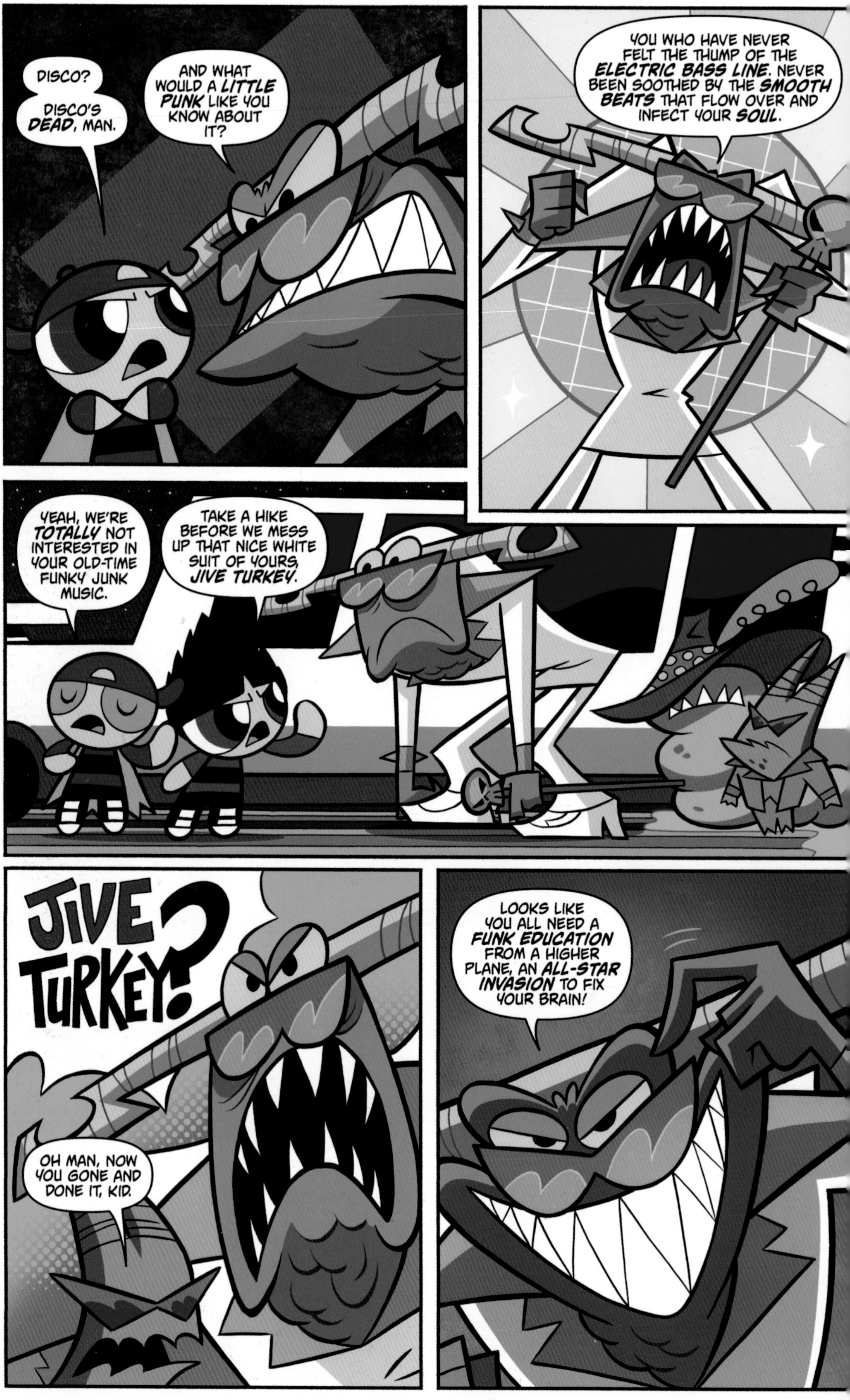
DISCO?
DISCO'S DEAD, MAN.
AND WHAT WOULD A LITTLE PUNK LIKE YOU KNOW ABOUT IT?
YOU WHO HAVE NEVER FELT THE THUMP OF THE ELECTRIC BASS LINE. NEVER BEEN SOOTHED BY THE SMOOTH BEATS THAT FLOW OVER AND INFECT YOUR SOUL.
YEAH, WE'RE TOTALLY NOT INTERESTED IN YOUR OLD-TIME FUNKY JUNK MUSIC.
TAKE A HIKE BEFORE WE MESS UP THAT NICE WHITE SUIT OF YOURS, JIVE TURKEY.
JIVE TURKEY?
OH MAN, NOW YOU GONE AND DONE IT, KID.
LOOKS LIKE YOU ALL NEED A FUNK EDUCATION FROM A HIGHER PLANE, AN ALL-STAR INVASION TO FIX YOUR BRAIN!

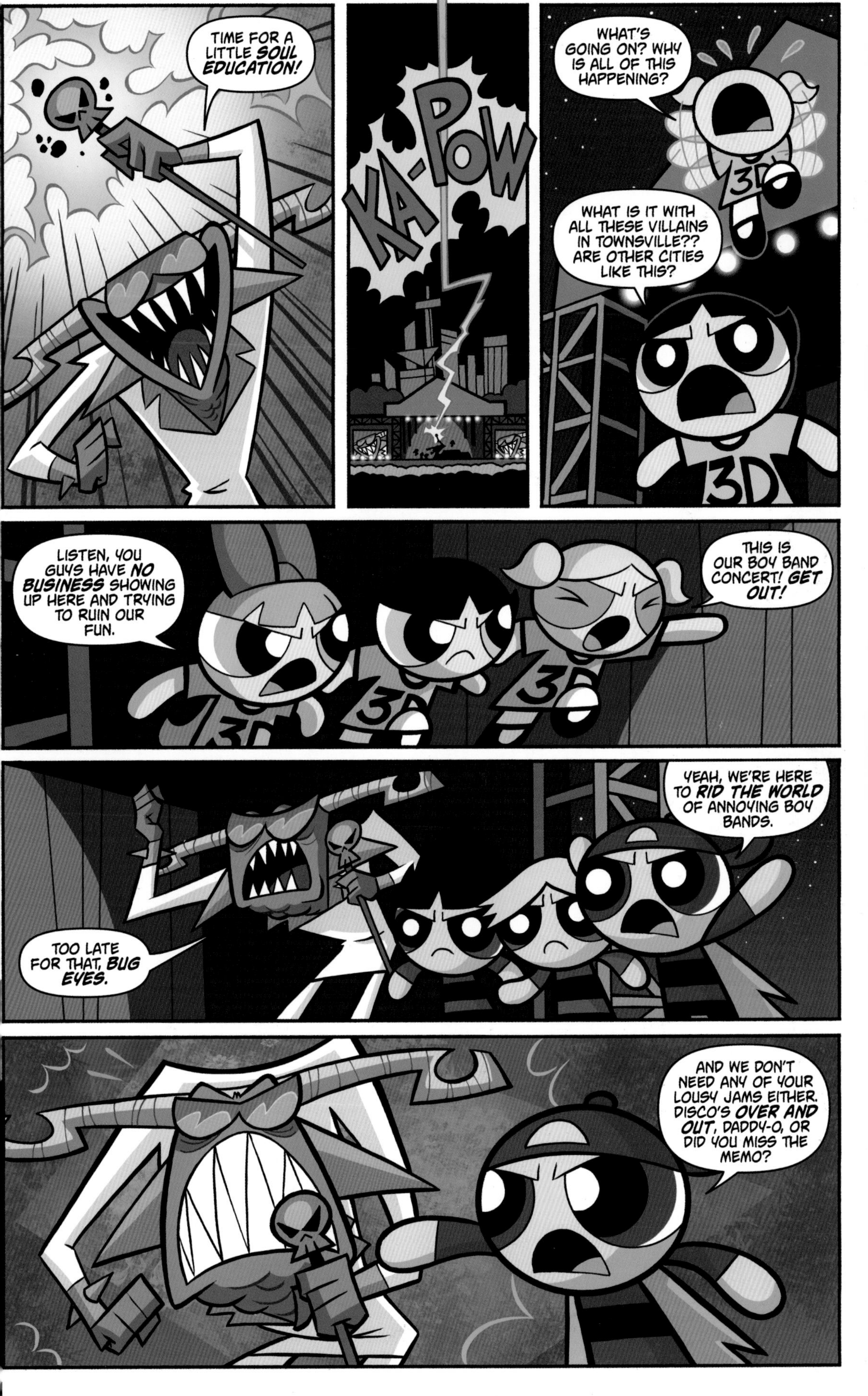

TIME FOR A LITTLE SOUL EDUCATION!
KA-POW
WHAT'S GOING ON? WHY IS ALL OF THIS HAPPENING?
WHAT IS IT WITH ALL THESE VILLAINS IN TOWNSVILLE?? ARE OTHER CITIES LIKE THIS?
LISTEN, YOU GUYS HAVE NO BUSINESS SHOWING UP HERE AND TRYING TO RUIN OUR FUN.
THIS IS OUR BOY BAND CONCERT! GET OUT!
YEAH, WE'RE HERE TO RID THE WORLD OF ANNOYING BOY BANDS.
TOO LATE FOR THAT, BUG EYES.
AND WE DON'T NEED ANY OF YOUR LOUSY JAMS EITHER. DISCO'S OVER AND OUT, DADDY-O, OR DID YOU MISS THE MEMO?

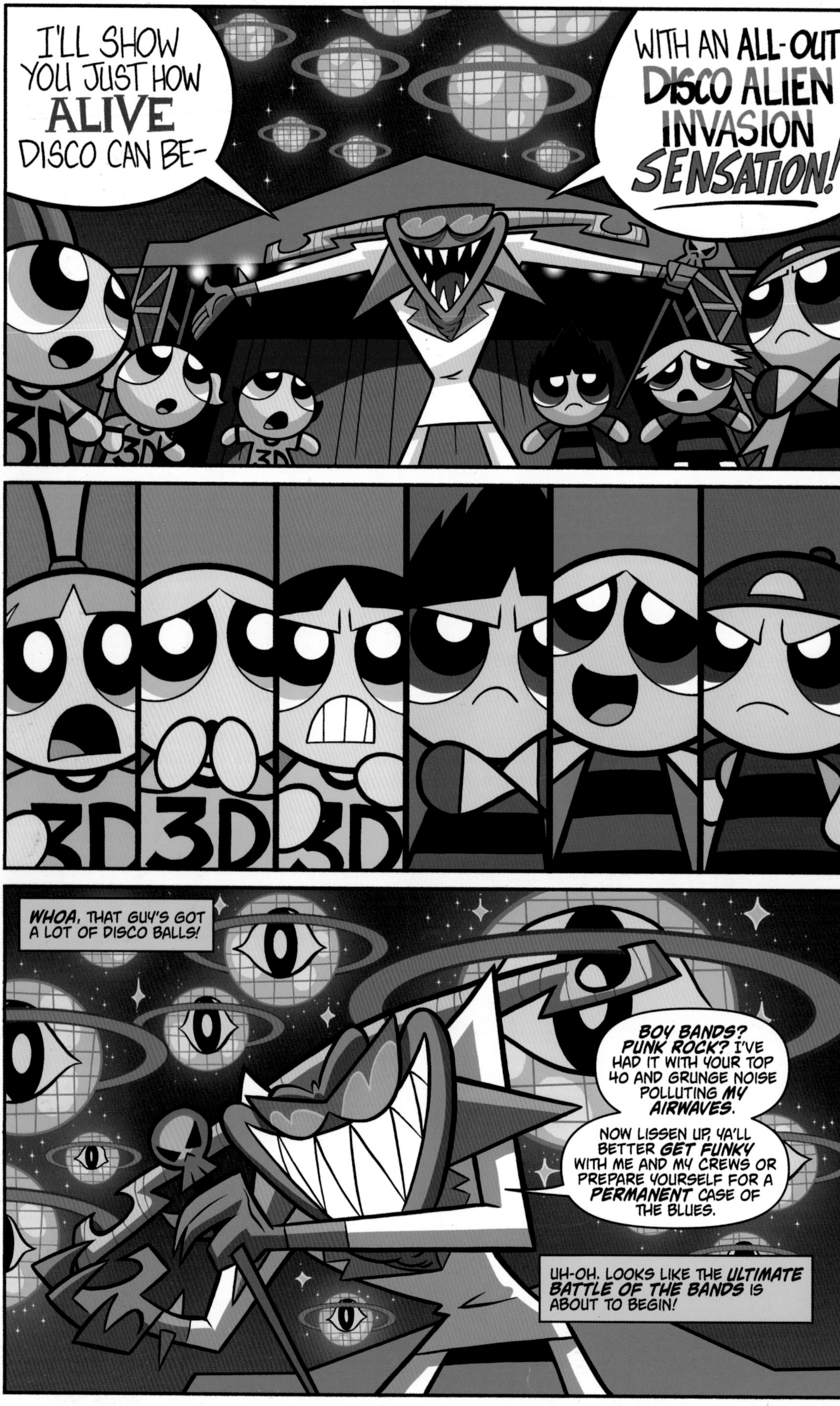

I'LL SHOW YOU JUST HOW ALIVE DISCO CAN BE-
WITH AN ALL-OUT DISCO ALIEN INVASION SENSATION!
3D
3D
3D
3D
3D
3D
WHOA, THAT GUY'S GOT A LOT OF DISCO BALLS!
BOY BANDS? PUNK ROCK? I'VE HAD IT WITH YOUR TOP 40 AND GRUNGE NOISE POLLUTING MY AIRWAVES.
NOW LISSEN UP, YA'LL BETTER GET FUNKY WITH ME AND MY CREWS OR PREPARE YOURSELF FOR A PERMANENT CASE OF THE BLUES.
UH-OH. LOOKS LIKE THE ULTIMATE BATTLE OF THE BANDS IS ABOUT TO BEGIN!

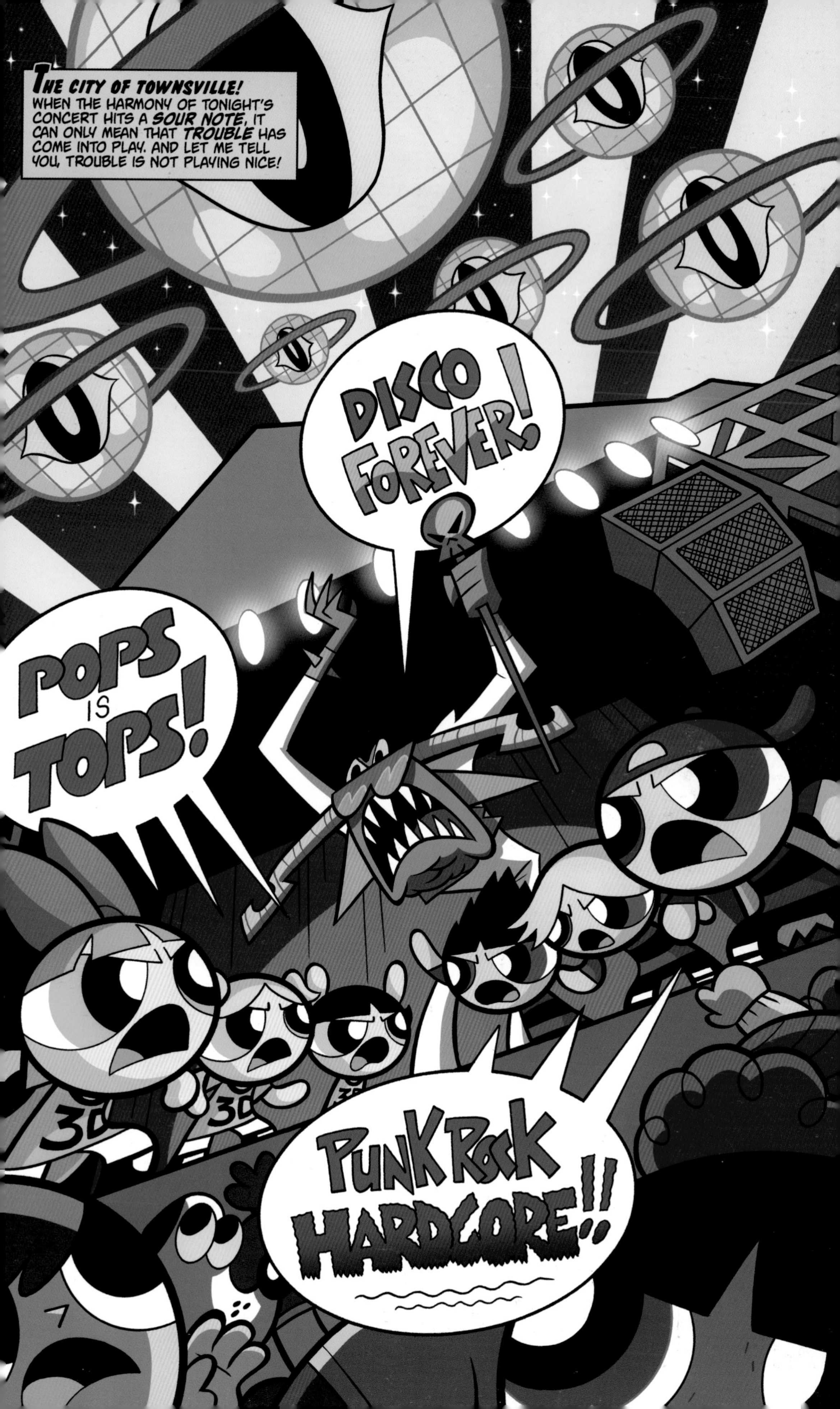
THE CITY OF TOWNSVILLE! WHEN THE HARMONY OF TONIGHT'S CONCERT HITS A SOUR NOTE, IT CAN ONLY MEAN THAT TROUBLE HAS COME INTO PLAY. AND LET ME TELL YOU, TROUBLE IS NOT PLAYING NICE!
DISCO FOREVER!
POPS IS TOPS!
PUNK ROCK HARDCORE!!

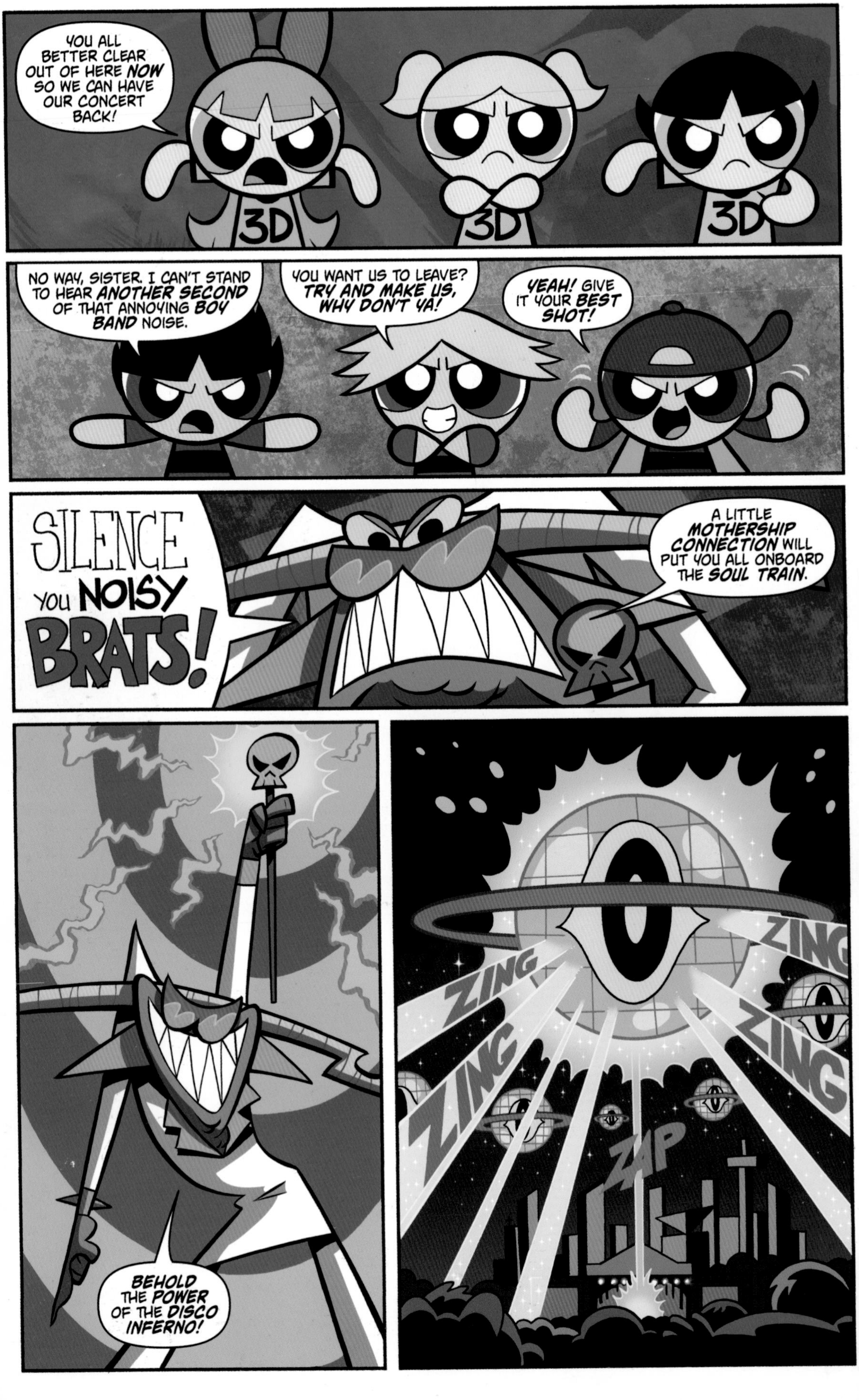

YOU ALL BETTER CLEAR OUT OF HERE NOW SO WE CAN HAVE OUR CONCERT BACK!
3D
3D
3D
NO WAY, SISTER. I CAN'T STAND TO HEAR ANOTHER SECOND OF THAT ANNOYING BOY BAND NOISE.
YOU WANT US TO LEAVE? TRY AND MAKE US, WHY DON'T YA!
YEAH! GIVE IT YOUR BEST SHOT!
SILENCE YOU NOISY BRATS!
A LITTLE MOTHERSHIP CONNECTION WILL PUT YOU ALL ONBOARD THE SOUL TRAIN.
BEHOLD THE POWER OF THE DISCO INFERNO!
ZING
ZING
ZING
ZING
ZAP

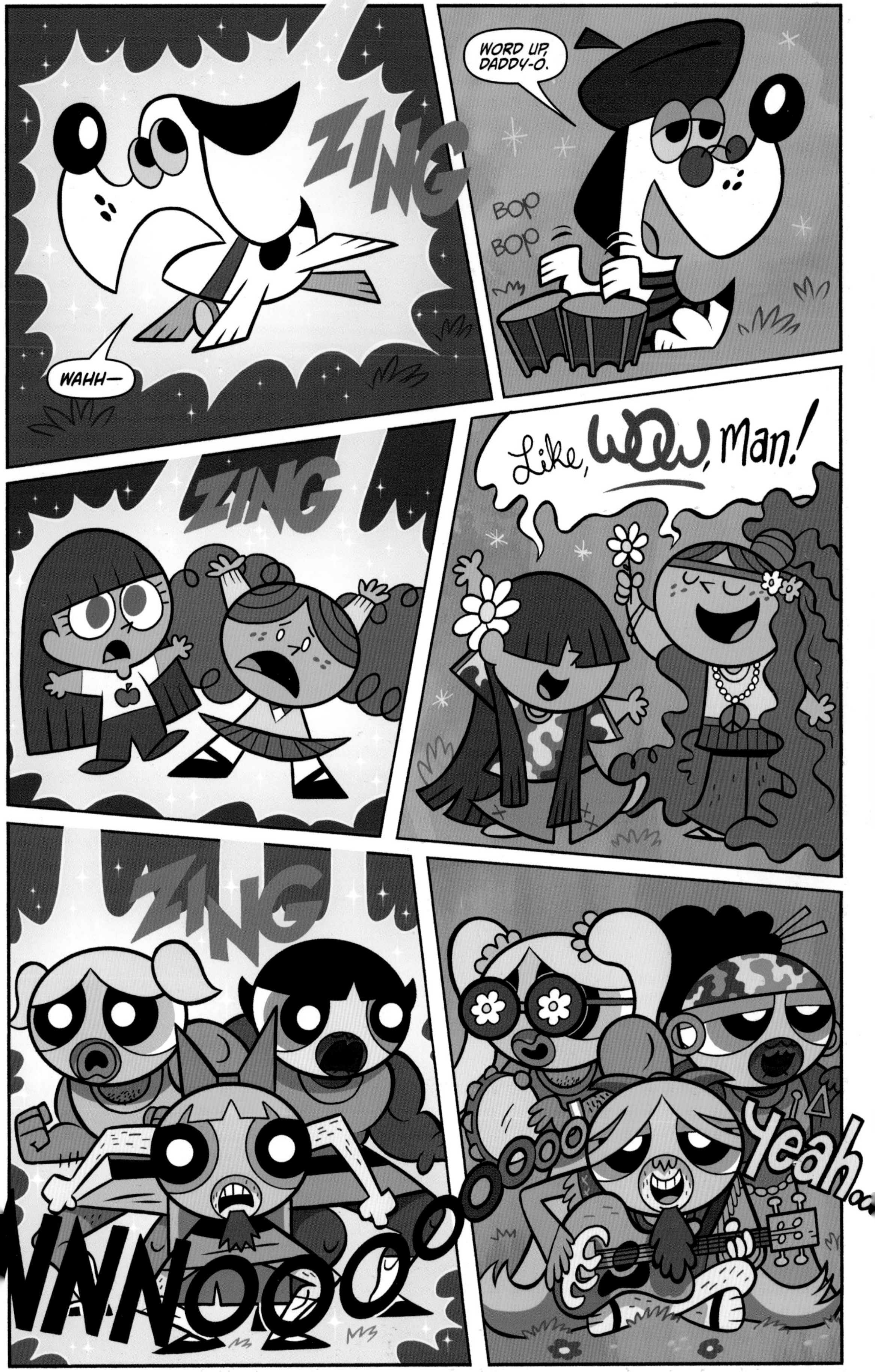
ZING
WAHH—
WORD UP, DADDY-O.
BOP BOP
ZING
Like, WOW, Man!
ZING
NNNOOOOOOOOOOO
Yeah...

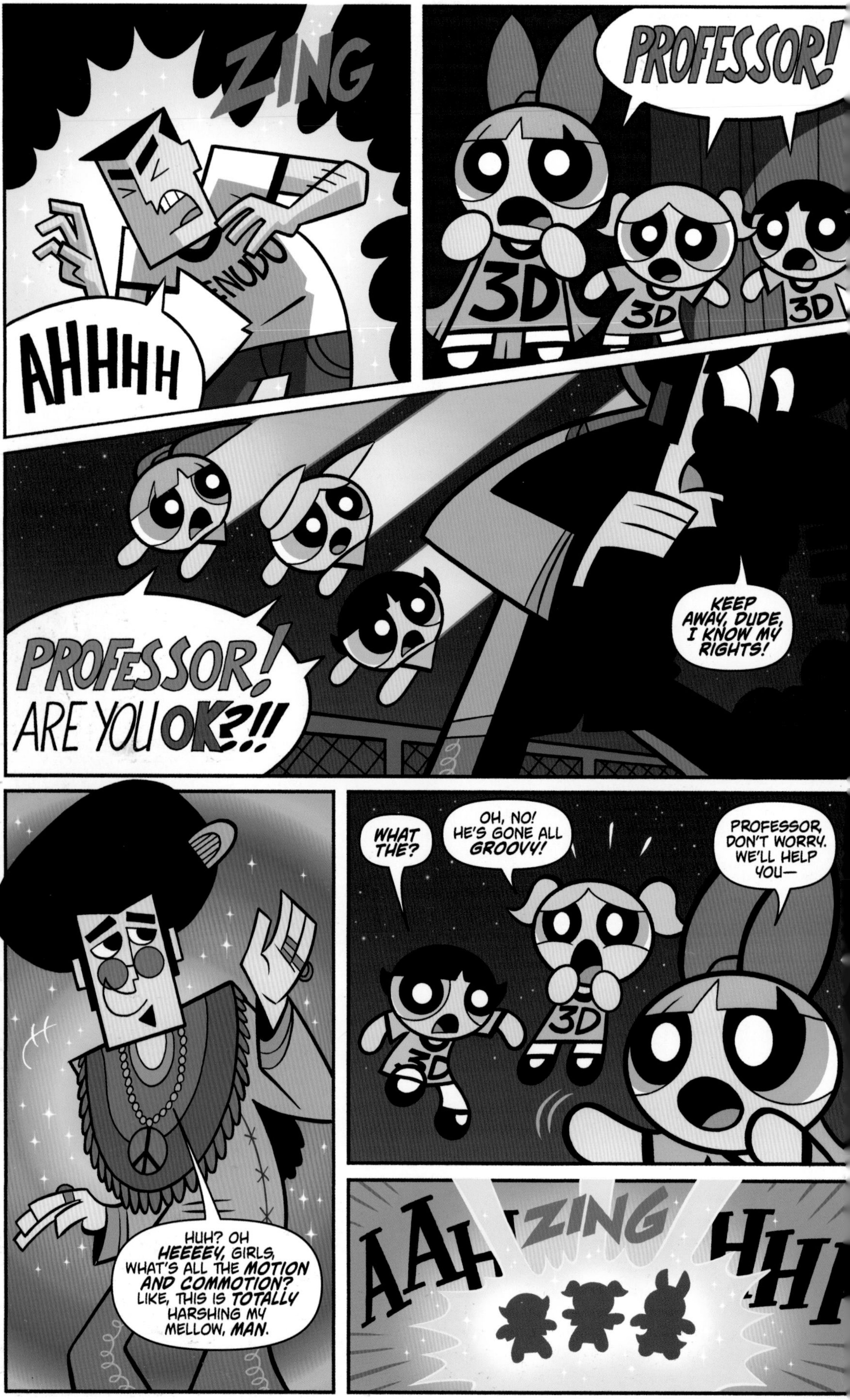
ZING
AHHHH
PROFESSOR!
PROFESSOR! ARE YOU OK?!!
KEEP AWAY, DUDE, I KNOW MY RIGHTS!
HUH? OH HEEEEY, GIRLS, WHAT'S ALL THE MOTION AND COMMOTION? LIKE, THIS IS TOTALLY HARSHING MY MELLOW, MAN.
WHAT THE?
OH, NO! HE'S GONE ALL GROOVY!
PROFESSOR, DON'T WORRY. WE'LL HELP YOU—
AAH ZING HHH

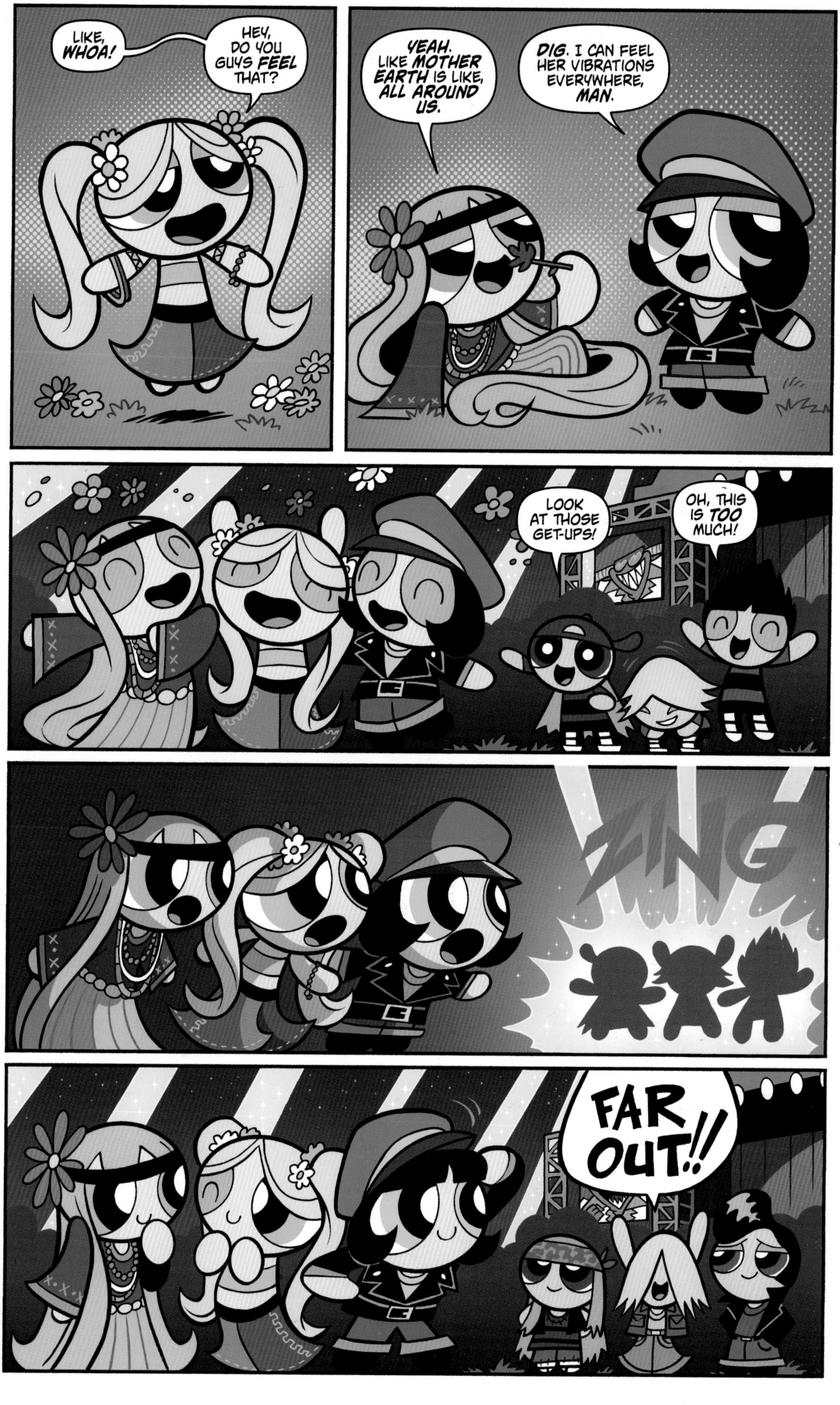
LIKE, WHOA!
HEY, DO YOU GUYS FEEL THAT?
YEAH. LIKE MOTHER EARTH IS LIKE, ALL AROUND US.
DIG. I CAN FEEL HER VIBRATIONS EVERYWHERE, MAN.
LOOK AT THOSE GET-UPS!
OH, THIS IS TOO MUCH!
ZING
FAR OUT!!

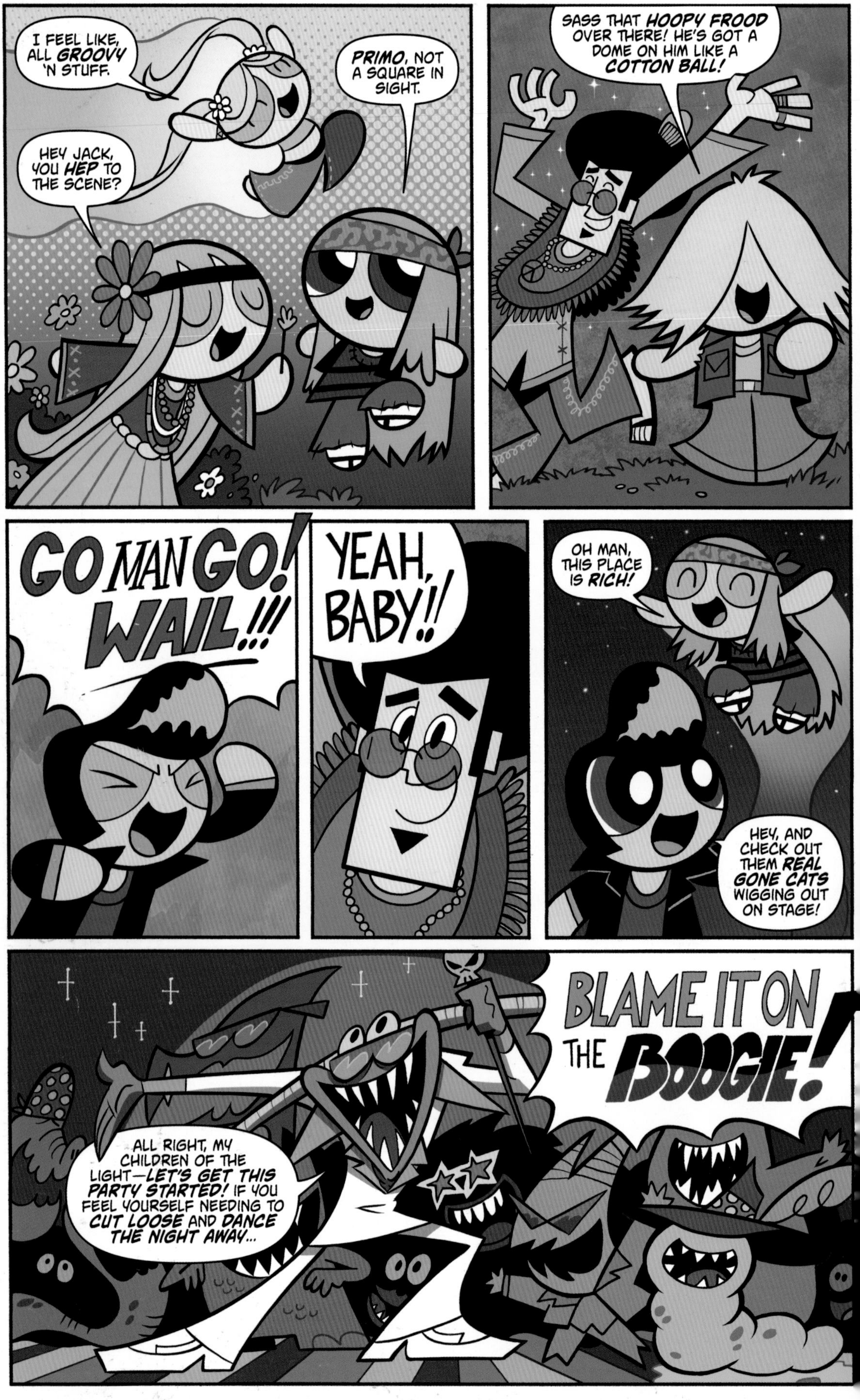
I FEEL LIKE, ALL GROOVY 'N STUFF.
PRIMO, NOT A SQUARE IN SIGHT.
HEY JACK, YOU HEP TO THE SCENE?
SASS THAT HOOPY FROOD OVER THERE! HE'S GOT A DOME ON HIM LIKE A COTTON BALL!
GO MAN GO! WAIL!!!
YEAH, BABY!!
OH MAN, THIS PLACE IS RICH!
HEY, AND CHECK OUT THEM REAL GONE CATS WIGGING OUT ON STAGE!
BLAME IT ON THE BOOGIE!
ALL RIGHT, MY CHILDREN OF THE LIGHT—LET'S GET THIS PARTY STARTED! IF YOU FEEL YOURSELF NEEDING TO CUT LOOSE AND DANCE THE NIGHT AWAY...

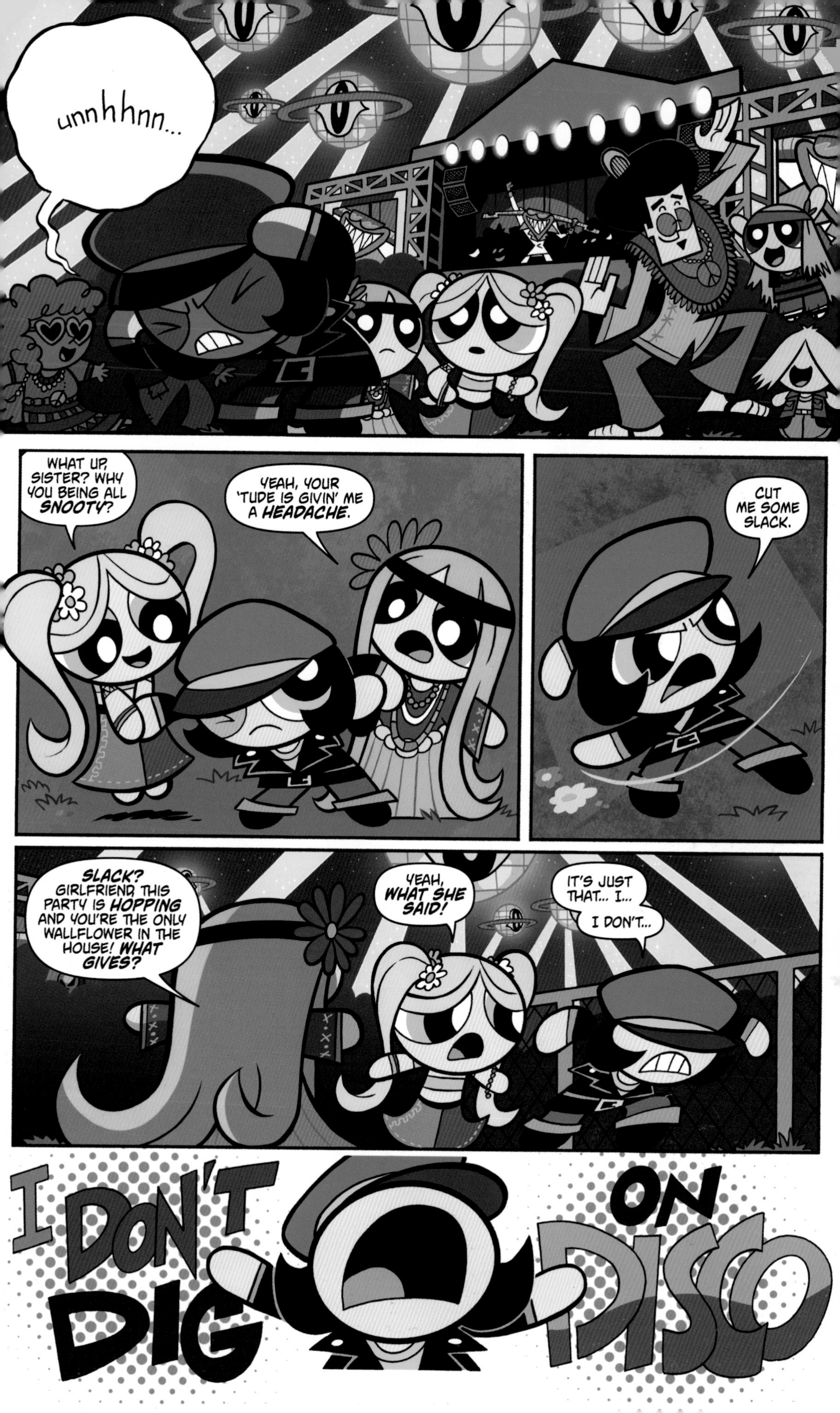
unnhhnn...
WHAT UP, SISTER? WHY YOU BEING ALL SNOOTY?
YEAH, YOUR 'TUDE IS GIVIN' ME A HEADACHE.
CUT ME SOME SLACK.
SLACK? GIRLFRIEND, THIS PARTY IS HOPPING AND YOU'RE THE ONLY WALLFLOWER IN THE HOUSE! WHAT GIVES?
YEAH, WHAT SHE SAID!
IT'S JUST THAT... I...
I DON'T...
I DON'T DIG ON DISCO

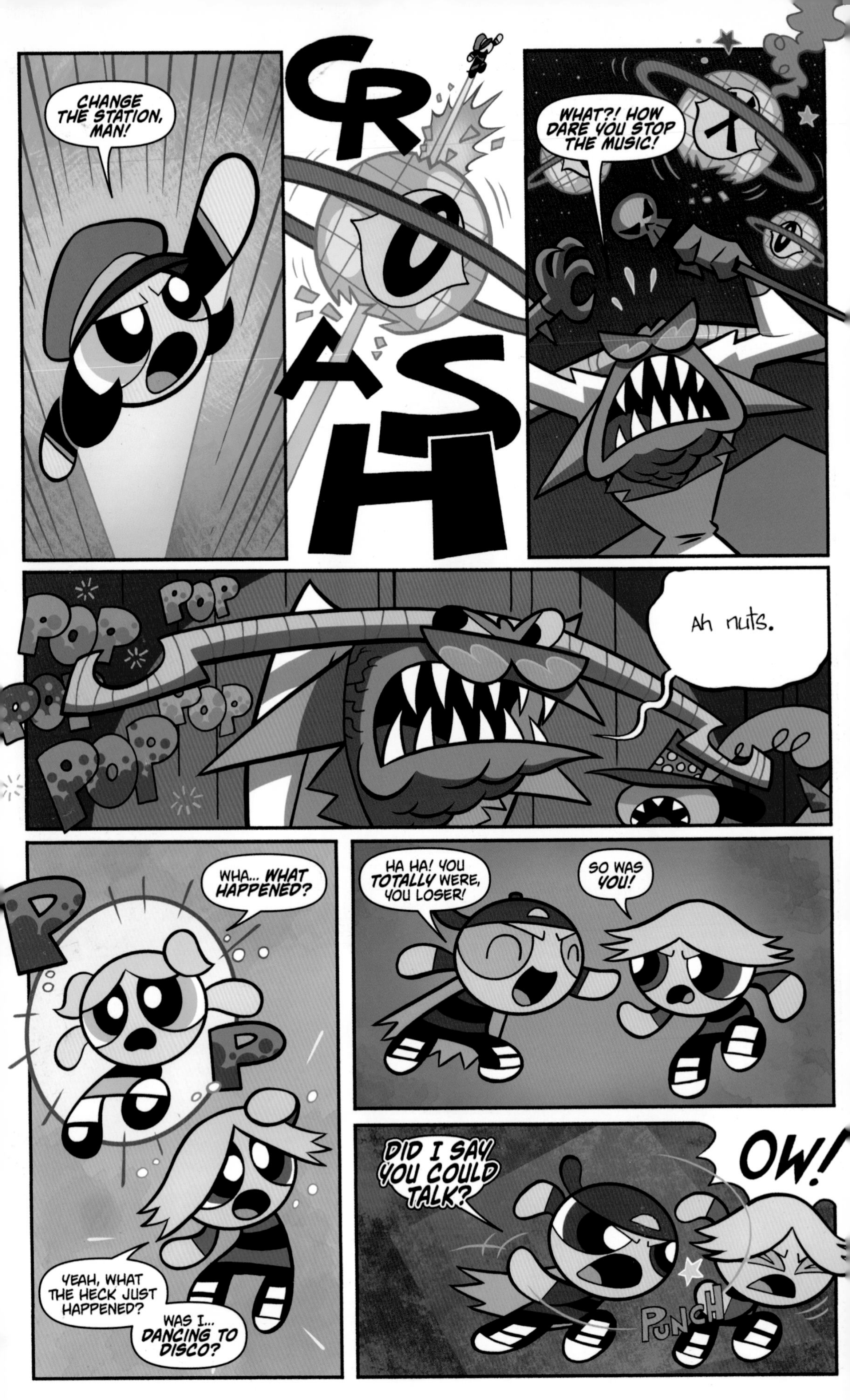

CHANGE THE STATION, MAN!
CRASH
WHAT?! HOW DARE YOU STOP THE MUSIC!
POP POP POP POP POP
Ah nuts.
P P
WHA... WHAT HAPPENED?
YEAH, WHAT THE HECK JUST HAPPENED?
WAS I... DANCING TO DISCO?
HA HA! YOU TOTALLY WERE, YOU LOSER!
SO WAS YOU!
DID I SAY YOU COULD TALK?
OW!
PUNCH

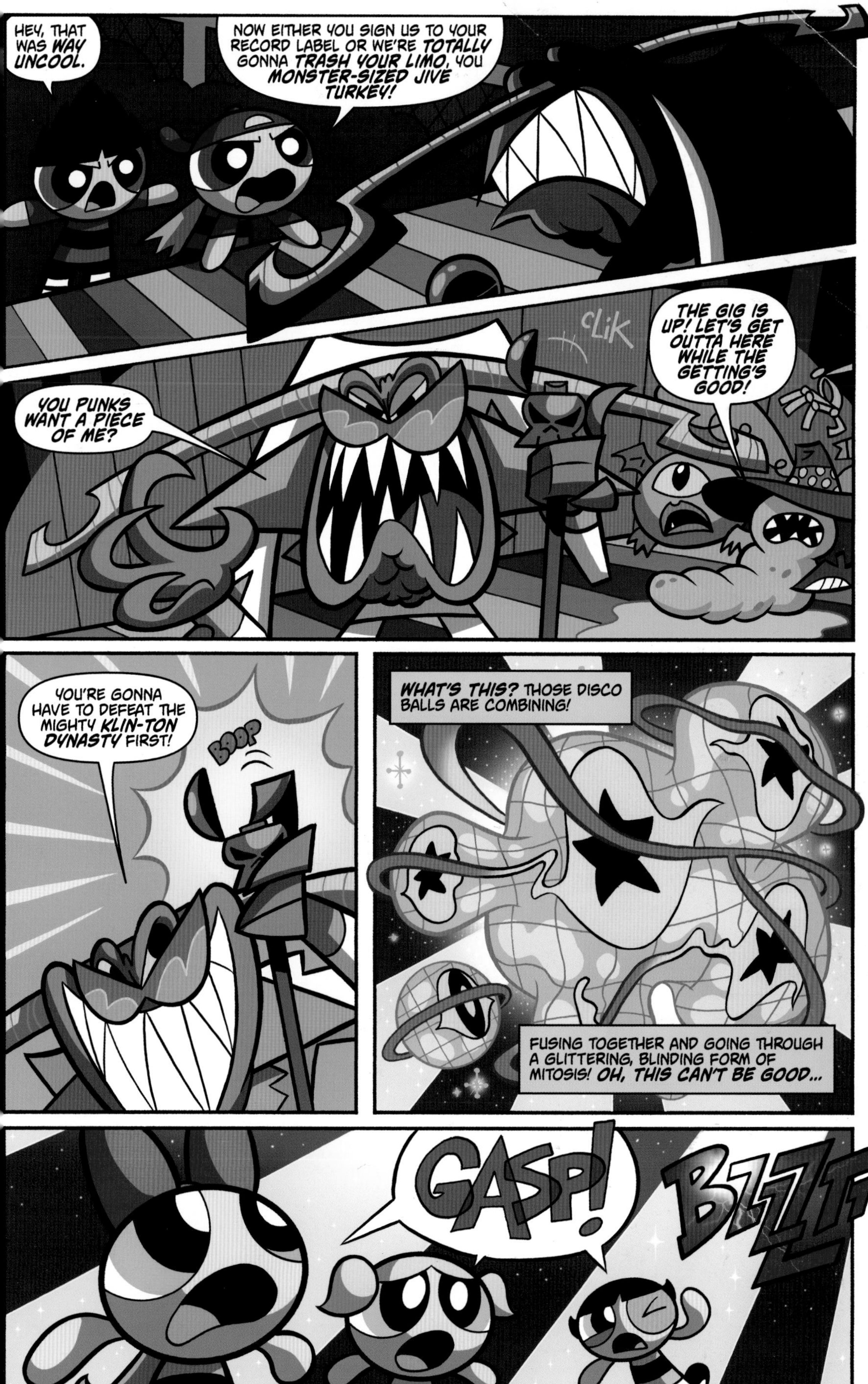
HEY, THAT WAS WAY UNCOOL.
NOW EITHER YOU SIGN US TO YOUR RECORD LABEL OR WE'RE TOTALLY GONNA TRASH YOUR LIMO, YOU MONSTER-SIZED JIVE TURKEY!
CLIK
THE GIG IS UP! LET'S GET OUTTA HERE WHILE THE GETTING'S GOOD!
YOU PUNKS WANT A PIECE OF ME?
YOU'RE GONNA HAVE TO DEFEAT THE MIGHTY KLIN-TON DYNASTY FIRST!
BOOP
WHAT'S THIS? THOSE DISCO BALLS ARE COMBINING!
FUSING TOGETHER AND GOING THROUGH A GLITTERING, BLINDING FORM OF MITOSIS! OH, THIS CAN'T BE GOOD...
GASP!
BZZTT

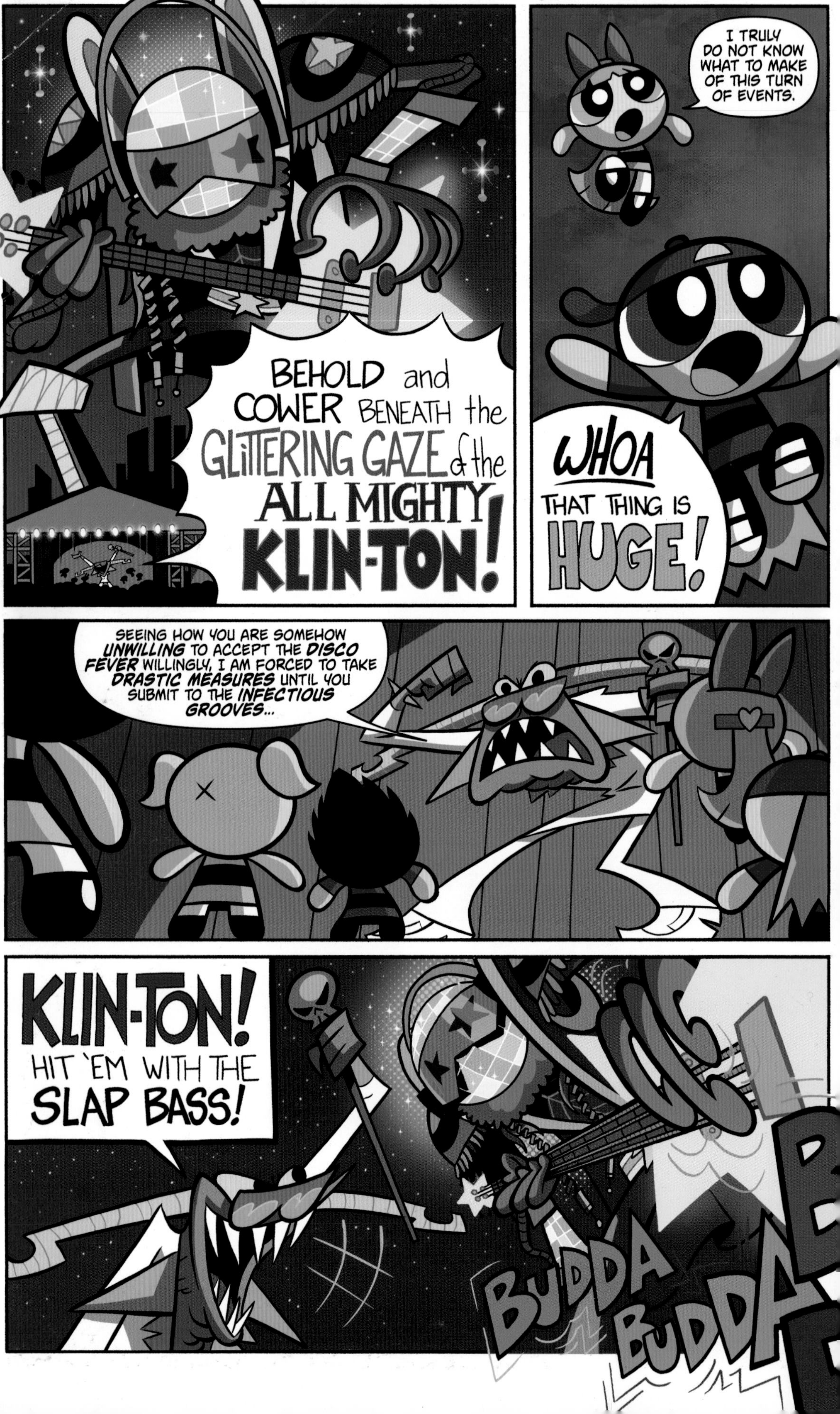
BEHOLD and COWER BENEATH the GLITTERING GAZE of the ALL MIGHTY KLIN-TON!
I TRULY DO NOT KNOW WHAT TO MAKE OF THIS TURN OF EVENTS.
WHOA THAT THING IS HUGE!
SEEING HOW YOU ARE SOMEHOW UNWILLING TO ACCEPT THE DISCO FEVER WILLINGLY, I AM FORCED TO TAKE DRASTIC MEASURES UNTIL YOU SUBMIT TO THE INFECTIOUS GROOVES...
KLIN-TON! HIT 'EM WITH THE SLAP BASS!
BUDDA BUDDA

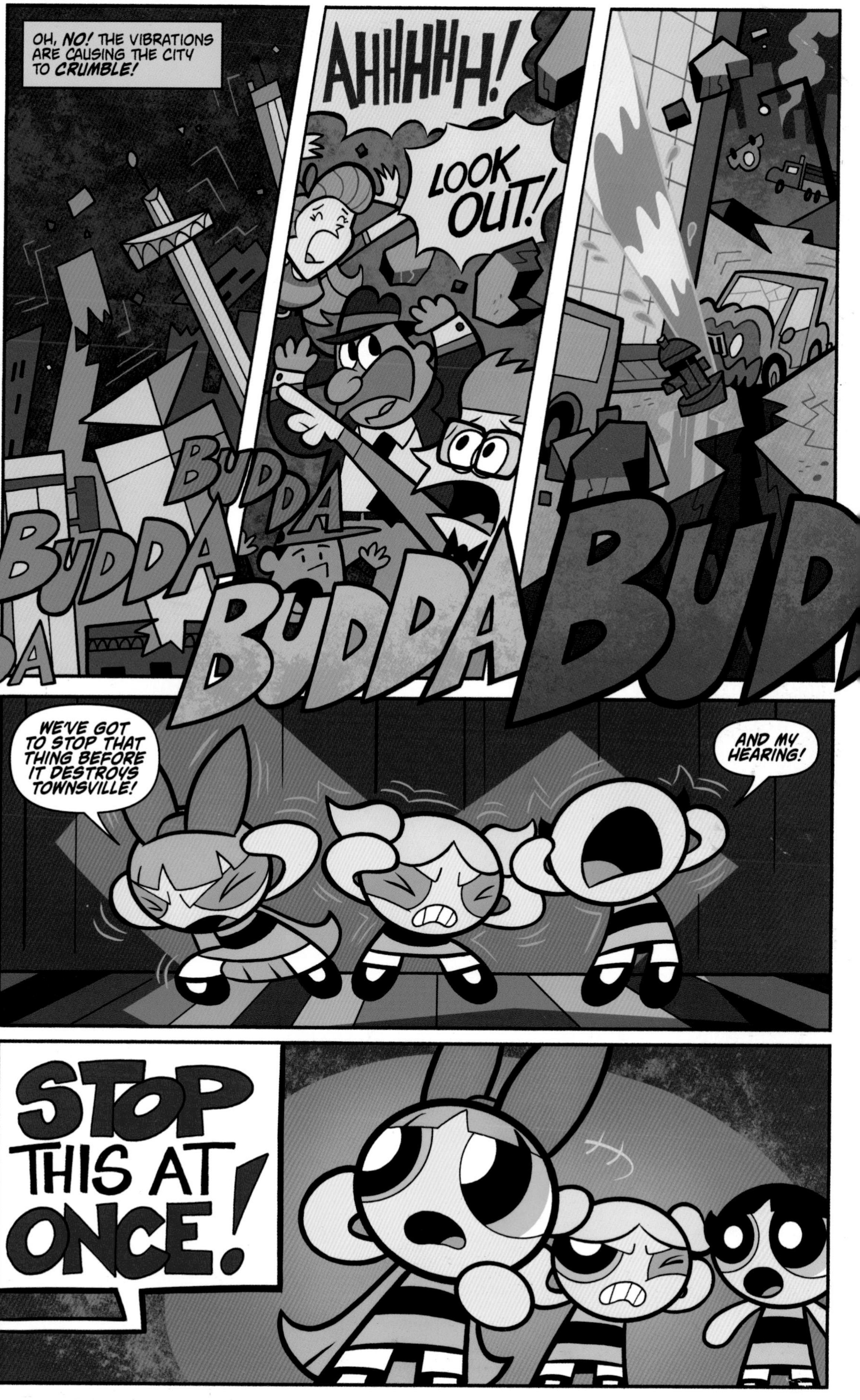
OH, NO! THE VIBRATIONS ARE CAUSING THE CITY TO CRUMBLE!
AHHHHH!
LOOK OUT!
BUDDA
BUDDA
BUDDA
BUDDA
BUD
WE'VE GOT TO STOP THAT THING BEFORE IT DESTROYS TOWNSVILLE!
AND MY HEARING!
STOP THIS AT ONCE!

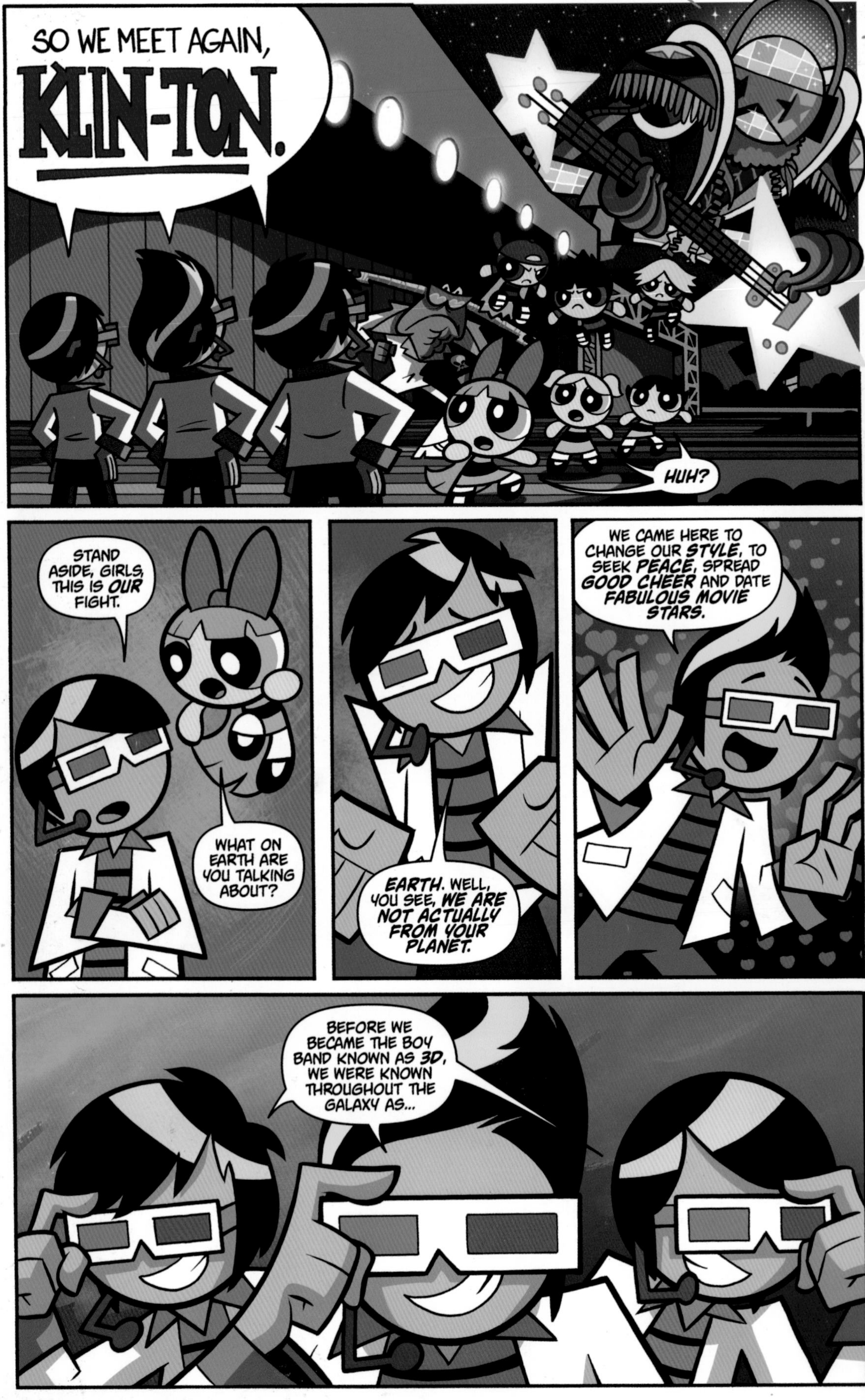
SO WE MEET AGAIN, KLIN-TON.
HUH?
STAND ASIDE, GIRLS, THIS IS OUR FIGHT.
WHAT ON EARTH ARE YOU TALKING ABOUT?
EARTH. WELL, YOU SEE, WE ARE NOT ACTUALLY FROM YOUR PLANET.
WE CAME HERE TO CHANGE OUR STYLE, TO SEEK PEACE, SPREAD GOOD CHEER AND DATE FABULOUS MOVIE STARS.
BEFORE WE BECAME THE BOY BAND KNOWN AS 3D, WE WERE KNOWN THROUGHOUT THE GALAXY AS...

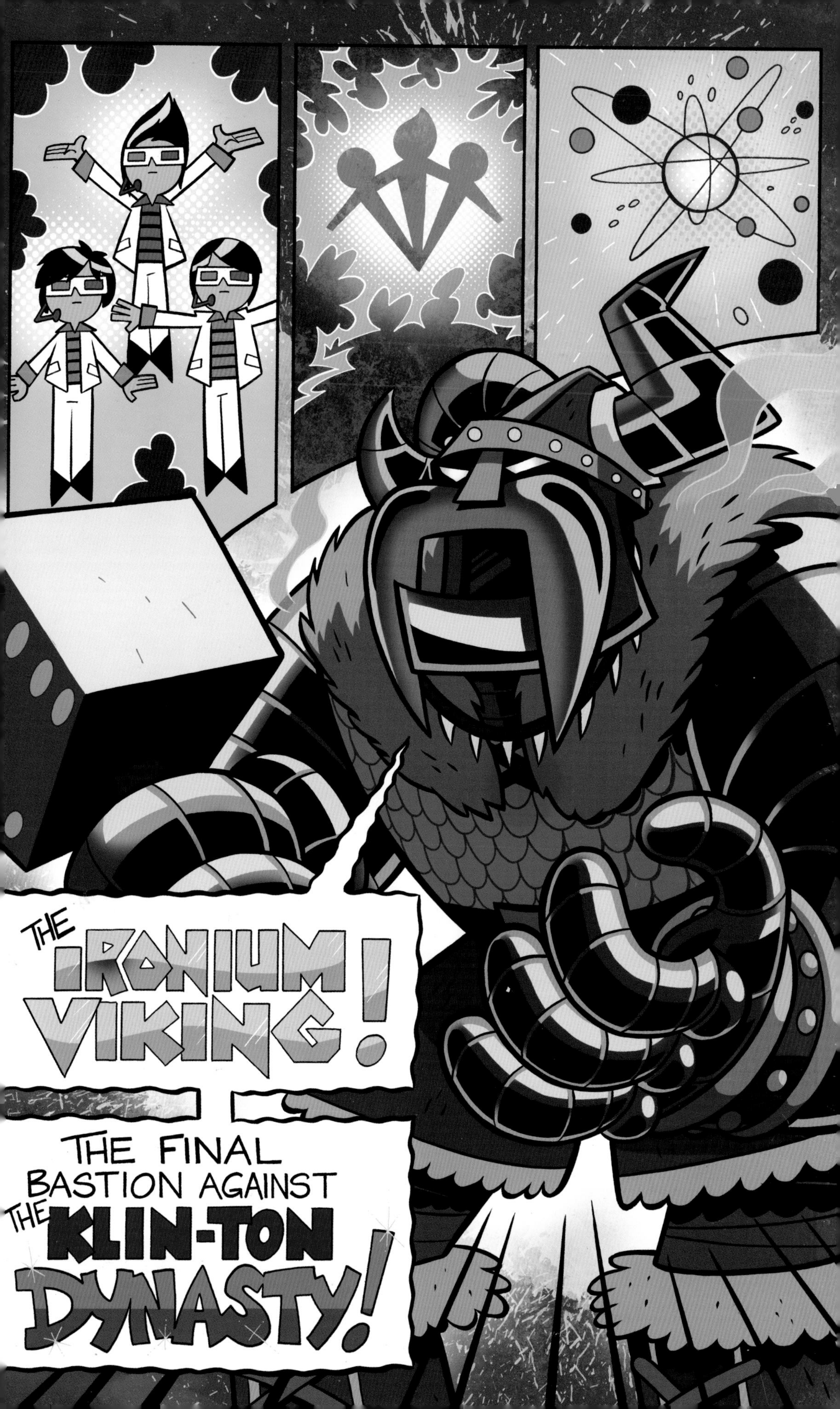
THE IRONIUM VIKING!
THE FINAL BASTION AGAINST THE KLIN-TON DYNASTY!

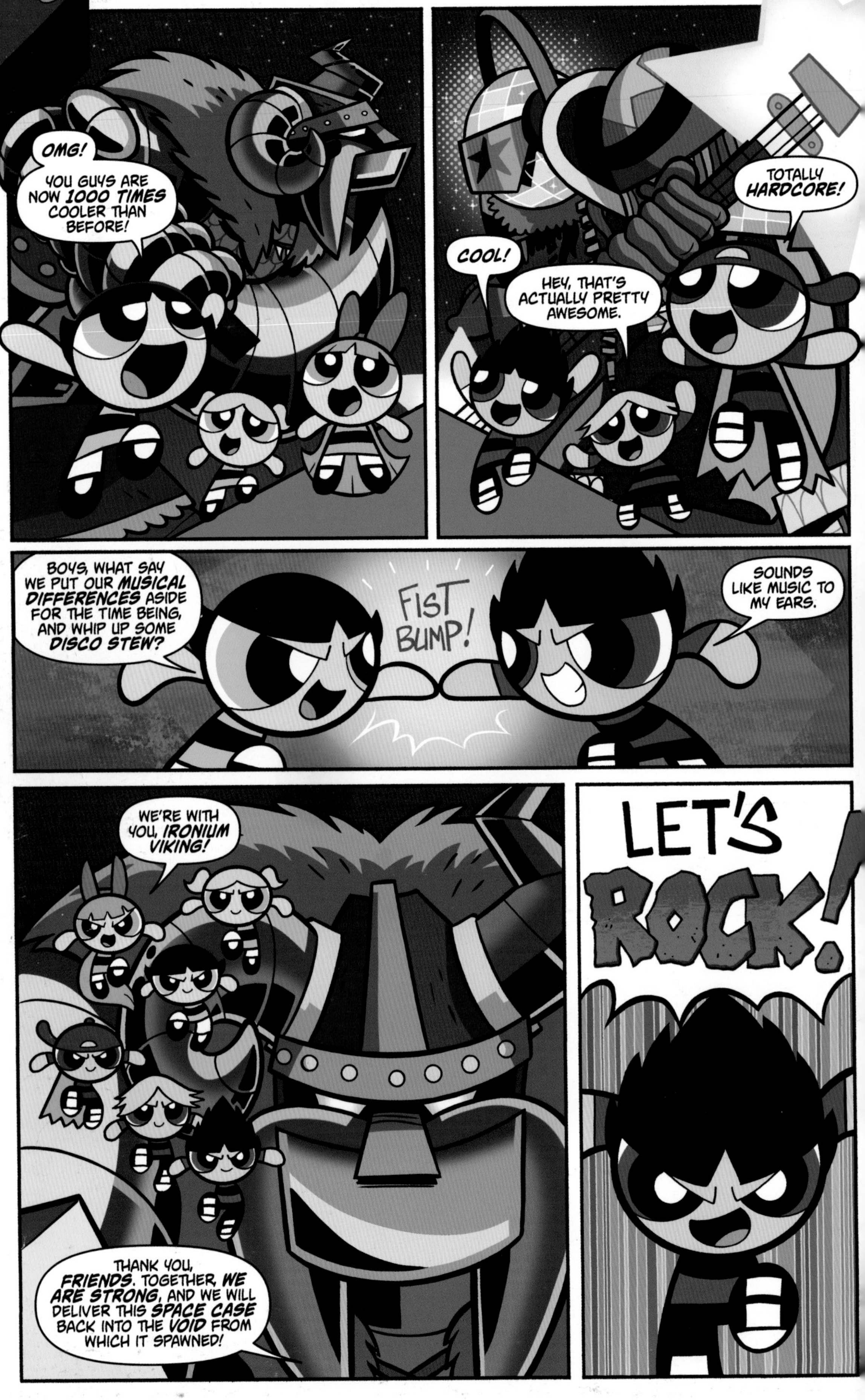
OMG!
YOU GUYS ARE NOW 1000 TIMES COOLER THAN BEFORE!
TOTALLY HARDCORE!
COOL!
HEY, THAT'S ACTUALLY PRETTY AWESOME.
BOYS, WHAT SAY WE PUT OUR MUSICAL DIFFERENCES ASIDE FOR THE TIME BEING, AND WHIP UP SOME DISCO STEW?
FIST BUMP!
SOUNDS LIKE MUSIC TO MY EARS.
WE'RE WITH YOU, IRONIUM VIKING!
THANK YOU, FRIENDS. TOGETHER, WE ARE STRONG, AND WE WILL DELIVER THIS SPACE CASE BACK INTO THE VOID FROM WHICH IT SPAWNED!
LET'S ROCK!

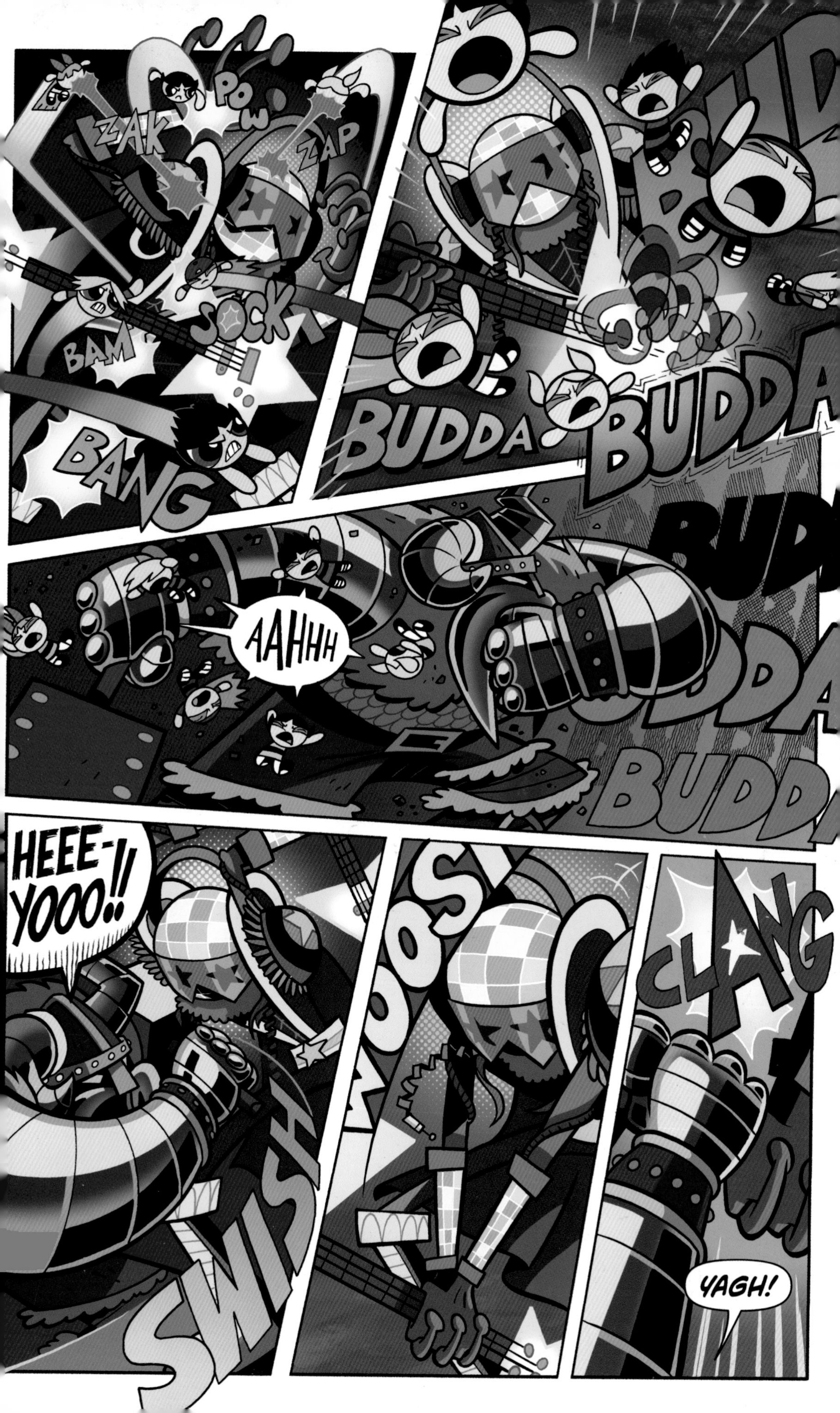
ZAK
POW
ZAP
SOCK
BAM
BANG
BUDDA
BUDDA
BUD
BUDDA
BUDDA
AAHHH
HEEE-YOOO!!
SWISH
WOOSH
CLANG
YAGH!

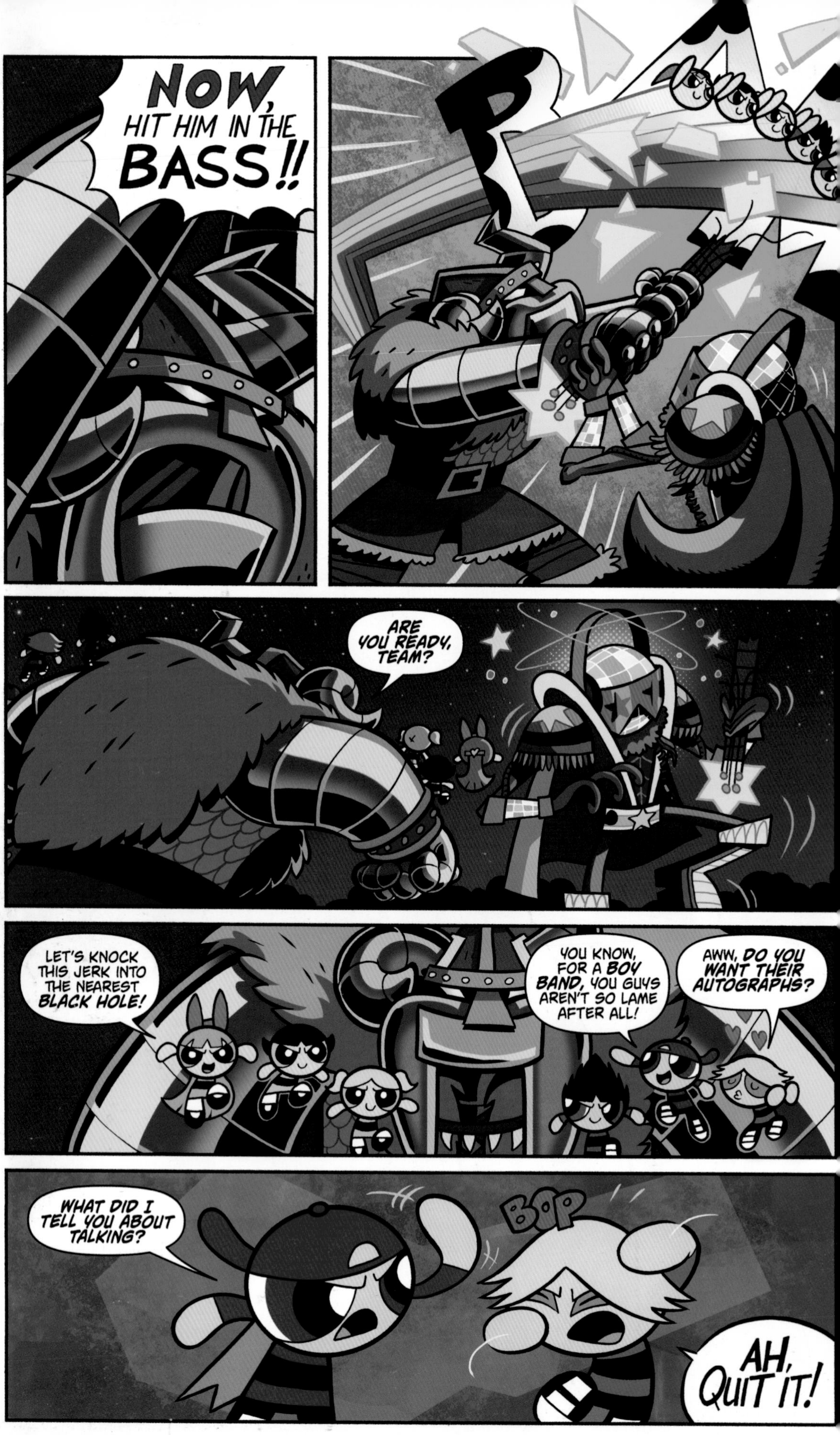
NOW, HIT HIM IN THE BASS!!
ARE YOU READY, TEAM?
LET'S KNOCK THIS JERK INTO THE NEAREST BLACK HOLE!
YOU KNOW, FOR A BOY BAND, YOU GUYS AREN'T SO LAME AFTER ALL!
AWW, DO YOU WANT THEIR AUTOGRAPHS?
WHAT DID I TELL YOU ABOUT TALKING?
BOP
AH, QUIT IT!

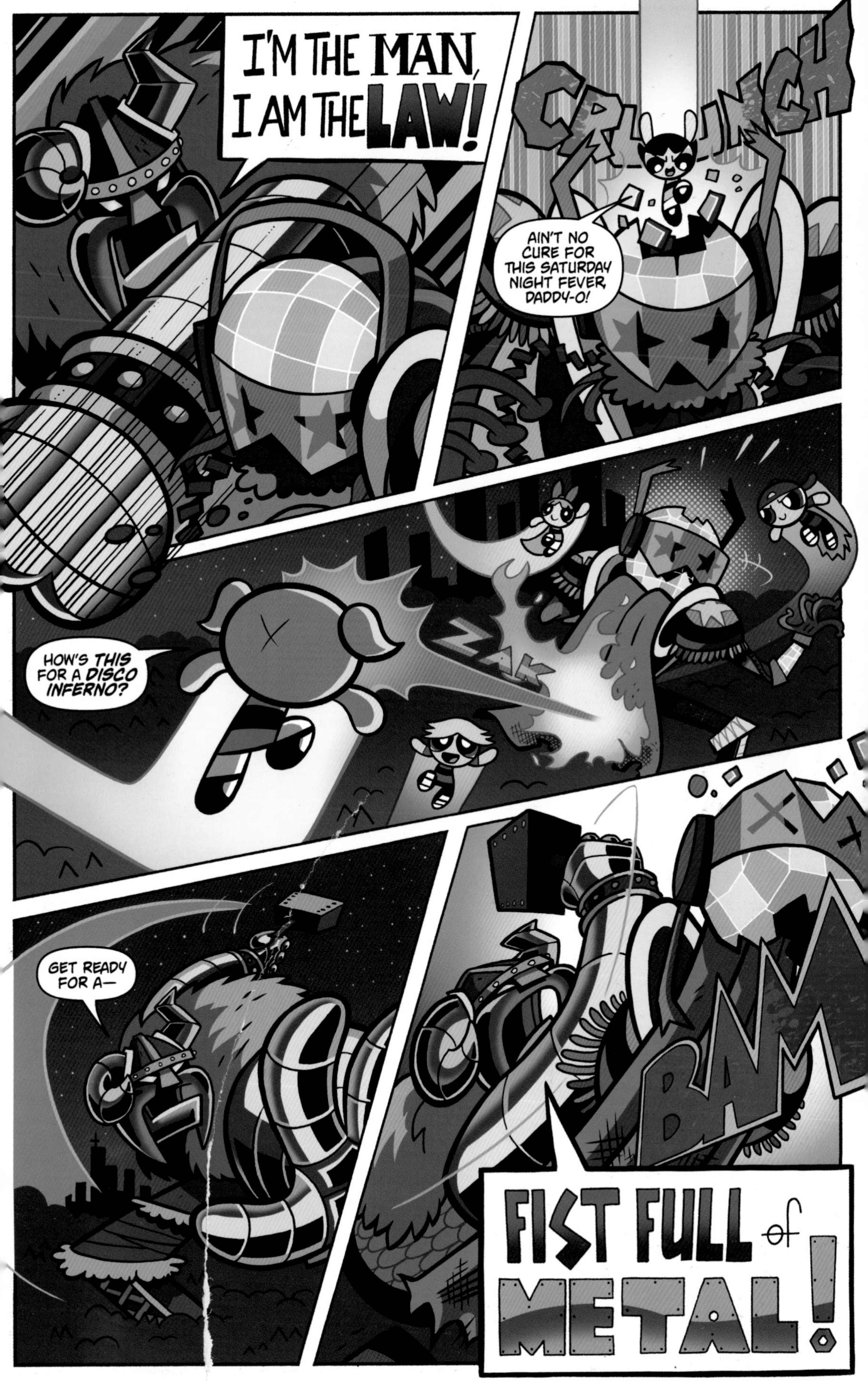
I'M THE MAN, I AM THE LAW!
CRUNCH
AIN'T NO CURE FOR THIS SATURDAY NIGHT FEVER, DADDY-O!
HOW'S THIS FOR A DISCO INFERNO?
ZAK
GET READY FOR A—
BAM
FIST FULL of METAL!

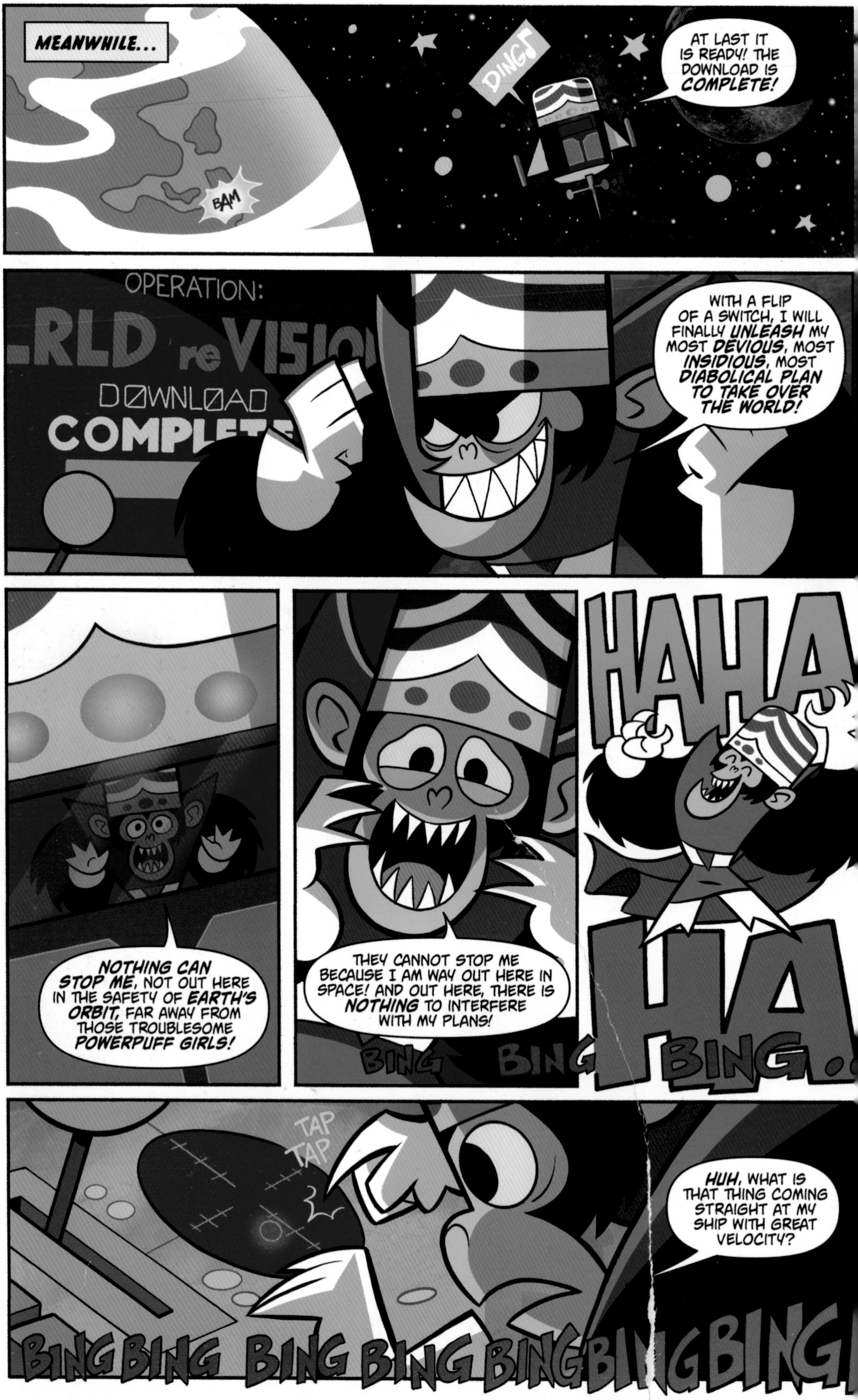

MEANWHILE...
DING♪
BAM
AT LAST IT IS READY! THE DOWNLOAD IS COMPLETE!
OPERATION:
DOWNLOAD
WITH A FLIP OF A SWITCH, I WILL FINALLY UNLEASH MY MOST DEVIOUS, MOST INSIDIOUS, MOST DIABOLICAL PLAN TO TAKE OVER THE WORLD!
NOTHING CAN STOP ME, NOT OUT HERE IN THE SAFETY OF EARTH'S ORBIT, FAR AWAY FROM THOSE TROUBLESOME POWERPUFF GIRLS!
THEY CANNOT STOP ME BECAUSE I AM WAY OUT HERE IN SPACE! AND OUT HERE, THERE IS NOTHING TO INTERFERE WITH MY PLANS!
HAHA
HA
BING BING BING..
TAP TAP
HUH, WHAT IS THAT THING COMING STRAIGHT AT MY SHIP WITH GREAT VELOCITY?
BING BING BING BING BING BING BING

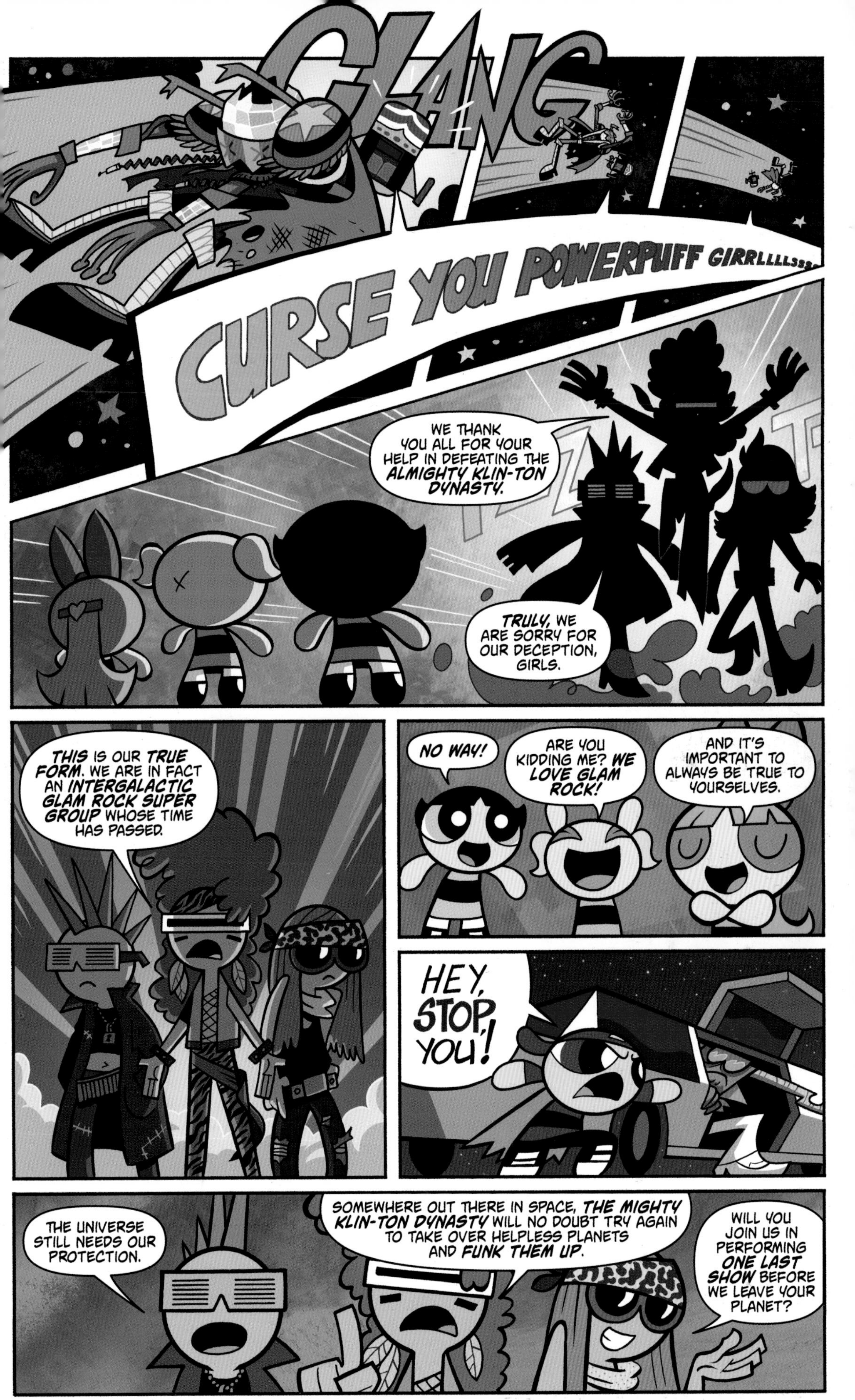
CLANG
CURSE YOU POWERPUFF GIRRLLLLsss
WE THANK YOU ALL FOR YOUR HELP IN DEFEATING THE ALMIGHTY KLIN-TON DYNASTY.
TRULY, WE ARE SORRY FOR OUR DECEPTION, GIRLS.
THIS IS OUR TRUE FORM. WE ARE IN FACT AN INTERGALACTIC GLAM ROCK SUPER GROUP WHOSE TIME HAS PASSED.
NO WAY!
ARE YOU KIDDING ME? WE LOVE GLAM ROCK!
AND IT'S IMPORTANT TO ALWAYS BE TRUE TO YOURSELVES.
HEY, STOP, YOU!
THE UNIVERSE STILL NEEDS OUR PROTECTION.
SOMEWHERE OUT THERE IN SPACE, THE MIGHTY KLIN-TON DYNASTY WILL NO DOUBT TRY AGAIN TO TAKE OVER HELPLESS PLANETS AND FUNK THEM UP.
WILL YOU JOIN US IN PERFORMING ONE LAST SHOW BEFORE WE LEAVE YOUR PLANET?

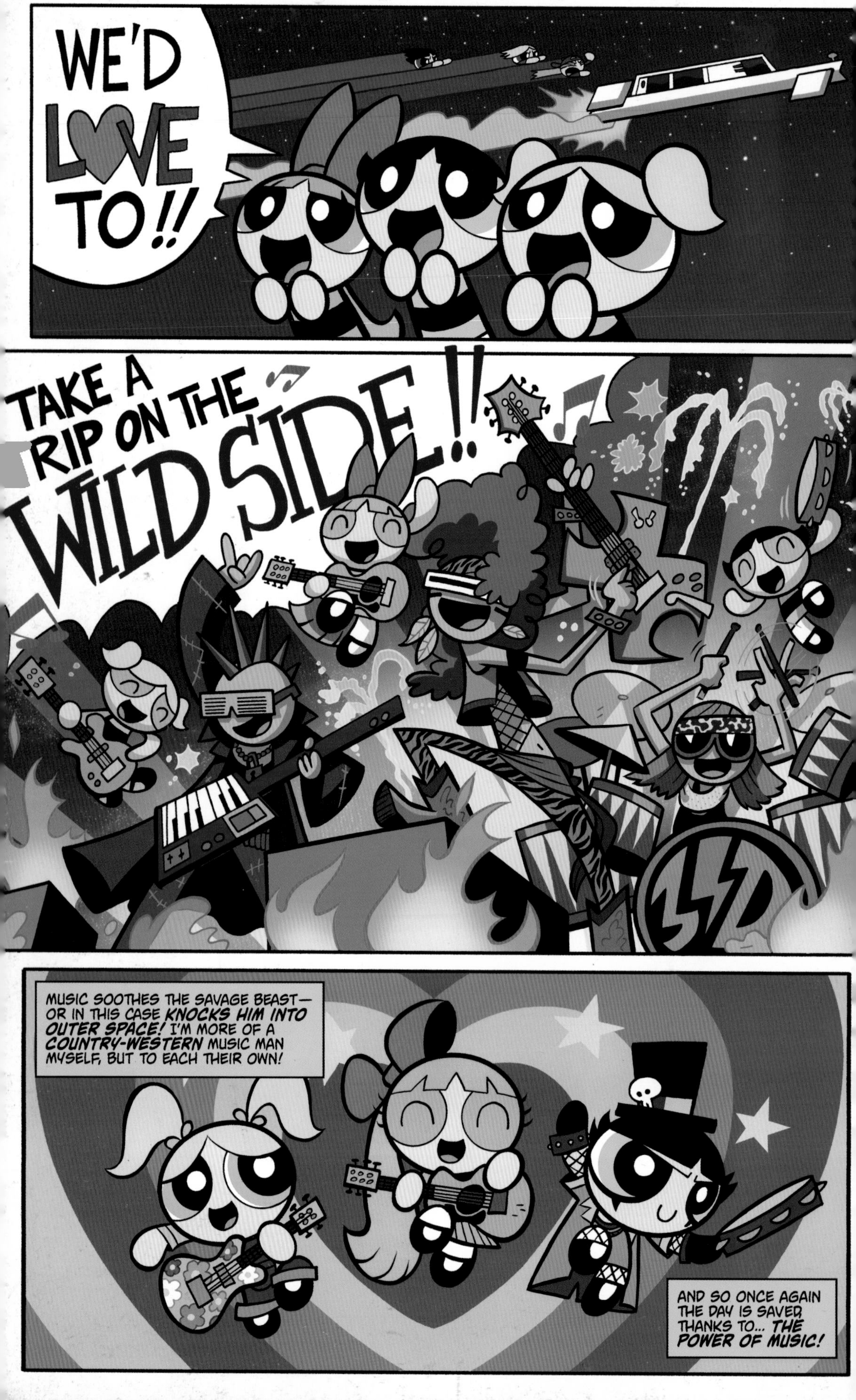
WE'D LOVE TO!!
TAKE A RIP ON THE WILD SIDE!!
MUSIC SOOTHES THE SAVAGE BEAST— OR IN THIS CASE KNOCKS HIM INTO OUTER SPACE! I'M MORE OF A COUNTRY-WESTERN MUSIC MAN MYSELF, BUT TO EACH THEIR OWN!
AND SO ONCE AGAIN THE DAY IS SAVED, THANKS TO... THE POWER OF MUSIC!

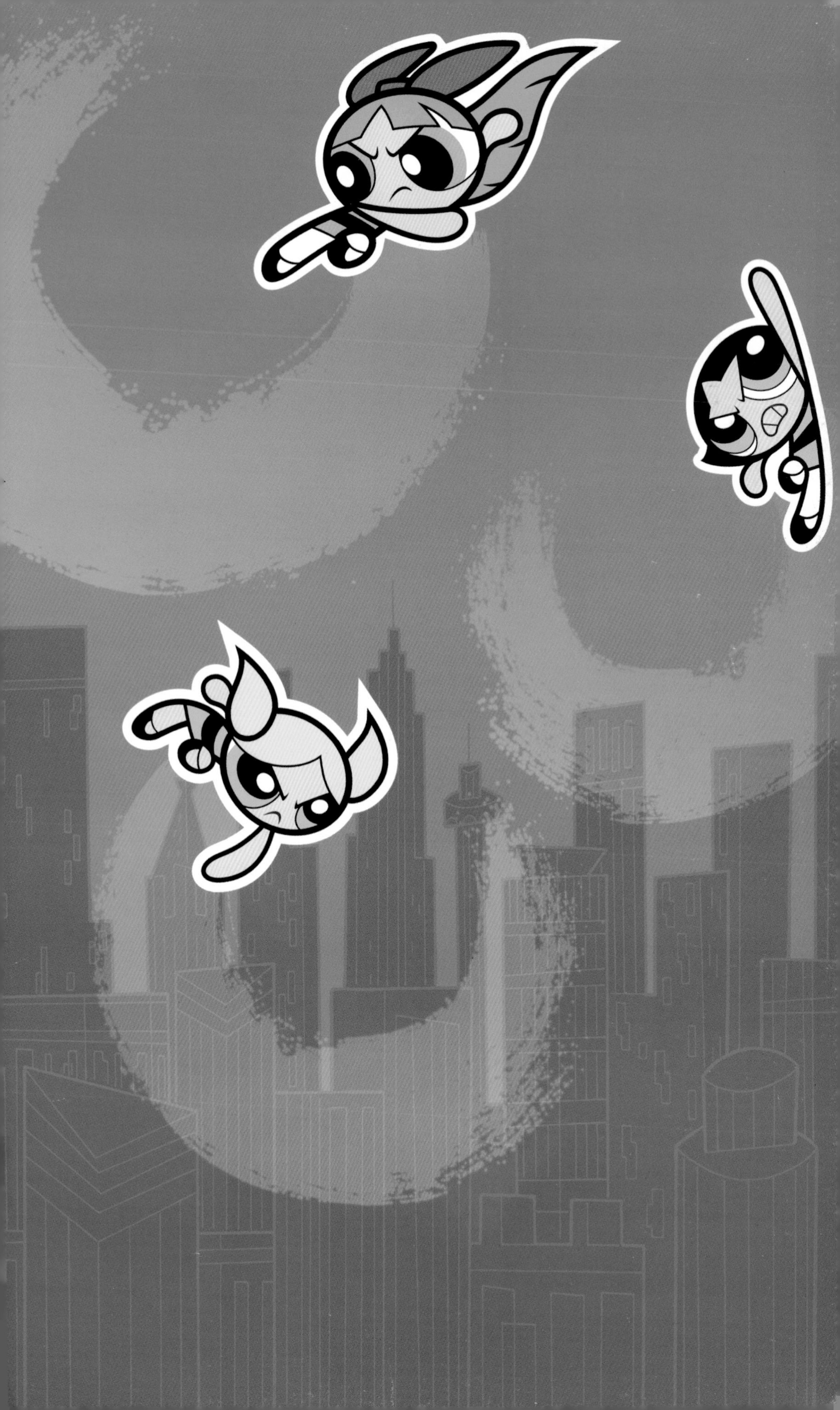

art by **Phil Moy**
colors by **Jason Lewis**

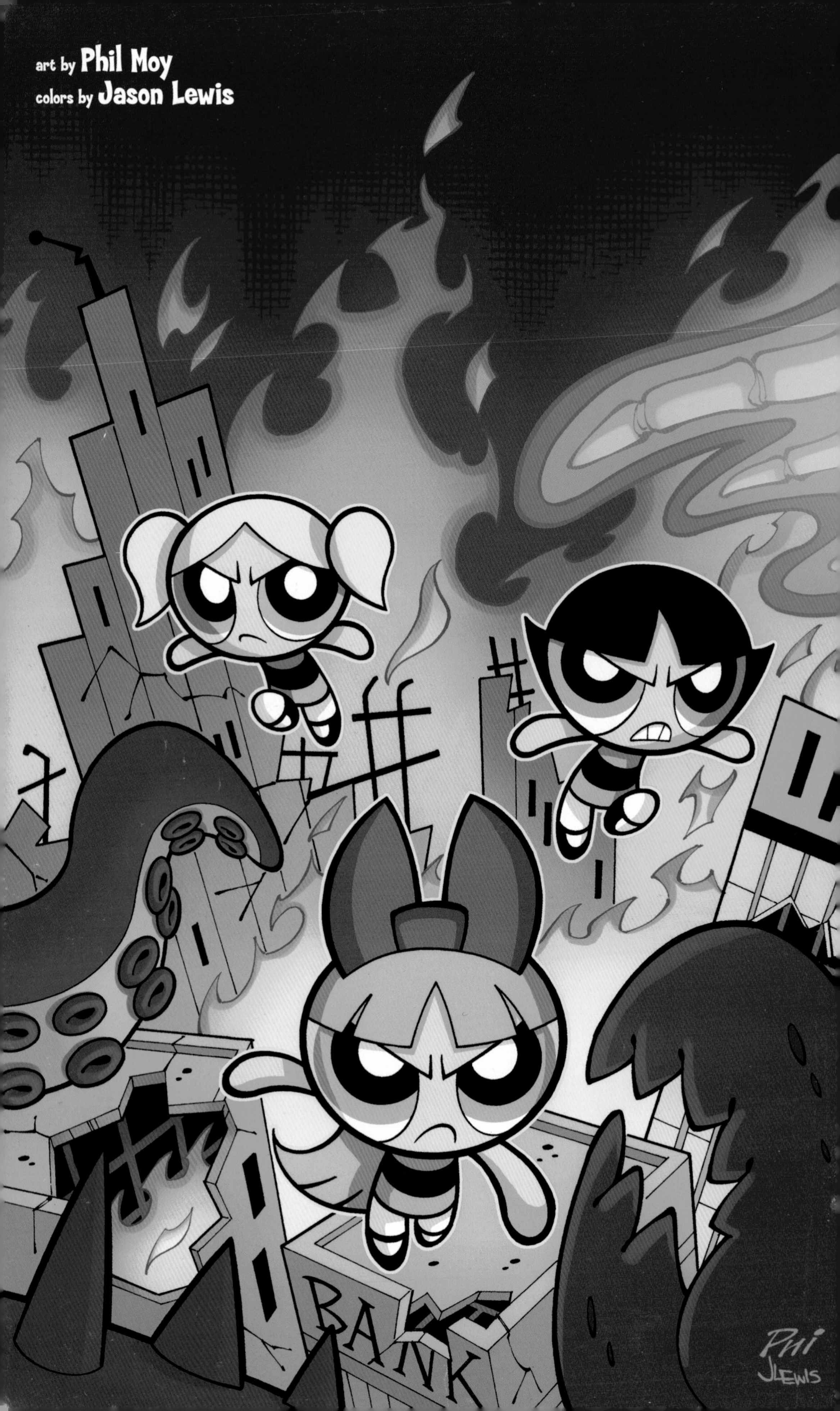
BANK
Phil
JLEWIS

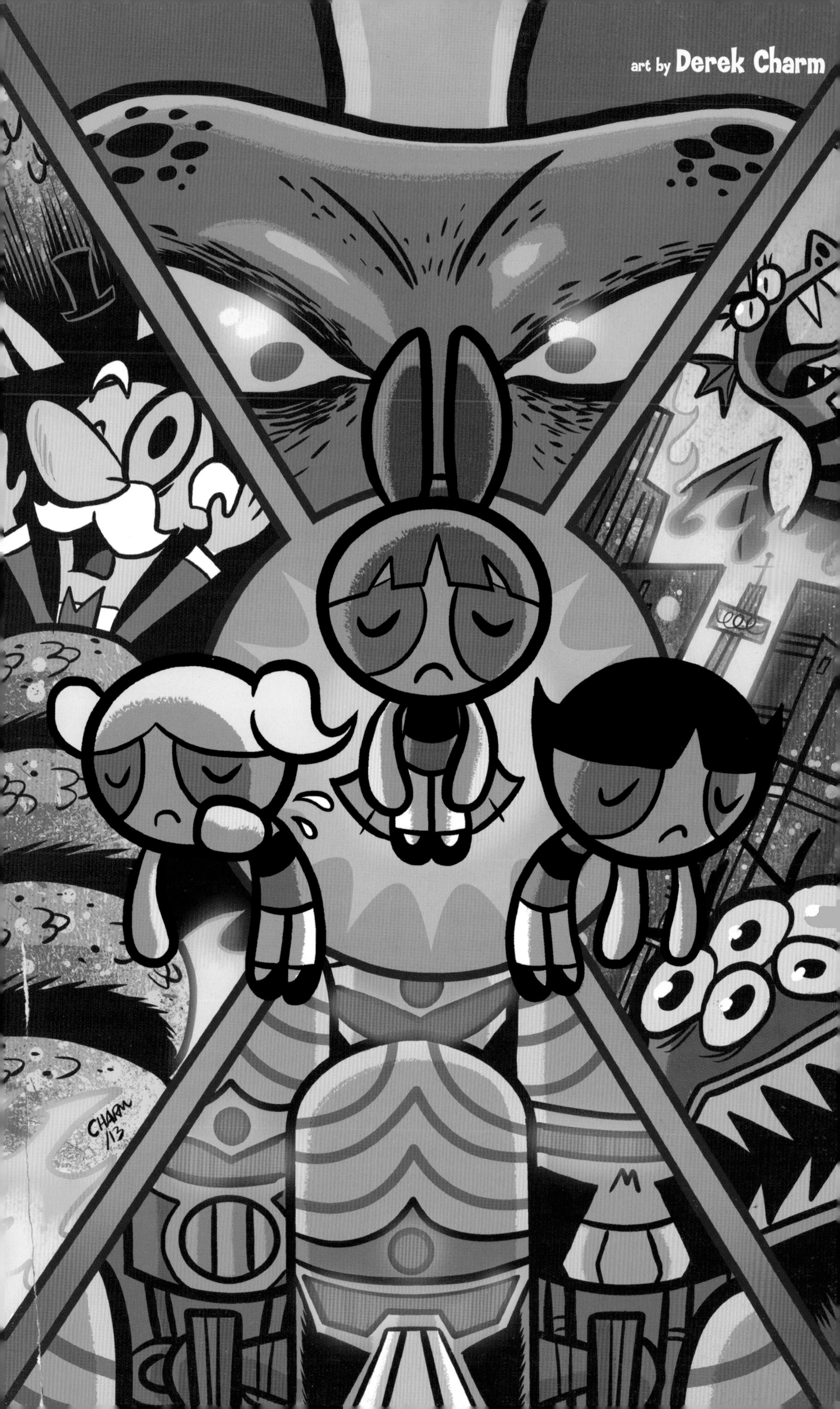
CHARM
/13
art by **Derek Charm**

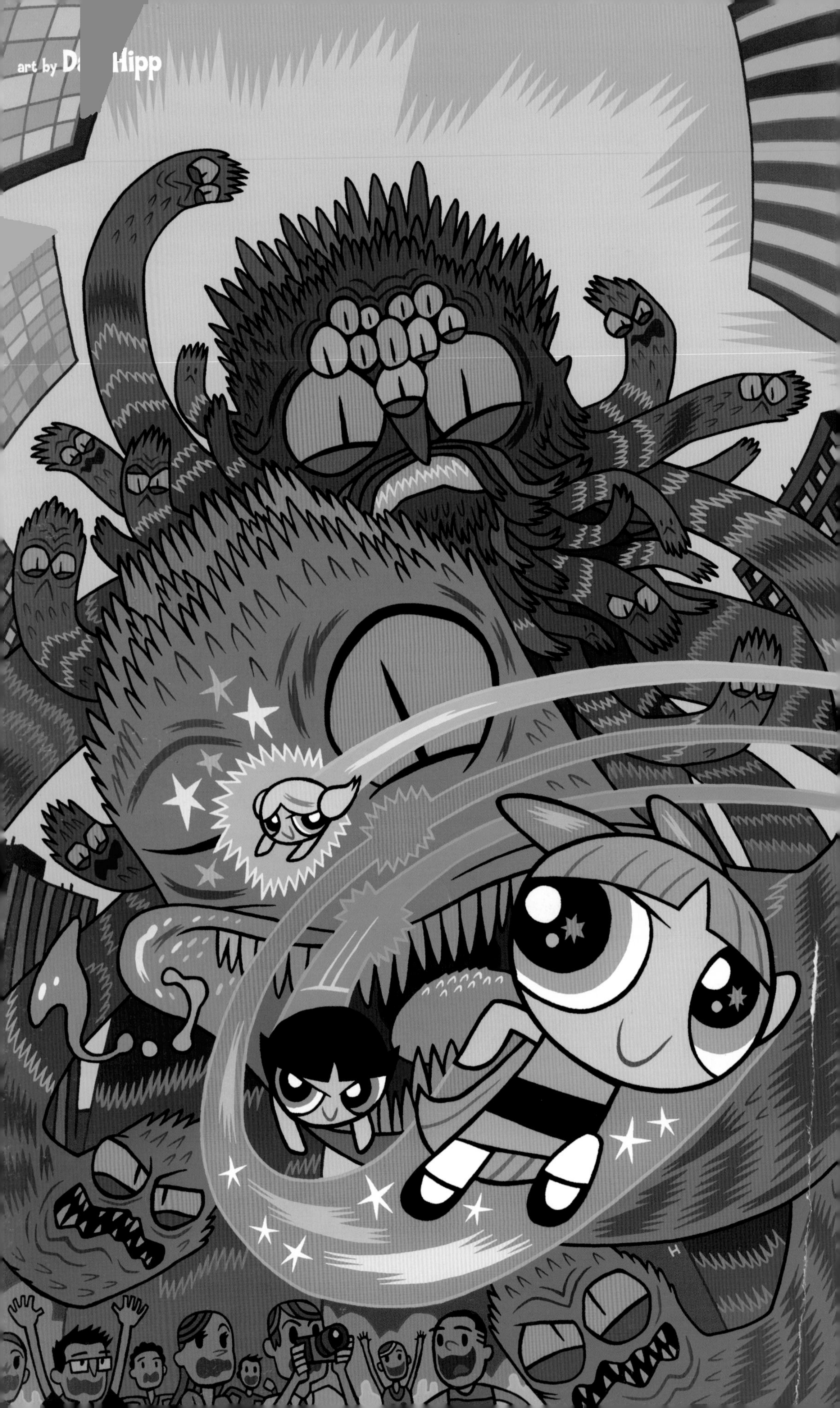
art by Da Hipp

art by Matt Kaufenberg

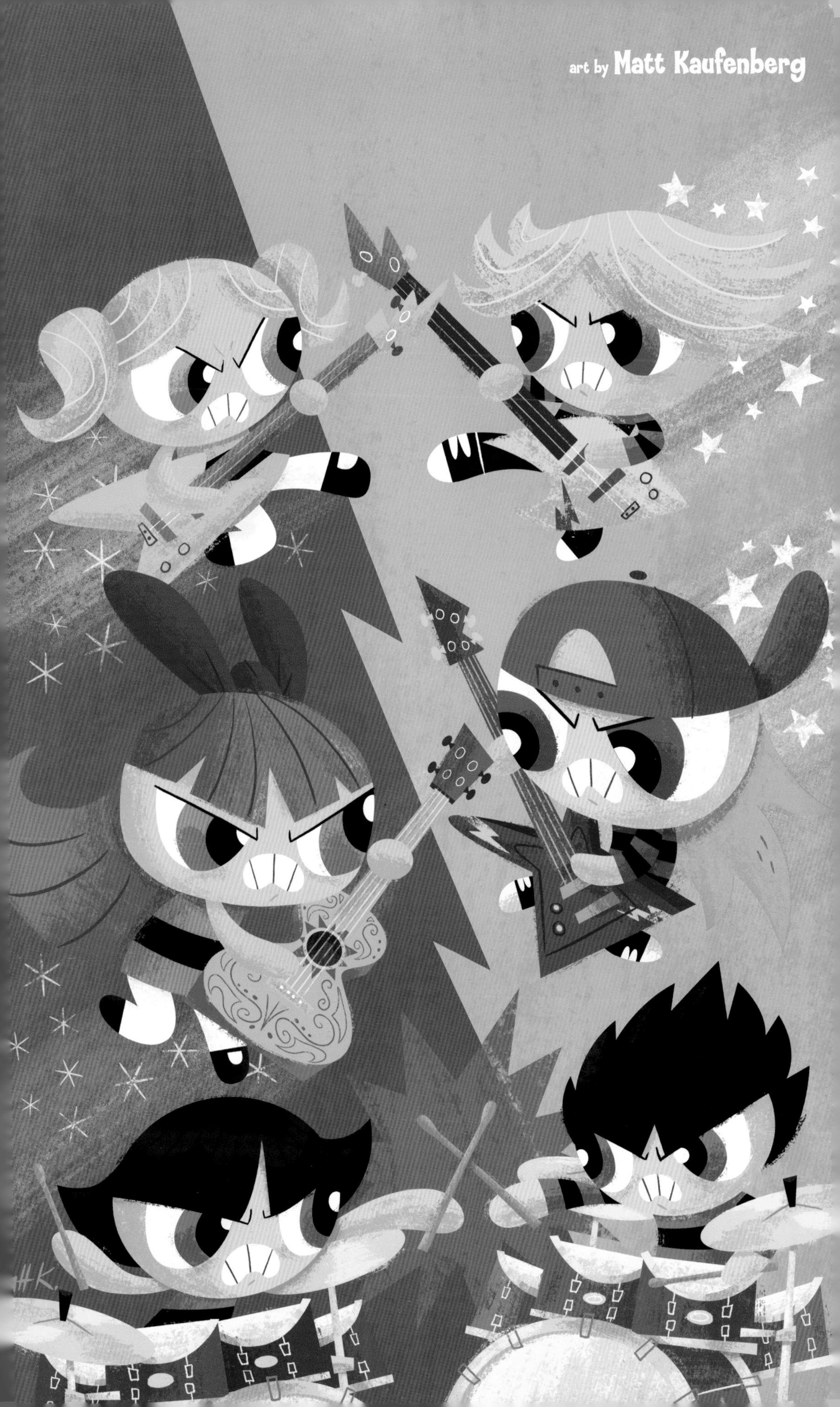

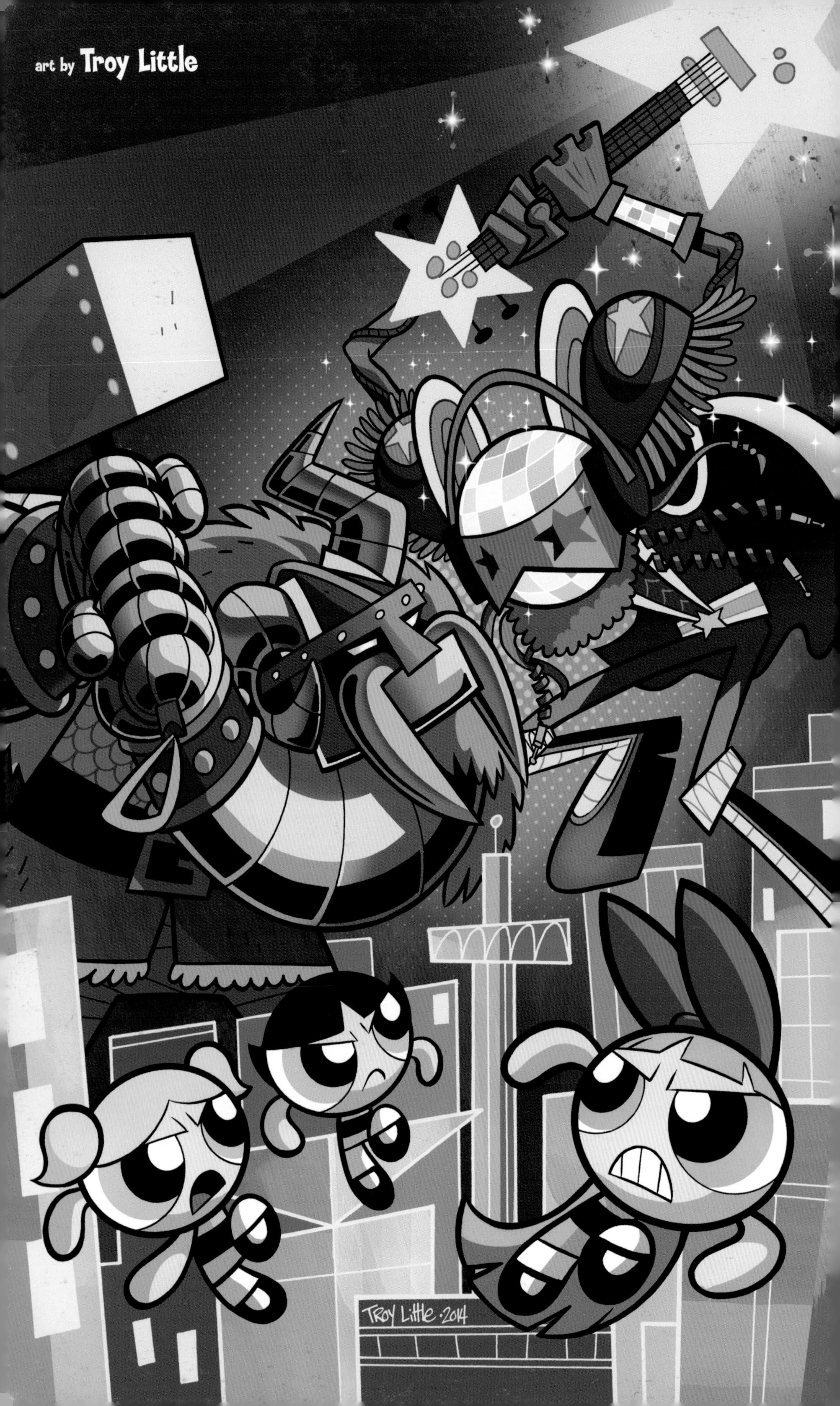
art by Troy Little
TROY LITTLE · 2014

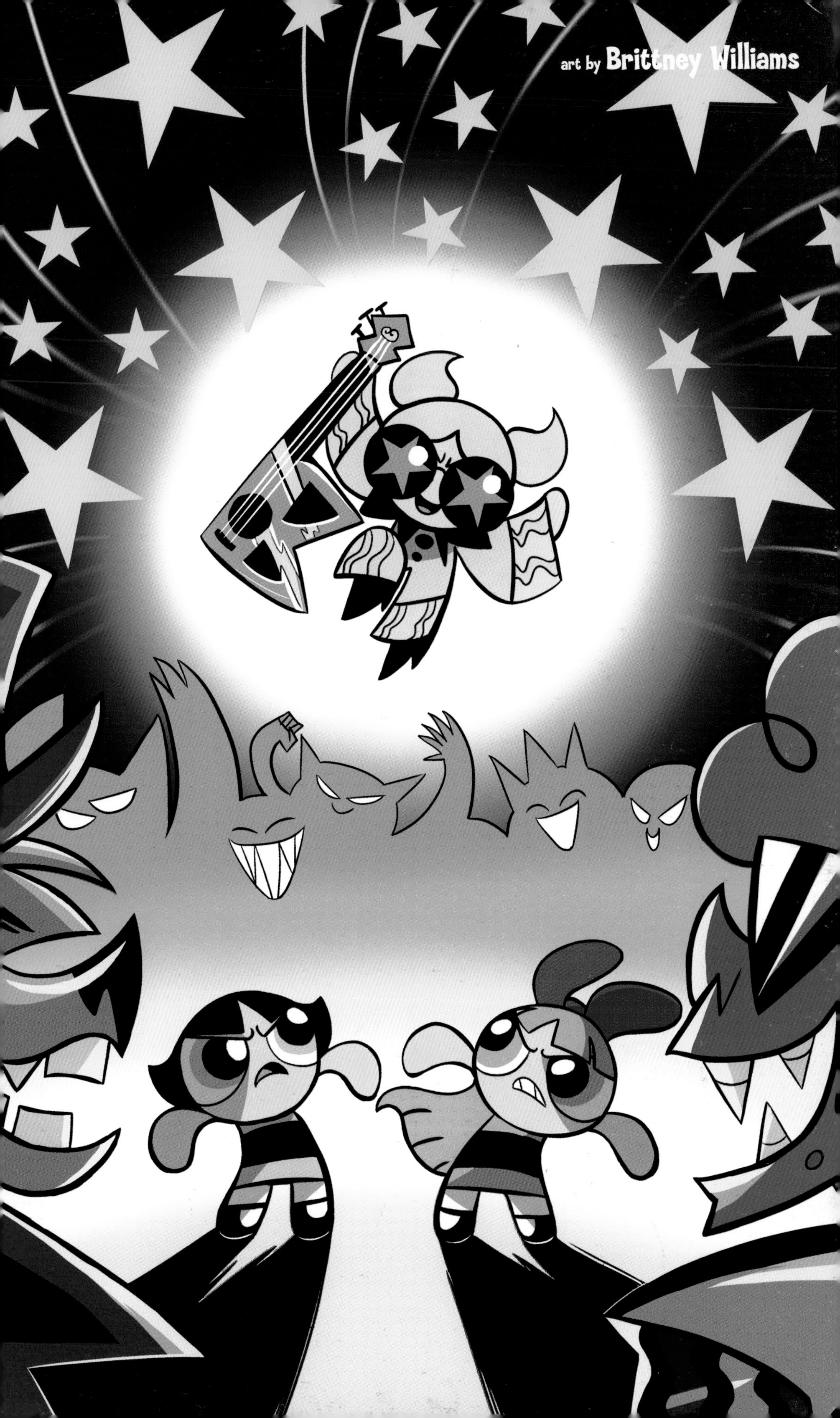
art by Brittney Williams

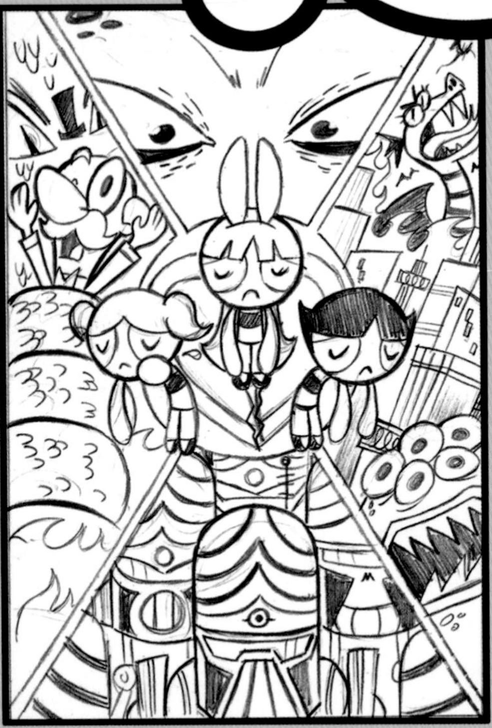

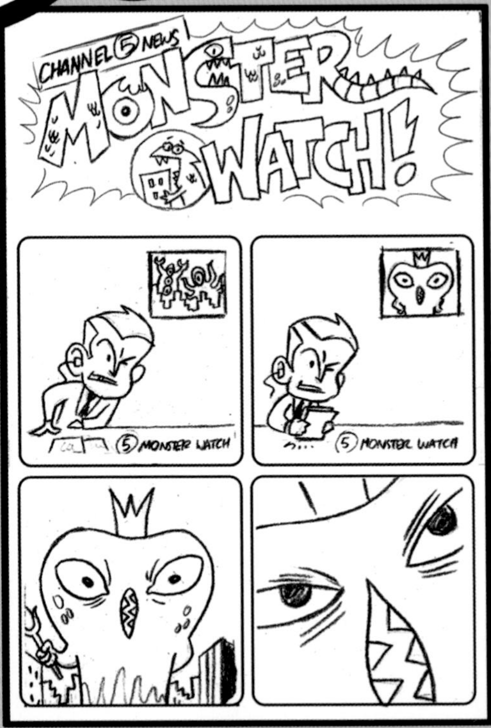
CHANNEL 5 NEWS
MONSTER WATCH!
5 MONSTER WATCH
5 MONSTER WATCH

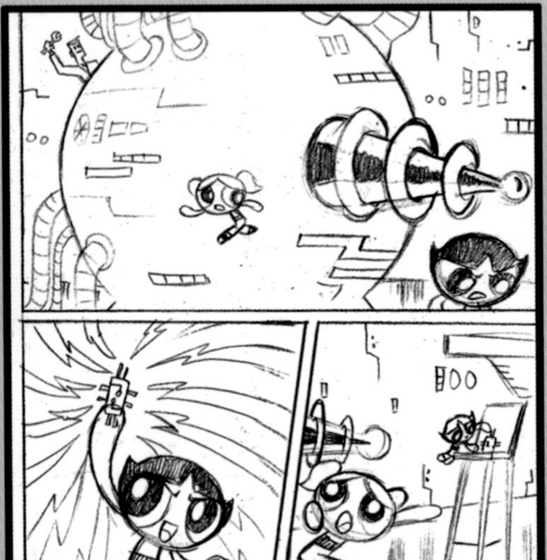

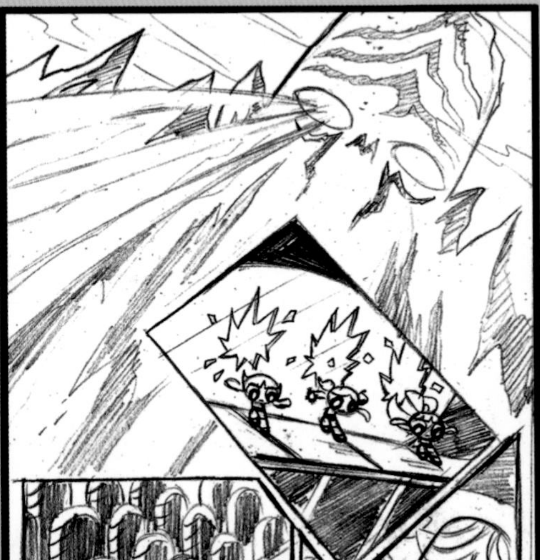

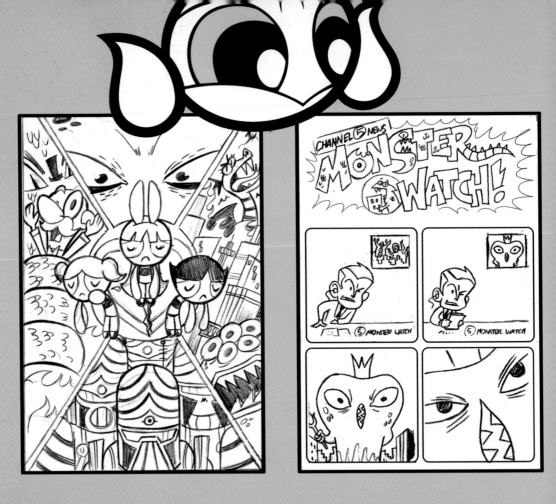

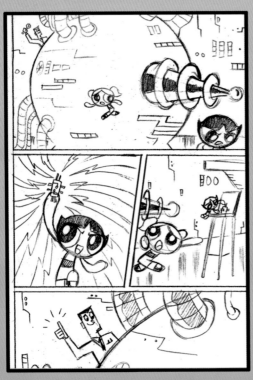

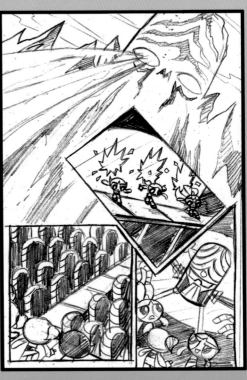

pencils by **Derek Charm**

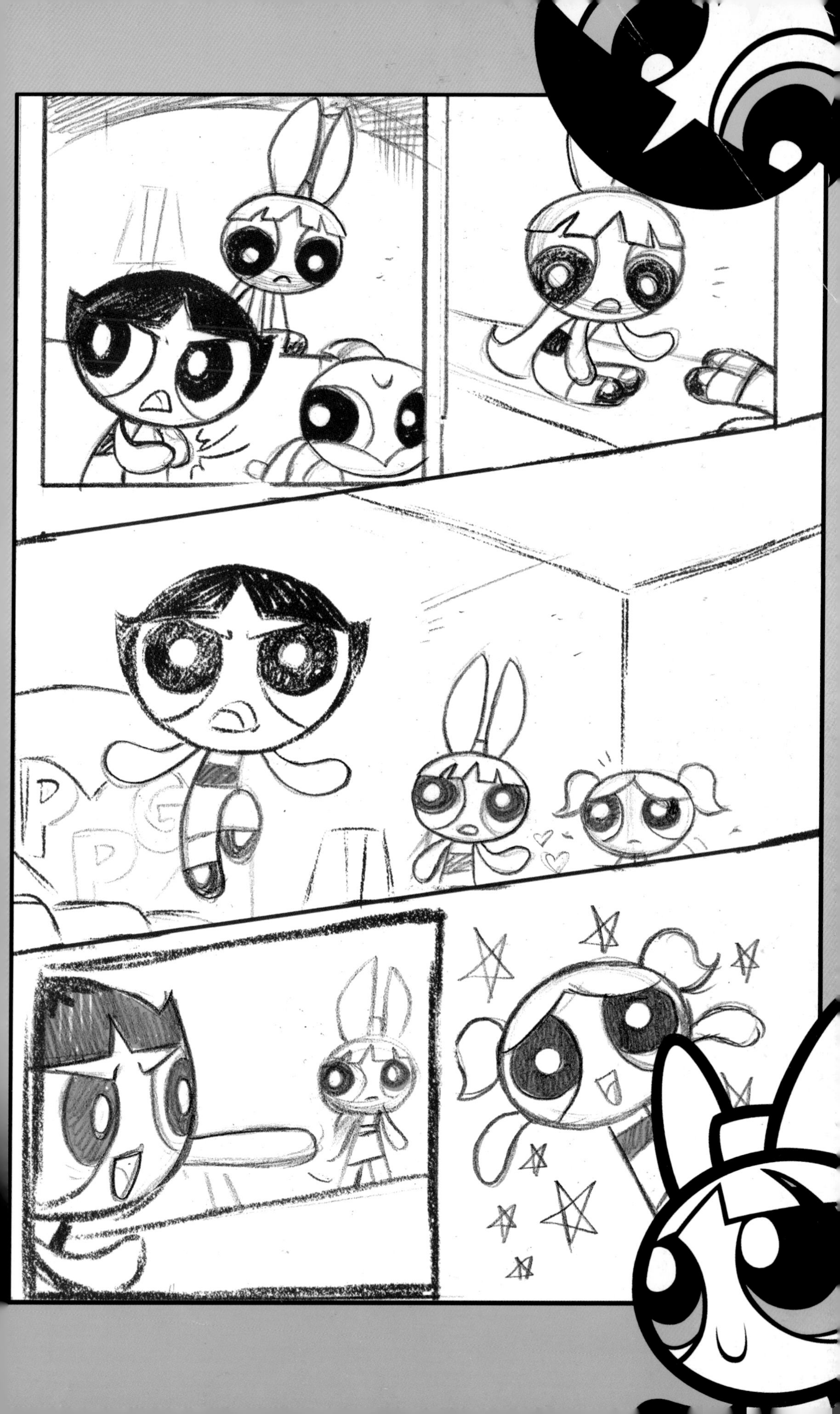

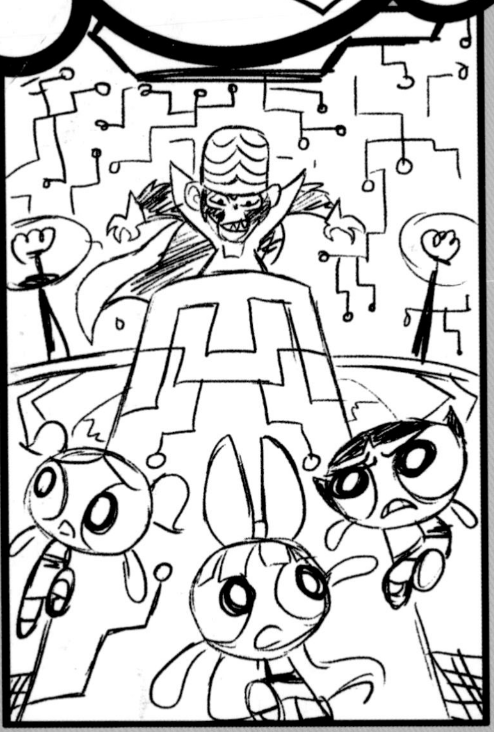

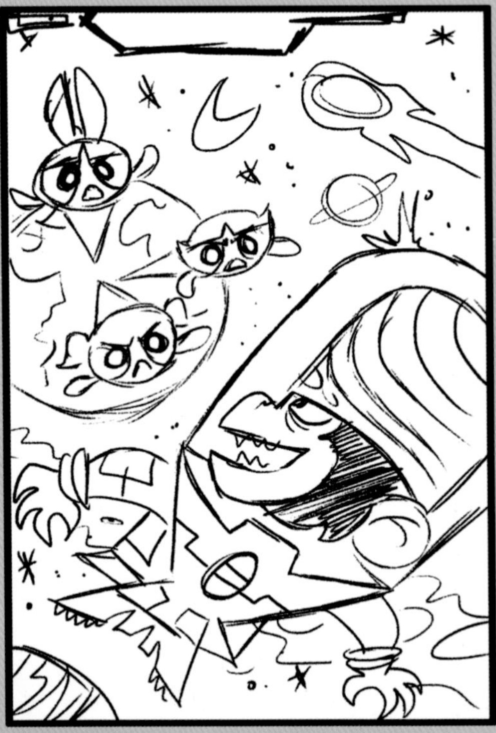

pencils by **Derek Charm**

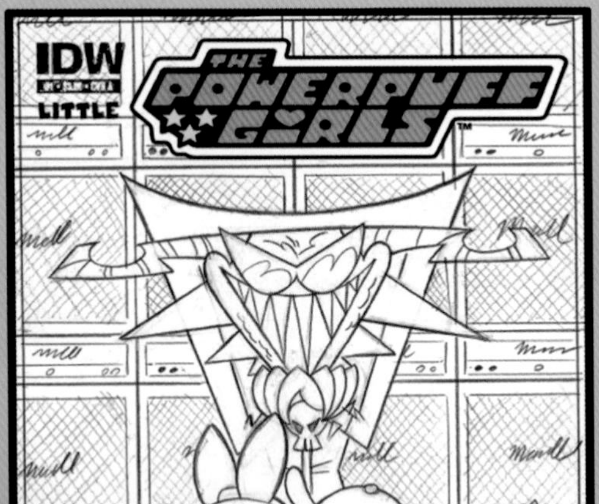
IDW
LITTLE
THE POWERPUFF GIRLS
THIS WEDNESDAY, TOWNSVILLE PARK!
ADMISSION ONLY $3.99!

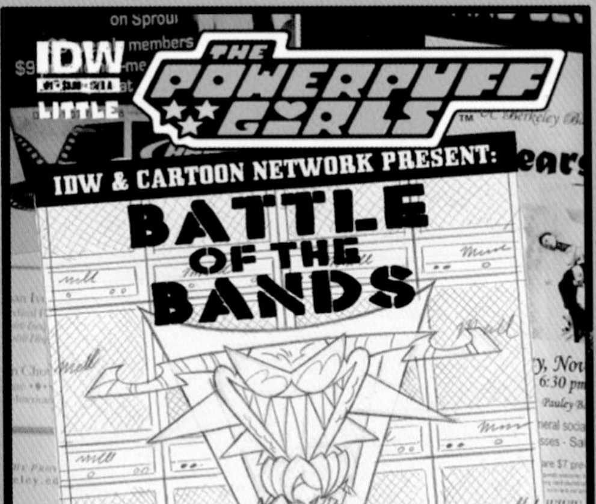
IDW
LITTLE
THE POWERPUFF GIRLS
IDW & CARTOON NETWORK PRESENT:
BATTLE OF THE BANDS
FEATURING:
· THE POWERPUFF GIRLS!
· THE ROWDYRUFF BOYS!
· BOOGIE MAN!
PLUS SPECIAL GUESTS!
THIS WEDNESDAY, TOWNSVILLE PARK!
ADMISSION ONLY $3.99!

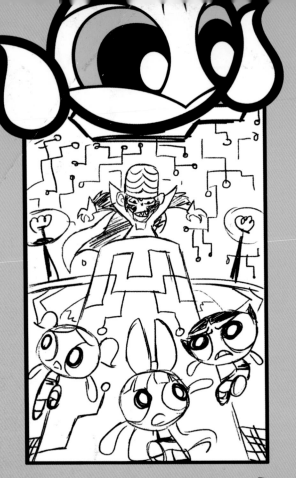

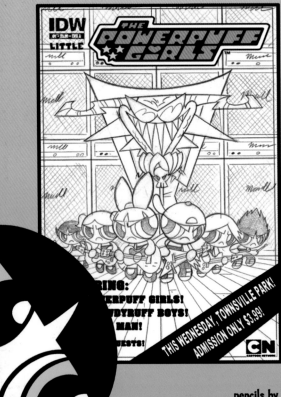

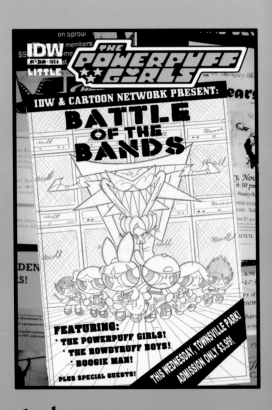

pencils by **Troy Little**

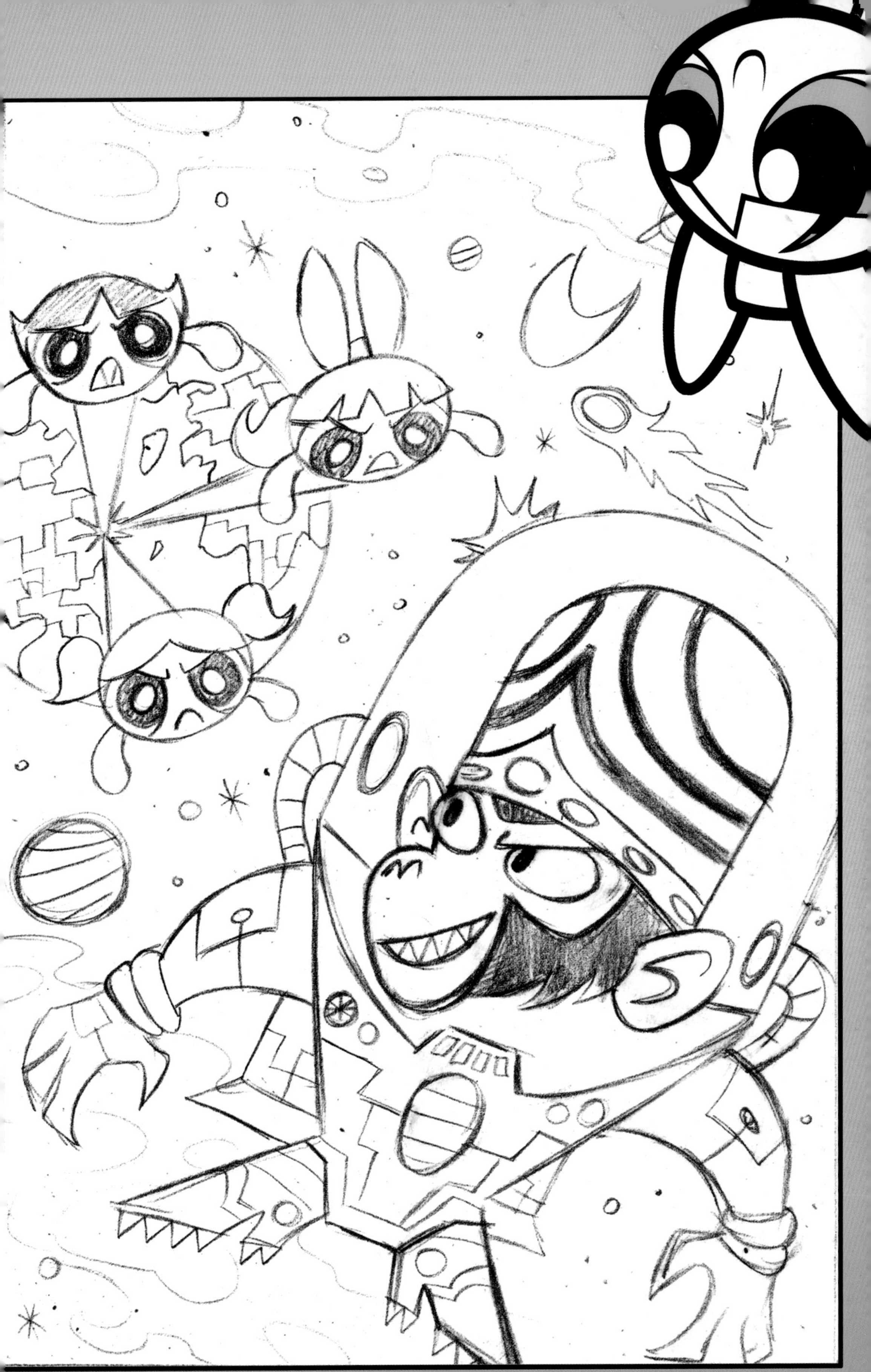

pencils by **Derek Charm**

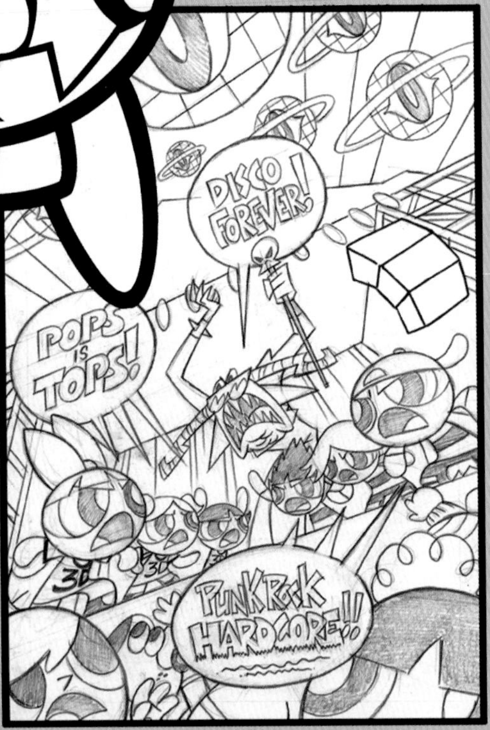
DISCO FOREVER!
POPS is TOPS!
PUNK ROCK HARDCORE!!!

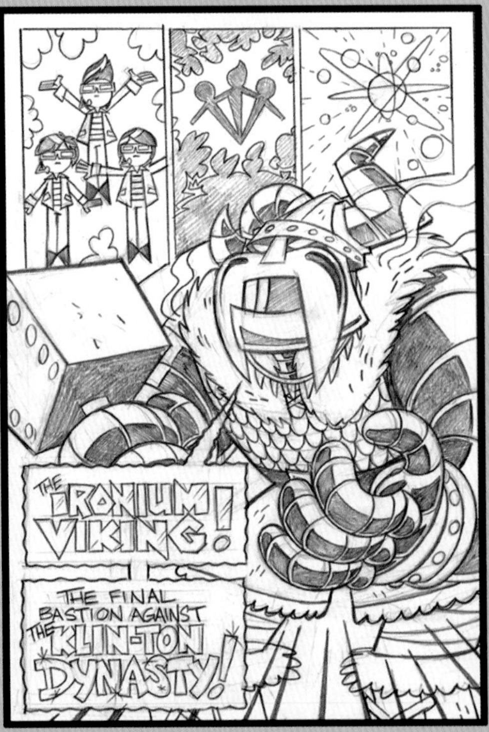
THE IRONIUM VIKING!
THE FINAL BASTION AGAINST THE KLIN-TON DYNASTY!

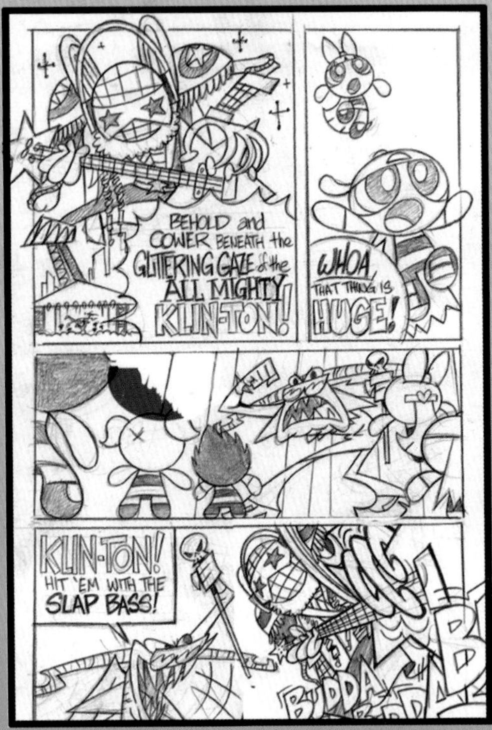
BEHOLD and COWER BENEATH the GLITTERING GAZE of the ALL MIGHTY KLIN-TON!
WHOA, THAT THING IS HUGE!
KLIN-TON! HIT 'EM WITH THE SLAP BASS!
BUDDA

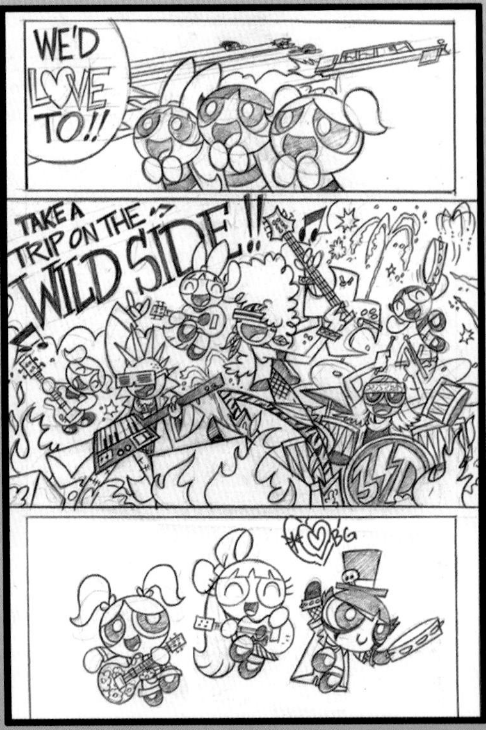
WE'D LOVE TO!!
TAKE A TRIP ON THE WILD SIDE!!

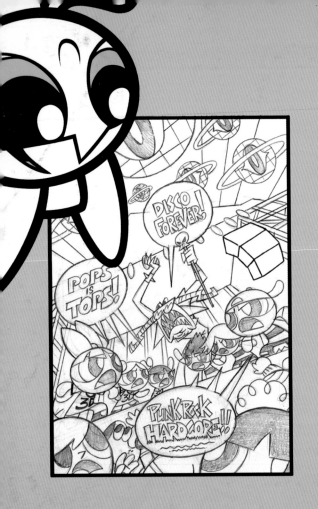

pencils by **Troy Little**

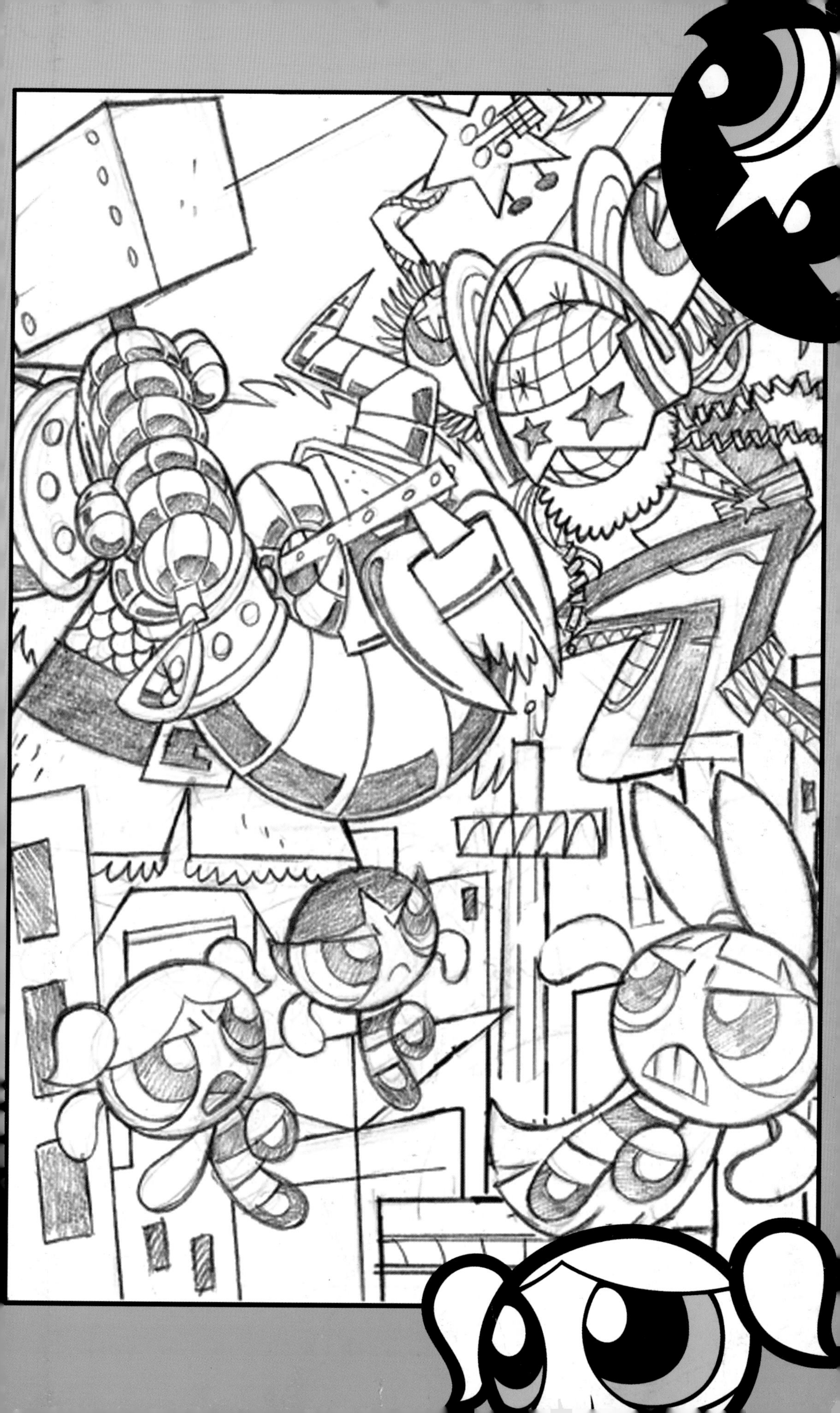

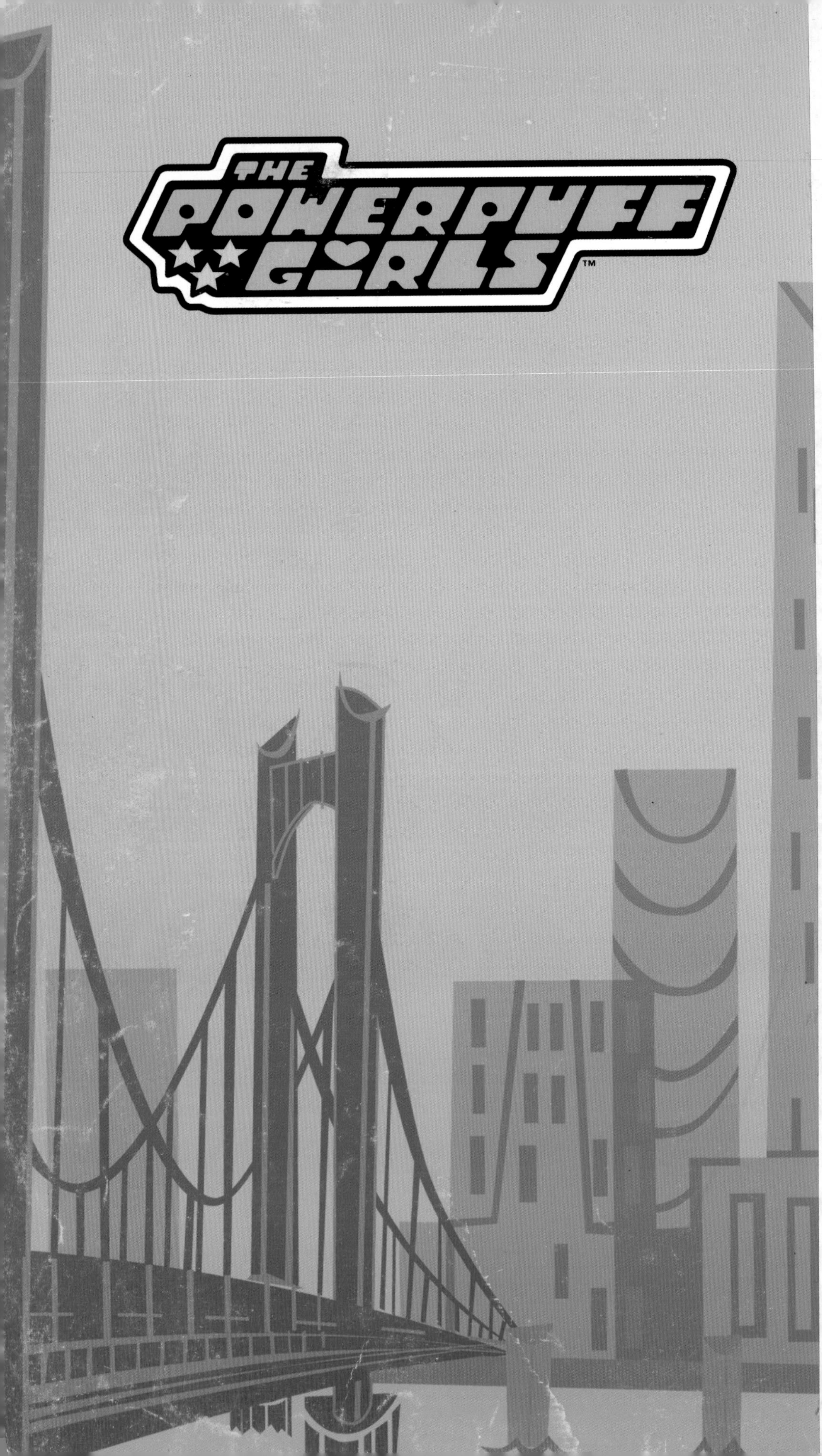
THE POWERPUFF GIRLS™